EDUCATIONAL FUTURES
RETHINKING THEORY AND PRACTICE
Volume 52

Scope
This series maps the emergent field of educational futures. It will commission books on the futures of education in relation to the question of globalisation and knowledge economy. It seeks authors who can demonstrate their understanding of discourses of the knowledge and learning economies. It aspires to build a consistent approach to educational futures in terms of traditional methods, including scenario planning and foresight, as well as imaginative narratives, and it will examine examples of futures research in education, pedagogical experiments, new utopian thinking, and educational policy futures with a strong accent on actual policies and examples.

Policy, Discourse and Rhetoric

How New Labour Challenged Social Justice and Democracy

Edited by

Marie Lall

SENSE PUBLISHERS
ROTTERDAM/BOSTON/TAIPEI

A C.I.P. record for this book is available from the Library of Congress.

ISBN: 978-94-6091-815-5 (paperback)
ISBN: 978-94-6091-816-2 (hardback)
ISBN: 978-94-6091-817-9 (e-book)

Published by: Sense Publishers,
P.O. Box 21858,
3001 AW Rotterdam,
The Netherlands
https://www.sensepublishers.com/

Printed on acid-free paper

For Dave Gillborn, who introduced me to sociology of education
and for NWM, who died on the 1st of January 2012.
He believed that writing could change the world.

CONTENTS

ACKNOWLEDGEMENTS

Our profound thanks go to Michael Apple who inspired this volume, to Anne Gold for good advice, to Terence Edmonds for lending his art for the cover design, and to Viren Lall for his help throughout the editing and proof reading process.

LIST OF AUTHORS

Editor: Dr Marie Lall, FRSA is an Education Policy Studies specialist and a South Asia expert (India, Pakistan and Burma/Myanmar) specialising in political issues (with regard to the economy, geopolitics, foreign policy formulation, citizenship and Diaspora politics) and education (with specific regard to education policy, gender, ethnicity and social exclusion issues, the formation of national identity and its close links with citizenship). She has 18 years of experience in the region, conducting extensive fieldwork and having lived both in India and Pakistan. She has written widely on these topics and is the author/editor of 4 books, with two more forthcoming titles.

She is a Reader in Education and South Asian Studies at the Institute of Education, University of London. She is an honorary fellow at the Institute of South Asian Studies, National University of Singapore and was an associate fellow on the Asia Programme at Chatham House till 2011. She has had a number of short fellowships at world renowned universities in Australia, Germany, India and Pakistan. She received her PhD from the London School of Economics in 1999.

Julia Püschel is a doctoral candidate at the Graduate School of North American Studies (John-F.-Kennedy Institute, Free University of Berlin). During the academic year 2011/2012 she is a visiting scholar at the Graduate School of Princeton University's Economics department (New Jersey/USA). In her dissertation she analyses the impact of offshoring on wage inequalities in the United States. After having completed her M.A in Business Administration at the Free University of Berlin in 2008 she has worked as an academic assistant at the Economics department of the College of Europe (Bruges/Belgium) in 2008/2009. Julia's research interests include international economics and its implications for education policies, economic inequalities, European economic integration, and transatlantic relations.

Boris Vormann is a doctoral candidate in Political Science at the Graduate School for North American Studies (John-F.-Kennedy Institute, Free University Berlin). In 2005, Boris earned his undergraduate degree at the Technische Universität Dresden where he studied Educational Science, American and French Studies to become a teacher. He was employed as a research assistant at the Department of Educational Science until 2007. He was a Fulbright visiting scholar at the John C. Whitehead School of Diplomacy and International Relations (Seton Hall University, New Jersey) in 2007/2008 and completed his M.A. in American and French Studies at the TU Dresden in 2009 where he was honoured with the Lohrmann Medal. Boris Vormann's research interests include neoliberal policy reform and globalisation processes, education policies and socio-economic inequalities, as well as North American urban and security studies. Boris is a visiting scholar at New York

University in the academic year 2011/2012. His latest major publication was his co-editorship of 'Québec: Staat und Gesellschaft' (with Alain-G. Gagnon and Ingo Kolboom, Synchron Publishing, 2011).

Irene Brew-Riverson (BA Hons., P.G.C.E, MA) Irene is Lecturer and Dissertation Supervisor at The University of Westminster and The London South Bank University. Her role as an Advanced Practitioner at Westminster Kingsway College involves the interpretation of relevant policy documents that affect vocational learners in higher education and the provision and support of colleagues in course delivery in order to fulfil one of the college's key objectives of effectively widening educational participation in Inner London. She has worked with students from non-traditional backgrounds on a range of Higher Education courses in Business and Management since 1994. She has been involved in curriculum and course design and change in response to policy changes over the last fifteen years that have affected the provision of two-year higher level programmes for part time and full time students. Irene was one of the designers of one of the very first Foundation Degree Programmes in Hospitality at Westminster Kingsway College. She has subsequently contributed to the design of Foundation Degrees in Business and Management and Public Administration.

She is currently researching Widening Participation via Foundation Degrees for her EdD Thesis at the Institute of Education. Her work to date has involved a project examining the progression of Foundation Degree students onto honours programmes and the exploration of professional challenges faced by lecturers seeking to effectively widen participation.

Kathy Edmonds is Senior lecturer in Youth and Community Work at Glyndwr University, Wrexham and a Fellow of the Higher Education Academy. She has been a professional in the field of youth and community work for 27 years, in a variety of settings, both in the UK and abroad. She has worked with the Tate Liverpool for 20 years and has been on the Tate professional register as a Gallery educator since 2005 and has been instrumental in driving forward the gallery's pioneering work within the youth sector. Through co-tutoring on the *Opening Doors* course she has been providing professional development for people in the social care and health professions, using the gallery as a resource. She has had a chapter published in *The RHP Companion to Working with Young People*, and a number of articles on a range of youth work issues published in *Young People Now*. Her particular interests are Citizenship and youth work; Mobile youth work; and Youth culture and the arts. She is studying for a professional doctorate at the institute and her research area is Arts, Creativity and well-being.

Sophie Park MBChB M.Med.Sci (dist) MRCGP (dist) DCH DFFP is a practising GP and academic. She has worked within UCL Medical School for the last 5 years, having achieved a Masters in Medical Education at Nottingham University. She teaches for UCL, the London Deanery and the Institute of Education (IOE) at both undergraduate and postgraduate level in a variety of subjects relating to general practice and medical education. She co-ordinates community-based placements for undergraduates in Dermatology, Child and Women's Health, is course lead for the Consultation module, BSc in Primary Care at UCL and is a tutor on the Education and Technology in Clinical Practice MA, at the IOE. Sophie is currently studying for a professional doctorate in education at the IOE and has presented and been invited speaker at several international conferences on her related research exploring how undergraduate medical students develop their professional identity using narrative analysis. She contributed to the PasTest '*practical guide to Medical Ethics and Law*' and was recently contributory author and co-editor of a book with Developmedica entitled '*A Career Companion to General Practice*' (in press 2010).

Theophilus Tambi *BA Eng Lang & Lit., PGCE Adult Lit., MA Comp Lit., MEd Special/Inclusive Education* is a lecturer and programme leader in Special Education Studies. With over ten years of national and international experience working within special and inclusive education, he has also taught literacy and numeracy to students experiencing a variety of mild to profound disabilities and difficulties in learning both within general and specialist colleges. While working as Equality and Diversity Officer, responsible for the curricular and pastoral inclusion of students in one of the largest colleges in the North West of England, Theophilus worked directly within multiprofessional teams to address the tensions, complexities and challenges involved in policy rhetoric and interpretation. Theophilus is currently engaged in professional doctoral research - a theoretical, practice based and methodological journey that should culminate into an improved understanding of learners' needs and an evidence based strategy for addressing them.

Stephen Colwell is Senior Lecturer at Ravensbourne, a specialist University Sector College teaching communication media production. He spent 35 years as a media professional as a Film Editor, Writer, Producer and Director working in film and television making a wide range of factual programming for major Broadcasters. He began teaching in 2003 and has since become increasingly involved in research in his field. He completed an MA in Political Communication at Goldsmiths College in 2008 and at present he is working on a Doctorate in Education at the Institute of Education.

MARIE LALL

IDENTIFYING NEW LABOUR'S TROJAN HORSE

An introduction on how New Labour introduced neoliberalism into Britain's education system

This book reviews the major shifts in the education sector under New Labour between 1997 and 2009, analysing selected case study policies in order to articulate dominant discourses in recent policy-making which have helped establish a particular hegemony. It illustrates how, despite their label and previous history as supporters of socialist policies, New Labour chose a rhetoric of 'the Third Way', heavily influenced by the neoliberal. This dominant discourse, which with globalisation has been embraced by the majority of Western cultures[i], emphasises the role of the free market, the individual as consumer and the state as a regulator as opposed to a provider, with irrevocable effects on social justice. This book focuses particularly on the influence of a neoliberal agenda in education. It explores how competing discourses of social justice and democracy have been challenged and how through the use of particular language, engagement with these ideologies has evolved and, marketed as 'the common sense approach', is becoming widely accepted within most state sectors in the UK.

However this is not yet another book on New Labour and neoliberalism. This volume is different from the rest of the literature as it uses policy case study evidence to show the rhetorical nature of the commitment New Labour appeared to have been making to education and the gap between text and practice. It builds on Ball's Education Debate (2008), but widens the discussion to include issues such as higher education and citizenship amongst others. The book focuses on how neoliberalism was promoted through the discourse of the chosen policies in education, making neoliberalism the 'new common sense'. Unlike other books on that era, this one aims to review New Labour's time in government through specific policy texts.

Education is often only perceived as limited to policies relating to schools and higher education. However the book seeks to demonstrate that education as a sector is a much broader field and therefore the areas covered include key policies in citizenship and youth work, widening participation in higher education, the place of inclusive education in the curriculum, the undergraduate medical curriculum, and the attempt to harness creativity with regard to the media industry. The book emanates out of the Contemporary Education Policy optional module of the Institute of Education, University of London's Ed D

M. Lall (ed.), Policy, Discourse and Rhetoric: How New Labour Challenged Social Justice and Democracy, 1–14.

programme. The contributors are all specialists in their field, working as lecturers at various universities across the UK as well as working on their own doctorate. Two doctoral students working on neoliberal theory from another university were invited to join the project. The varied backgrounds of the contributors allowed for a wide range of disciplines and a detailed discussion of the crossover of issues, which enriches the debate. The contributors chose what they considered the key policy text of their area for analysis. By bringing 'their policy' to this book they also hope to bring the debate to a wider audience. In effect the broad selection of sectors demonstrates that New Labour's education policies were not only detrimental in traditional education settings, but also affected areas such as medicine and the media which are of importance to those who no longer are affected by what happens in institutions of learning and teaching. Despite the wide spectrum of policies, the coherence of the book is maintained through its structure of policy analysis that is replicated in every chapter and the discussion of the discursive materials relating to neoliberalism and education.

This introduction will briefly cover the rationale of use of the Policy Cycle, the tool around which the book revolves and the rationale for the selection of the key policy texts and moments. It also discusses the links between the various chapters and how the book moves from policies affecting young people through citizenship and youth work, to issues pertaining to special educational needs in schools, to the failed widening participation agenda in higher education. Beyond the scope of schools and higher education it then explains how the book moves on to discuss the effects of education policies in the professional arenas of the media and medical education and the relevance of these arenas in the wider education debate.

Why do we need to be aware of policy?

Policy is incredibly influential in determining how individuals interact, what they perceive to be 'good', and how they shape their lives in order to fulfil or move against cultural rewards for 'success'. Policy often reflects a conversation between influential players in its construction, including communities affected by that policy, business and media, although their power and influence negotiating the focus and impact of policy, of course, varies. Policy will create and shape how society is desired to function and 'be' in certain contexts, influencing the language which people value, the actions which receive reward and the way in which people choose to express 'goodness' as a way of conforming or rejecting certain policy. Particular communities are often challenged and required to change by policy. Many feel threatened and isolated as a result. What this book highlights is the commonalities of these challenges within a particular timeframe. This book illustrates how a number of different policies produced during the reign of 'New Labour' represent the impact of influential ideologies, shaping the priorities and language which different services are expected to fulfil.

A TOOL TO FACILITATE A CRITICAL APPROACH - THE POLICY CYCLE

There are many different ways of critiquing policy in order to understand the ways in which it achieves (or does not achieve) its influence. We have chosen to use the Policy Cycle as a theoretical framework to analyse selected case study policies in order to discern dominant discourses in recent policies establishing and supporting a particular hegemony.

The 'Policy Cycle' as a concept and a theoretical framework was developed by Stephen Ball along with Richard Bowe and Anne Gold. (Bowe, Ball and Gold, 1992) The key question at the heart of the debate is the extent to which the state determines the policy making process and as a consequence the room available for other actors, especially those involved in implementation to re-interpret the policy text in practice. In this analysis both the process and the extent to which the state determines policy content is key. This is particularly salient in today's globalising world, as the number of active actors involved in policy making is increasing and creating a more complex playing field.

There is some degree of difference between state controlled and state-centred explanations of the role of the state in policy formulation, however both see the state as the primary actor in making education policy and do not engage greatly with contributions to education policy made by actors outside the state. State control models would see the state as determining in all policy making. These models come from the Marxist tradition - influenced by theorists like Habermas, Althusser, Gramsci and Offe. These authors stressed the structural constraints and the power of the state. State-centred explanations of policy making however, see the state as dominating but also acknowledge other influences. Dale (1989) argues that the state has to fight to secure active consent, to secure hegemonic control and as a result there are inherent contradictions and conflicts with different levels of the state. However both positions argue that a central position should be allocated to the state in policy analysis, because the state is more than just another actor as it is able to employ legitimate coercion, shape institutional features, define and enforce conditions of ownership and control, and secure active consent.

On the other hand, Bowe et al. (1992) argue that the state-centred models are too simple and too linear and that they neglect the agency of anything other than the institutions of the state. They criticise the state control approach for the detachment of the policy generation from implementation, which reinforces tidy, managerial, linear models. Its focus on macro-based theoretical analysis, 'silence' the voices of teachers, students and parents. They argue that we need to understand the histories and ideologies of the people who receive policy texts, and what drives them to implement policy in the way that they do. Bowe et al. stress that the policy process does not just begin when the policy is launched and received as a text by the people who have to implement it. Even the production of the text itself is not one static moment, but a process. Texts themselves are the products of compromises and power struggles. They have interpretational and representational history and 'policy sediment' builds up around them, which in effect means that there are never really any completely 'new' policies'.

The notion of a Policy Cycle is therefore where policy is made and remade in different contexts. Each of the three contexts described below have public and private arenas of action and each involves compromise, and in some cases even the repression or ignoring of certain interest groups altogether. By taking a policy through the various contexts of the Policy Cycle, the origins of the policy, the voices which are reflected in the policy and the effects of the policy interpretation become clearer.

- *Context of influence* is where interest groups struggle over the construction of policy discourses and where key policy concepts are established. Important influences are networks of influence, the relationships between civil servants and ministers, the micro-politics within parties, and the role of unions and Local Education Authorities where they are present. There is also the overriding context of a democratic society and the need to appeal to the electorate; Which voices are heard is crucial.
- *Context of policy text production* is where texts represent policies. Texts have to be read in relation to time and the site of production, and with other relevant texts. This context is one of policy compromise and misunderstandings. Since authors can't control the meanings of their texts, the process of interpretation and re-interpretation is key. (Bowe et al. 1992) Another feature of the context is that text writers have to be careful not to be too radical in order to stay in power. In order to ensure re-election the middle classes cannot be asked for too many sacrifices.
- *Context of practice* is where policy is subject to interpretation, recreation and practice on the ground. In general the policy in action does not reflect what was originally envisioned either in the context of influence not in the context of text production.

In his 1994 book, Ball added two more contexts in apparent recognition of the need for a feedback loop from the context of practice at micro level back to the context of influence at macro level:

- *Context of outcomes* is where the impact of policies on existing social inequalities is seen. This context's analytical concern is with the issues of justice, equality and individual freedom. Policies are analysed in terms of their impact upon and interactions with existing inequalities and forms of injustice.
- *Context of political strategy* is where one identifies political activities which might tackle the inequalities which have been identified in the Context of Outcomes. In effect this is the feedback loop into the Context of Influence.

Whilst the Policy Cycle framework does not explain how policy gets done, it is a way of thinking about policy, a way of researching policy and a way of theorising policy. As such the authors of the various chapters have used it as a starting point, a flexible schema which they developed, extended and changed according to their needs and areas of work.

By using this framework we are able to examine the ideologies and discourses which are common to a number of different policies, affecting multiple disciplines, professionals and students during the New Labour terms in office. In particular, we focus upon the prominence and impact of neoliberalism.

Neoliberalism and its tensions

David Harvey defines neoliberalism as 'a theory of political economic practices that proposes that human well-being can be advanced by liberating individual entrepreneurial freedoms and skills within an institutional framework characterised by strong private property rights, free markets and free trade.' (Harvey 2005, 2). This theory, based on 19th century English liberalism (see the first chapter in this volume) resulted in politically guided neoliberal measures that include amongst other things de-regulation, privatisation, commercialisation of public services and the use of market proxies, reinforcing the profit motive. Neoliberalism also promotes the importance of individual entrepreneurial freedom, competition, choice, and initiative, believing that these features can be effectively achieved through a free market (Harris, 2007; Harvey, 2005). The assumption behind the promotion of free markets is that the laws of demand and supply will encourage higher quality at competitive prices. The role of the state in this context is to regulate the market without intervening in it, while consumers choose the alternative that suits them best using the information produced by the market (Olssen and Peters, 2005). In this context the state has to provide an institutional framework to safeguard the capitalist system, but does not directly provide services or intervene. These ideas are not new. Hayek in his 'A Road to Serfdom' (1944) argued early on that state intervention needed minimising as it fosters a 'dependency culture'. Instead the focus should be on individuals making their own choices and gains in market economy – where services are not provided collectively and paid for by the state but provided privately by a range of competitive providers. Competition between these providers would ensure the high quality of their services, individual consumers would make their own choices, and individual effort, talent and hard work would be the key to success. Structural inequalities are not recognised as impediments.

Neoliberalism can be identified as the predominant ideology of the last decades (Giroux, 2002); in effect the new 'common sense' that has replaced the social democracy of the post-war era. It has penetrated education (Harris, 2007) changing the purpose of education itself (Bartlett et al., 2002; Wolf, 2002). Education currently is seen as a main condition for economic success, central to any modern economy. (Gamanikov 2009) Often forgotten is that education is relevant for the development of citizenship values (see chapter 2 in this volume), and for the sake of learning (McGregor, 2009; Wolf, 2002). Although it brings economic benefits it also brings an essential contribution to the public good

(Margison 1993 in McGregor, 2009). Neoliberal ideology not only changed the purpose of education, but it also changed the structure of education systems (Bartlett et al., 2002; Wolf, 2002). Through the implementation of neoliberal policies, education was opened to the market assuming the features just described. This has meant that there are private providers entering into the education system in a context of deregulation, which constitutes the commercialisation and marketisation of education (Ball, 2007; Verger, 2008).

The debate over the role of the state led to reforms across all UK public services. Over the last 20 years the way the public sector has been managed has changed markedly - there has been a shift away from old-style bureaucratic administration. The elevation of effectiveness and efficiency as the sole criteria of legitimacy reflects the increasing dominance of an ethic of managerialism and a concomitant emphasis upon measuring and improving performance (see chapter 1 in this volume). This new way of perceiving public services also gave rise to an 'accounting logic,' promoting a general perception that what is visible and quantifiable is what is important. However professional 'outputs' are not easily standardised and measurable:

> 'In various guises, the key elements of the education reform 'package' – and it is applied with equal vigour to schools, colleges and universities - are embedded in three interrelated policy technologies: the market, managerialism and performativity.' (Ball 2003)

As the role for the state has changed from provider to regulator, there has been the loss of a distinctive public sector. It is important not to suggest a 'golden age' of public sector administration. There are lots of criticisms that can be (and were) made, for example, issues of professional discretion and judgement, the lack of client consultation, the slow and weighty bureaucracy, the hierarchy and the lack of accountability. But the reforms leading to a change from public sector bureaucracy to managerialism have also affected the character, ethos, values and behaviour of individuals and organisations. Today the discussion of education focuses not so much on the transformations in peoples' lives brought about by education, or the quality of their educational experiences, but the number of qualified students, the savings made in the delivery of services and the proportion of students going on into higher education.

The effects of neoliberalism on social justice and education

> 'It is clear therefore that with increased market logic there is also an increase in democratic deficit and with it a reduction of the social justice agenda, especially in the public sector arena as new inequalities are created.' (Lall and Nambissan 2011 p.7)

The effects of the reforms across the UK education sector have led to substantial change. The new policy discourse is restricting both for head teachers managing the schools and teachers in the classroom (Harris: 2007). With regard to schooling the focus has shifted to an instrumentalist thinking with measurable outputs. Schools aim to raise achievement in order to compete with each other through league tables. The influx of new educational providers such as academies has led to increased opportunities for students from poorer backgrounds to attend different types of schools. Nevertheless, as Roberts (2001 in Reay, 2006) argues, this transformation has created the illusion of a fairer society while it creates a stratification along the system which relegates the working classes to different trajectories than middle classes (Reay, 2006). The underlying assumption is that free markets allow parents to choose the school that aligns with their expectations and needs. The possibility of choosing a school would act as a natural selection process through which unpopular schools will be forced to change or to close if they do not adapt to clients expectations (Ball, 1993). However the rhetoric of choice assumes that all parents have equal cultural capital and are equally informed and capable of making such a choice for their children. The middle classes benefit whilst the lower classes have to make do with the leftovers (Leathwood, 2004; Reay, David and Ball, 2005). This has also affected those with Special Educational Needs, where a rhetoric of inclusive education has not resulted in equitable education provision for all. (See Chapter 3 in the volume)

There have been similar effects in the higher education sector: Marketisation across the sector has made performativity and accountability cornerstones of higher education policies today. Increasing the number of institutions has led to a stratified system with 'first' and 'second class' universities providing a different quality learning experience and catering to different sections of society. The pressure to increase the number of students, account for how time is spent and the general concern with national and international rankings are all effects of the changing understanding of what higher education stands for. The role of the university is no longer that of a 'public interest institution' but being sites of 'knowledge production' in light of the economic imperatives of the 'knowledge economy.' (see Chapter 4 in this volume)

New Labour's Britain

'The driving force of third way politics is globalisation.' (Fairclough 2000, p.27)

The acceptance of New Labour's vision of the neoliberal global economy underpinned third way politics. Chapter one will give a detailed analysis on how New Labour adopted neoliberalism and how the Third Way paved the way for market politics. It is however important to remember that the Third Way objectives did not immediately mean a market centred approach. The neoliberal vision and rhetoric developed gradually over the three New Labour terms. The Third Way promised to tread a middle ground where social justice was not to be abandoned. In light of globalisation New Labour proposed to create a dynamic knowledge-based economy founded on individual empowerment and opportunity, where the government's role was to support and the power of the market was to be harnessed to serve the public interest. A strong civil society would help enshrine rights and responsibilities and a modern government would be based on partnership and decentralisation (adapted from Blair, T., 1998). For education this meant increased investment, continued emphasis on human capital creation and the standards agenda as well as investment in higher education. Specialist schools, and school diversity was to be increased as well as parental involvement encouraged. Education services were to be privatised and business involvement encouraged, especially in disadvantaged areas. New Labour worked out partnership arrangements between the government, civil society and the private sector in areas which needed regeneration. New Deal for Communities as well as Education Action Zones were flagship programmes of the time.

New Labour's time in office is characterised by two phenomena: a policy epidemic (Levin, 1998; Ball 2008) – in international convergence of ideas with an ever increasing number of texts appearing, focusing on the same themes of efficiency and effectiveness (especially but not limited to education); as well as a steady move of policies as well as education officials, senior civil servants and think tanks to the political right (Gibton, 2011). It can be argued that neoliberalism as a political and social ideology became a driver for an ever increasing number of policies which were developed under New Labour. The shift to a neoliberal hegemony happened by stealth as New Labour presented 'consultation' as a key to a participative mode of societal governance. Members of the public and civil society organisations were invited to be involved in policy consultation, creation and application. However 'consultation' was often sent out of schools or conducted just before the holidays. As Jones and Gammell (2009) observe, consultation is 'far from an idyllic state of benign democracy with stakeholder organisations and the general public happily rejoicing that governments and quangos condescend to ask then their opinions' but a 'half way house between mass participation... and the traditional way we always took important decisions.' New Labour also relied on particular policy advisors, most of whom were not politicians, but people who were perceived as 'stars', such as Chris Woodhead and Michael Barber. Whose voice was being heard and whose were being ignored is often not taken into account when looking back at the consultation practice.

Policies are key instruments in helping the government establish the 'common sense' of the day. In order to unpick the move towards a neoliberal rhetoric in New Labour policy and to understand how the new hegemony was established, it is important to return to some key policy texts of the time. Only policy analysis will allow us to answer how the discourse differed from the practice on the ground and how those who wrote the policies intended to convince the practitioners that their commitment to social justice was best served by an increasingly neoliberal agenda. In order to do this, each chapter applies the Policy Cycle as a theoretical and analytical framework to the chosen policy texts.

THE CHAPTERS

We think of education too often as simply school and higher education. This volume shows that education goes beyond these traditional spheres and also lies within youth work, medical education, creativity and the media. It was critical to cover areas outside of mainstream education in order to show how far education policy still impacts on society at large, even when not everyone is at an educational institution. Parents of course are affected by their children's lives at school, as are those who are studying in Higher Education (HE). Teachers and lecturers are directly affected as well. However the inclusion of the medical curriculum raises questions with regard to the relationship we all have with our doctors and the issue of creativity and media influences anyone who watches TV, listens to the radio or reads a newspaper. The media of course is also used by policy makers to communicate, interpret and re-interpret policy. Today the media's influence on political strategy and also on professional practice is greater than ever. The book's purpose is to give sample policy texts to show the historical and political relevance of New Labour education policy to illustrate what went before them and what has followed. The contributors to this book combine their own professional experience and theoretical expertise in contemporary education policy, to make explicit these ideologies. They use recent examples of policy and practice within their own professional field seeking, through increased awareness, to widen the reader's choice in action within their own settings and contexts.

The book's opening chapter gives the historical and political backdrop of neoliberalism and subsequent chapters explore the field of policymaking in education under the New Labour government.

Chapter 1 - *Grey Zones of the Market – Public Services, Education Policies and Neoliberal Reform in the United Kingdom* by Julia Püschel and Boris Vormann covers the origins of neoliberalism, and the different theories and the linkages to contemporary public policy. Using Stephen Ball's 'Policy Cycle' as an analytical tool this chapter examines the grey zones of neoliberal market theory with a particular emphasis on the UK model (Ball 1992). The first section outlines the basic tenets of neoliberal theory and examines its implications for public services and education policies. Based on the foundational texts of neoliberal theory (Friedman, van Hayek) – which, themselves, were produced in a specific, locatable context (context of influence) – they emphasise the historical and geo-political specificity of neoliberalisation processes – their context of policy text production. Public services and, more specifically, education policies appear as compromises in the free market model: as quasi-markets. After addressing the emergence of neoliberalism as a hegemonic discourse from the fringes of public policy debates and outlining its fundamental principles, they discuss the development of public services in the UK during the initial phase of 'roll-back' neoliberalism (Brenner et al. 2010). The second part of the chapter examines educational policies in the context of practice and context of outcomes. Drawing on neoliberal theory as posited in its foundational texts, as well as on real political shifts in the United Kingdom, two central categories are identified for an analytical assessment of educational policies and their contradictions: 'Competition & Choice' and 'Managerial Re-Organisation.'

From there the volume moves on to youth work and the role of education in creating citizenship.

In Chapter 2 – *Young people's engagement in society: how Government policy has ignored the role of youth work in citizenship education* Kathy Edmonds takes as a focus a critical analysis of part of the Governance of Britain Green Paper 'Britain's future: the citizen and the state' (2007), on citizenship and national identity; in particular young people's engagement in society. Government policy is focussed on the delivery of citizenship education only through schools. Edmonds concern is that if the government is serious about enabling young people's engagement in society as "active citizens" and encouraging them to vote, then why is the audience for this education policy selected only through formal education, namely schools and teachers? Where is the voice of youth work and young people? The chapter examines whose voice has been heard and who has influenced the agenda on citizenship, whilst identifying any gaps, and exploring why very few youth work professionals or practitioners get to have a say in the creation of policy, yet are expected to deliver and implement policy initiatives. The chapter explores the perceived lack of representation of youth work, starting with an overview of the concept of citizenship and its role in political literacy; and highlighting the differences in understanding between those on the right and left of the political spectrum on what being an "active citizen" means. The role of informal education through youth work looks at the characteristics of this style of work; whilst citizenship in practice looks at how policy is enacted or addressed. The literature reviewed identifies different models and changes to practice, from top down to bottom up, which can, through including youth worker's and young people in the discussion on citizenship education, impact on improved access and participation for young people; leading, Edmonds believes, to an improved relationship between society and young people.

From there the book moves into schools, looking in particular at children with special educational needs and how they have been affected by the changing policy rhetoric. Again this was chosen as being a less 'visible' policy effect, yet one which should be a central concern for anyone concerned with social justice.

In Chapter 3 – *Special Education Needs and inclusion – a critical appraisal* Theo Tambi explores the Special Educational Needs and Disability Act (SENDA) 2001, the key New Labour policy for inclusive education. To date, SENDA 2001 is arguably the single most important pieces of legislation underpinning the provision of services for learners experiencing disabilities and difficulties. This high level of importance is also matched by the level of controversies and, sometimes, contradictions associated with this legislation. One of the trends in special education studies today is the growing gap between policy and practice or between rhetoric and reality. This implies that the introduction of SENDA in 2001 does not mean that all the policy objectives have been accomplished. The policy analysis focuses on how the text reflects the neoliberal agenda of the day. The chapter argues that SENDA 2001 as a policy has its roots in a Conservative agenda, but was realised by Labour. It is inferred here that unless policy is analysed in this rigorous fashion, a lot of misjudgement and misappropriation of effort would be incurred in attempts to improve educational provision for learners experiencing disabilities and difficulties.

Higher education has been a key policy debate under New Labour, especially the Widening Participation agenda which shows that so many more students now have access to HE. However the claims remain contested and in Chapter 4 - *Widening Participation in Higher Education and Social Class - The 'mystery' of unchanging levels of engagement.* Irene Brew-Riverson analyses part of the DFES 2003 White Paper 'The Future of Higher Education', which deals with the expansion of Higher Education to meet the needs of the United Kingdom (UK). The promotion of Foundation Degrees as viable and supposedly valuable alternative higher education qualifications is a central part of the analysis. The key policy discourse of widening access is presented as one that has resulted in the increased participation of students from professional backgrounds - eighty percent study for a degree (Galindo-Rueda cited in Reay, David and Ball, 2005) whilst only fifteen percent of people from unskilled backgrounds are so engaged. The issue of a more appropriate 'habitus' (Bourdieu cited in Bowl, 2003) for middle and upper class families is cited as one of the reasons for the continuing improvements in engagement amongst the privileged to the disadvantage of those less privileged. The positioning of students as consumers in the higher education market place with the responsibility for their own success (Leathwood, 2003) is interrogated in the light of the fundamental lack of a level playing field because of the complexities that characterise the lives of many non-traditional entrants into the higher education sphere. The Labour Government's neoliberal stance is presented as an abdication of responsibility from a social -justice perspective on issues such as the payment of tuition fees and the kinds of institutions available to those from more non-traditional backgrounds. The concept of stakeholder analysis using the dimensions of power and interest (Mendelow, 1991 cited in Johnson, Scholes and Whittington, 2006) is used to critically examine the political context within which policy is developed. It sheds light upon the reason why some stakeholder voices are not articulated. The chapter ends with an analysis of the effects of Lord Browne's review and proposals for the HE sector.

The book now moves on to policy in relation to creativity in business and on the curriculum for medical undergraduates, and the impact in H.E. In Chapter 5 –

Education, Creativity and the Media: an analysis of the ideology of the Cox Review Stephen Colwell analyses the ideological stance of the Cox Review of Creativity in Business. He also uses Schumpeter's analysis of the decline of capitalism and a contemporary reading of Hegelian Historicism to argue that the elevation of the 'global competition narrative' and the promotion of business as the primary source of policy wisdom, direction and management of creativity represents a rationale that legitimises contingent and, by extension, de-legitimises absolute individual creative autonomy. He argues that by 2005 New Labour had moved decisively from its initial approach of encouraging creativity as a social good to fully embrace neoliberal hegemonic rationality expressed in an exploitation model of power relationships between 'Creatives' and Business articulated by the Cox Review. Colwell argues that Cox represents an ideology that potentially drives out those things that cannot be justified in commercial terms and articulates an entrenchment of subordination of the individual which shifts an already unequal power relationship decisively in favour of established commercial and political elites that advance a neoliberal agenda. Within this context the implications for Communication Media are explored with specific regard for the importance of individual autonomy for the functioning of a democratic public sphere.

In Chapter 6 - *The Industrialisation of Medical Education?* Dr. Sophie Park, a medical doctor, presents a critical analysis of the most recent revision of Tomorrow's Doctors (TD), published by the General Medical Council (GMC) in September 2009. TD details the curriculum to be taught throughout all undergraduate medical schools in the UK and is likely to have further impact internationally. In defining the curriculum (and indeed to what extent this is made explicit and standardised), this policy has enormous power both in its choices of delivery and content, to define the nature and purpose of medical education and evolving forms of 'professionalism'. The chapter begins by describing the relationships between various stakeholders involved in the consultation process and policy construction. It outlines the role of the General Medical Council (GMC) and explores competing perspectives on the curricula's core values and components for patients, the profession, and students. The changing nature of the NHS as employer and as a resource for medical education amid wider political change and privatisation is also discussed. Using Ball's context of influence, the chapter then seeks to critique the principles and qualities of some evolving and existing discourses which have shaped the new TD document. Using Wittgenstein's notion of 'linguistic philosophy' to explore the nature and function of language, the chapter next uses textual examples from consultation and TD policy material, to highlight examples of neoliberal influence and discusses how this might change the nature and definition of medical professionalism, both at undergraduate and postgraduate level. Finally, Park uses the context of political strategy to propose a breath for reflection, urging the reader to make a conscious choice in their use of language to support a particular discourse and hegemony within their professional context. While acknowledging Aristotle's dilemma between the abstract and particular nature of policy, or phronesis, this chapter urges readers to resist the temptation to over-stipulate the possible aspects of the particular, at the expense of facilitating space for the lesser-known, but essential aspects of professional practice.

In the *Afterword* Mike Apple assesses how professionals in the public sector can challenge the widening gap between the ruling class and the masses by replacing the language of the market with the language of equity, democracy and inclusivity.

What the chapters and the policies they analyse divulge is that New Labour did nothing to reverse the trends that had been set in motion in the 1980s. In fact the reforms set Britain on a neoliberal road. Whilst having to appeal to a middle ground of voters over the last 20 odd years, it is evident that the increased comfort and wealth of the middle classes, who have supported the Third Way, have left the voices of those less fortunate unheard. Consequently the effects of New Labour's policies on the social justice agenda have been catastrophic, paving the way for the new conservative/lib dem coalition which echoes the Thatcher/ Reagan politics of the 1970's and 80's with cuts to public services, the dismantling of the welfare state, the privatisation of key services such as education and health and the demise of collective opposition through Trade Unions.

This book provides a valuable review of the processes and time when British policy was being transformed. It is needed at this time as academia is being indoctrinated by the performativity driven culture, no longer allowing the space and time for the kind of in depth text analysis which is essential for the understanding of political and social trends and movements. It behoves us to raise questions that will provoke more thinking as to why the obvious reasons may not be the only ones behind, for example, the lack of social mobility and the yawning gap between the haves and have-nots in our society. Now is the time when educators, practitioners and policy makers need to be encouraged to move away from the prescriptive policy of neoliberalism, with its limited opportunities for social relations and the 'loss of public space for democratic interchange' (Monahan, 2005:152, in Ball, 2008) and to take up the challenge, of working together, with education as a dialogue between people and communities (Apple, 2006).

NOTES

[i] Neoliberalism is increasingly making headway in Asia as well. For an example on the effects of globalisation and neoliberalism on India see Lall and Nambissan (2011).

REFERENCES:

Ball, S.J. (1993). Education markets, choice and social class: The market as a class strategy in the UK and the USA. *British Journal of Sociology of Education, 14*(1), 3–19.

Ball, S. J. (1994). *Education Reform.* Buckingham: Open University Press.

Ball, S.J. (2007). *Education plc.* Oxon: Routledge.

Ball, S. J. (2008). *The Education Debate.* Bristol: The Policy Press.

Bartlett, L., Frederick, M., Gulbrandsen, T., & Murillo, E. (2002). The marketization of education: public schools for private ends. *Anthropology and Education Quarterly, 33*(1), 1–25.

Blair, T., (1998). *The Third Way: New Politics for a New Century.* London: The Fabian Society.

Brenner, N., Peck, J., & Theodore, N. (2010). Variegated neoliberalisation: Geographie, modalities and pathways. *Global Networks, 10*(2), 182–222.

Brown, & Lauder. (2003). *Globalisation and the Knowledge Economy: Some Observations on Recent Trends in Employment, Education and the Labour Market.* Cardiff: University of Cardiff.

Bowe, R., Ball, S. J., & Gold, A. (1992). *Reforming Education & Changing Schools.* London: Routledge.

Dale, R. (1989). *The State and Education Policy.* Milton Keynes: Open University Press.

Fairclough. (2000). *New Labour, New Language?* London: Routledge.

Gamarnikow, E. (2009). Education in network society: Critical reflection. In R. Cowen & A. M. Kazamias (Eds.), *International Handbook of Comparative Education* (Vol. 1, pp. 619–631). London: Springer.

Gibton. (2011, September). A Sociopolitical Analysis on ten years of education policy legislation in England: Senior policy maker's views. Presentation at BERA, Institute of Education, University of London.

Giroux, H. A. (2002). Neoliberalism, corporate culture, and the promise of higher education: The university as a democratic public sphere. *Harvard Educational Research, 72*(4), 425–463.

Harvey, D. (2005). *A Brief History of Neoliberalism.* Oxford: OUP.

Harris, S. (2007). *The Governance of Education: How Neo-liberalism is Transforming Policy and Practice.* London & New York: Continuum. Hayek (1944).

Hill, D. & Rosskam, E. (Eds.). (2008). *The Developing World and State Education: Neoliberal Depredation and Egalitarian Alternatives.* Routledge.

Lall, M., & Nambissan, G. (2011). *Education and Social Justice in the Era of Globalisation – Perspectives from India and the UK.* New Delhi: Routledge.

Leathwood, C. (2004). A critique of institutional inequalities in higher education: (or an alternative to hypocrisy for higher education policy). *Theory and Research in Education, 2*(1), 31–48.

McGregor, G. (2009). Educating for (whose) success? Schooling in an age of neoliberalism. *British Journal of Sociology of Education, 30*(3), 345–358.

Olssen, M., & Peters, M. A. (2005). Neoliberalism, higher education and the knowledge economy: From the free market to knowledge capitalism. *Journal of Education Policy, 20*(3), 313–345.

Reay, D., David, M., & Ball, S. (2001). Making a difference?: Institutional habituses and higher education. [Online]. *Sociological Research Online, 5*(4). Available at: http://socresonline.org.uk/5/4/reay.html

Reay, D. (2006). The zombie stalking English schools: Social class and educational inequality. *British Journal of Educational Studies, 54*(3), 288–307.

Verger, T. (2008). *Cuando la Educación Superior se Convierte en Mercancía. Hacia una Explicación del Fenómeno de la Mercantilización en las Universidades.* Barcelona: Observatori del Deute en la Globalització.

Wolf, A. (2002). *Does Education Matter?* London: Penguin Book.

Marie Lall
Reader in Education and South Asian Studies,
Institute of Education, University of London

JULIA PÜSCHEL & BORIS VORMANN

1. GREY ZONES OF THE MARKET

Public Services, Education Policies, and Neoliberal Reform in the United Kingdom

Beginning in the late 1970s, the restructuring of public services in general and the reform of education systems in particular has been the object of policy initiatives in most North Atlantic countries. Following the legitimation crisis of the Fordist-Keynesian mode of regulation, national governments have sought to prioritise the market as an instrument for economic distribution and accumulation (Bonal 2003). The objective of minimising public expenditures under the constraints of fiscal austerity as well as under the impact of a new free-market orthodoxy have led to a re-casting of the role of the state in the provision and funding of public services (Dale 2000). The creation of a 'small, strong state' – to view unfold from afar the new ethos of choice, freedom, and competitiveness – has produced its own contradictions (Gamble 1988, Sassen 2006). Particularly in those fields where the neoliberal ideal of free markets could only be approximated by "quasi-markets" (Levačić 1995), schisms between public rhetoric and social reality become most obvious.

Using Stephen Ball's 'Policy Cycle' as an analytical tool this chapter examines the grey zones of neoliberal market theory with a particular emphasis on the UK model (Ball 1992). The first section outlines the basic tenets of neoliberal theory and examines its implications for public services and education policies. Based on the foundational texts of neoliberal theory (Friedman, van Hayek) – which, themselves, were produced in a specific, locatable context (*context of influence*) – we emphasise the historical and geo-political specificity of neoliberalisation processes, their *context of policy text production*. Public services and, more specifically, education policies appear as compromises in free market theory – as quasi-markets. After addressing the emergence of neoliberalism as a hegemonic discourse from the fringes of public policy debates and outlining its fundamental principles, we discuss the development of public services in the UK during the initial phase of 'roll-back' neoliberalism (Brenner et al. 2010). The second part of the chapter examines educational policies in the *context of practice* and *context of outcomes*. Drawing on neoliberal theory as posited in its foundational texts, as well as on real political shifts in the United Kingdom, two central categories

Marie Lall (ed.), Policy, Discourse and Rhetoric: How New Labour Challenged Social Justice and Democracy, 15–40.

are identified for an analytical assessment of educational policies and their contradictions: 'Competition & Choice' and 'Managerial Re-Organisation.'

THE HISTORICITY OF NEOLIBERAL THEORY

In contrast to 'globalisation processes' – an analytical category to grasp the historical rise in the mobility of people, goods, capital and information as well as the relativisation of nation-state power – neoliberalism is best conceptualised as a set of theoretical assumptions about individuals and society which envisions and asserts a certain role for the political vis-à-vis an abstract and seemingly universal category: the market. Despite its claims for universality, the theoretical fundament on which neoliberalism rests is deeply grounded in history, building largely on 19th century English free-trade and laissez-faire economics (Palley 2004, 1). The dominance of liberalism waned in the 20th century when the size of government was considerably enlarged due to the drastic setbacks of the Great Depression that suddenly unveiled the shortcomings of unregulated markets. Advocating a more active role of the state in stabilising the economy by stimulating and managing aggregate demand with macroeconomic tools, the theories of John Maynard Keynes set up the frame for Fordist growth after World War II. Based on a nexus of mass consumption and mass production, economic growth in Europe and North America rested on a compromise between capital and labour which found its institutional materialisation in the Welfare State. With the disintegration of the Fordist model that resulted from a slowdown in productivity growth and the failure of reconciling high profit rates and high wages during the 1970s, a more conservative strand gained momentum (see Eichengreen 2007: 252; Brenner & Theodore 2008: 2f.).

It is important to underline that the surge of neoliberalism from the fringes of public policy debates was historically contingent. Some methodological clarifications might be useful at this point. The notion of contextual determinancy, which goes beyond a simple binary concept of structure and agency, guides our methodological framework for this chapter. We use Stephen Ball's 'Policy Cycle' as a matrix for our argument.[2] In a first step, we discern the 'context of influence' in order to identify the central struggles for the emergence of the neoliberal discourse as the hegemonic paradigm, and examine how these ideological presuppositions are translated in situational contexts of policy text production. The second part of this chapter deals with different contexts of practice, mainly by outlining parallels and divergences of Conservative and New Labour policies, leading to partially contradictory contexts of outcomes and, an aspect we analyse to a lesser degree, contexts of political strategy (Bowe, Ball & Gold 1992; Ball 1994; Lall 2007).

The context of influence of neoliberalism's foundational texts is reflected in their key presumptions. Some of neoliberalism's underlying suppositions can only be identified as such if one takes into account the context in which they came to undermine the Fordist compromise of capital and labour. Gaining wide-spread influence only in the crises of the 1970s, Friedrich August van Hayek's 1944 book 'the Road to Serfdom' was an acrimonious criticism of totalitarianism and of what he saw as a tendency of socialism: a drift into despotism. In the Cold War context, Milton Friedman's understanding of 'Capitalism and Freedom' (1962), was influenced by his deep-seated mistrust for central planning and government intervention. Like van Hayek, Friedman understood the market as a superior means of coordinating interests – a rationale that stresses the inevitable lack of knowledge of central planners. Not only did governments seem to assume responsibilities that curtailed individual freedom: they endangered democracy through the centralisation of both political and economic power. In England, Friedman's arguments were echoed in pamphlets published by authors of the New Right who deemed the market the "best device for registering individual preferences and allocating resources to satisfy them" (Harris & Seldon 1979, 5 cited in Gewirtz 2002, 9). In sum, these pamphleteers highlighted the notion of consumer sovereignty as their prime guiding principle (Gewirtz 2002, 9).

Harking back to Mendeville's fable of the bee, to utilitarian conceptions of the rational, utility-maximizing actor, and to Adam Smith's classical notion of the 'invisible hand', van Hayek, Friedman, and other neoliberal proponents consequently refuted the role that Keynes had assigned to the state, and reemphasised the perils of state-power and the paramount importance of (economic and individual) freedom (Palley 2004, 4). Resulting from these considerations, a set of economic policies was moulded into a theory of neoliberalism that needs to be viewed as the point of origin for the production of policy texts and that David Harvey defines as

> [...] a theory of political economic practices that proposes that human well-being can best be advanced by liberating individual entrepreneurial freedoms and skills within an institutional framework characterised by strong private property rights, free markets, and free trade. (Harvey 2005, 2)

What is described by the notion of neoliberalisation processes, then, is an increased reliance on the market in the most diverse fields of social practice; a shift in the public-private divide toward the latter (Sassen 2006). More precisely this has meant the liberalisation of trade, the privatisation of publicly owned companies and the deregulation of financial, labour and product markets.

This line of thought gained momentum when Friedrich August von Hayek and Milton Friedman won the Nobel Prize in 1974 and 1976 respectively, when American think tanks pushed for the neoliberal revolution, and when the crises of the 1970s (OPEC oil crisis, stagflation, fiscal austerity) called into question the meaningfulness of Keynesian economic policies and urged for alternatives. In the British context, the education system was seen as both a symptom of and, as we

17

discuss further below, an antidote to these crises. More deep-seated structural adjustment problems arising in the midst of economic restructuring and post-Fordist, global production systems had redirected attention toward the education system (Gewirtz 2002, 10f.).

The successful imposition of neoliberal strategies in the United Kingdom and the United States under Margaret Thatcher and Ronald Reagan – the neoliberal roll-back of Keynesian institutions – is a story similarly well-documented and analysed as is the international projection of neoliberal doctrine through powerful institutions and organisations (Brenner et al. 2010, Harvey 2005).[3] Rather than to its historical trajectory, however, we should pay closer attention to the implications that neoliberalism bears for the role of government. This is not only a theoretical task, although neoliberal ideology suggests that its truth claims are universally verifiable, as Pierre Bourdieu has argued and as can be witnessed in the all-out reliance on the market as a neutral, unhistorical and efficient instrument for resource allocation (Bourdieu 1998).[4] Neoliberalisation processes are determined in the political field – in the contexts of policy text production and the context of practice – even though the retrenchment of the state creates constraints that, in turn, delimit the state's capacity to act. The precise form of neoliberalism's 'ecological dominance', as Jessop and Sum put it, has depended just as much on extra-economic factors such as political culture, pre-existing institutions, and historical power relations (Jessop & Sum 2006, 284). In sum, neoliberal development has been contested and institutional settings have created local and national path dependencies for its trajectory.

While the 'state' has a certain (clearly limited) role in neoliberal *theory*, its function in different political landscapes can differ quite dramatically. It suffices to point to the different Welfare traditions of the decentralised Anglo-Saxon, 'liberal' systems, and the centralised, 'corporatist-statist' Welfare types in continental Europe (Esping-Andersen 1990), or, for that matter, to the different educational traditions (McLean 1995, Karsten 1999) in order to understand the concept of 'variegated neoliberalisation' (Brenner et al. 2010). While a state's point of origin differs – and hence does its development under neoliberalism – its new role denotes a re-orientation in a new context of liberalised global competition. The 'competitive state,' to use Cerny's (1997) terminology, has to "facilitate a regulative framework in which the national economy can compete in the international market [...]" (Bonal 2003, 163).

The Welfare State, developed in the context of a *national* totality, has come under attack in globalisation processes that re-direct the efforts and objectives of societies with a view to the global as the "broadest horizon of action" (Jessop 2003, 4). International competitiveness becomes the central determining goal of public and economic policy leading to a commodification of those elements of the public realm that had been shielded from global market forces during the Fordist era, such as public health, education, and infrastructure (Cerny 1997). International competitiveness, as Xavier Bonal argues, has been achieved "by developing internal competitive modes of governance" so that the "[d]istribution of goods and services and modes of public administration are now guided by the adoption of market mechanisms within the state" (Bonal 2003, 163).

In the provision or financing of these goods and services, the role of the state also differs according to the challenge at hand. It should not be forgotten that despite the ideal of marketisation, the neoliberal state, too, is tacitly supposed to meet a plethora of tasks. Its fundamental role is that of providing an institutional framework guaranteeing "the quality and integrity of money," as well as the functioning of the market and to set up those "military, defence, police, and legal structures and functions required to secure private property rights" (Harvey 2005, 2). In addition to these tasks, the neoliberal state has assumed a new role as a coordinator for the provision of public goods and services – the grey zones of market theory and neoliberalism.

Public Services and 'Market Failures'

Public goods and services are broadly defined as serving a *public interest.* [5] In this understanding it is the purpose – serving the 'public interest' – that is essential, not the provider which can generally be either, the government or private actors (see e.g. OECD 2008).[6] The duties and capacities of the Welfare State are, themselves, by no means clearly defined – and depend as much on the pre-existing (institutionalized) political culture of a society as on the degree of importance attributed to the market after neoliberal reform.[7] As public goods and services are commonly defined by their objective, and not the apparatus of provision: what exactly constitutes a *public interest?* Obviously, a definition is subject to debate. As Newman and Clarke have noted, "things, sites, people, ideas […] are not permanently or intrinsically public: their construction as public matters involves political struggles to make them so" and, as a consequence, certain goods and services "may also be de-publicised, and de-politicised" (Newman and Clarke 2009, 3).

Agreeing that a certain good or service does serve a public interest does not imply an agreement on the appropriate organisational design for providing this good or service. According to Adam Smith's notion of the 'invisible hand,' markets can be an efficient mechanism of provision – justifying their superiority in the allocation of resources in many fields. However, in the case of so-called market failures, necessary assumptions of the first and second theorems of welfare economics – which express the belief in the efficiency of market allocations – are violated. In other words, for these specific cases, unregulated markets are not the most adept mode of resource allocation so that state intervention is justified. Generally, *market failures* are presumed to include *externalities, information asymmetries, market power,* and *public goods* – which are often interrelated.

In order to overcome these failures governments can make use of various instruments such as state ownership and public procurement, regulation and subsidies. Let us briefly look at those types of market failure that will re-appear in our discussion of neoliberal education reform that is *externalities*, and *information asymmetries*. *Externalities* are benefits or costs that occur to a third party which did not engage in an economic transaction. Thus, the overall benefits or costs are not fully reflected in prices and the market mechanism fails.[8] Another assumption for the efficient operation of (perfectly competitive) markets is that of complete information. Buyers and sellers are aware of all relevant pieces of information about the quality and the price of the product. However, in reality there are often *information asymmetries*, with one party knowing more than the other party, which hampers informed decisions and consequently contradicts the notion of a rational actor (Stiglitz 2000, 80f.).[9]

Although these market failures are widely acknowledged, handling them has remained a matter of interpretation and creed. The Great Depression of the 1930s has generally shifted political opinion towards greater acknowledgement of market failures. This broad consensus started to erode during the late 1960s. A set of theoretical and, more importantly, empirical contributions from economic and political scientists at the University of Chicago, which we have already referred to, increasingly cast doubt on the taken-for-granted notion of the 'benevolent dictator.' Public officials, too, started to be seen as individual utility-maximisers in public choice theory, so that the possibility of government failures through conflicting individual interests was highlighted. From this vantage point, it would depend on the assumed scope of each failure, whether government intervention in 'failing' markets would actually enhance efficiency (Stiglitz 2000, 6f.). While these arguments have, indeed, led to caricature postures, pitting market fanaticism against state-adhering doctrine,[10] in practice, the UK Conservative governments of the 1980s and 1990s as well as New Labour, have leaned toward the former stance, taking the predominant view of strongly criticising the inefficiency and inertia of government bureaucracy (Clark 2002, 774f.).

Despite the elusiveness of the concept of the public interest and how it can be attained, discursive tendencies in longer historical periods can be more readily identified so that notions of what is 'public' and what is not become more visible when we contrast different contexts of policy text production, i.e. Keynesian vs. Post-Fordist, or different contexts of practice, i.e. specific government agendas. This is true, also, for the analysis of developments in the United Kingdom.

Famously – or notoriously, depending on political taste – Margaret Thatcher claimed that there "is no such thing as society, only individual men and women and their families." Accordingly, the scope of what was understood to constitute a public interest was relatively narrow and provision and funding of previously public goods and services was 'rolled back' during the Thatcher era (Brenner et al. 2010). Martin McLean and Natalia Voskresenskaya have emphasised 'privatisation' as a central component of Thatcher's approach to reform. It is worth quoting their assessment in full length as it succinctly links political orientations to policy action under Thatcher:

> Privatization involved 'rolling back' the state by disbanding agencies in the economic spheres, including nationalized productive enterprises such as gas and electricity, and reducing the power of allocation over social benefits in health, education, public housing, and legal services of inter-mediary 'gatekeeping' bodies. Individual choice was to be paramount as constraints on direct dealings between consumers and producers were removed. (McLean & Voskresenskaya 1992, 76f.)[11]

The emphasis on privatisation as well as the significant impact of public choice theory in Thatcher's policy decisions has contributed to the general perception of the United Kingdom as a "classic case of doctrinaire neoliberalism" (Clark 2002, 774). Under New Labour the commitment to the social and the 'public' resurged, at least rhetorically. This was mirrored in a different approach towards public goods and services with the public interest being, again, defined in broader terms. This putative re-expansion of the public, however, did not signify a return to 'Old Labour,' to socialist principles, or to the model of the Keynesian Welfare State. The "modernizing government" initiative under Tony Blair's government explicitly emphasised market efficiency, consumer choice, and competition in its reform of public services (Clark 2002, 775).

The new pro-market stance and rhetoric stressing government failure has created a new approach to these grey zones of the market – which is by no means as clear-cut as it might seem. A cacophony of key terms has held the public policy debate hostage since the first reforms in the 1980s. Newman and Clarke list "[...] efficiency and effectiveness, activation, personalisation, partnership, markets, social enterprise, social justice, choice, citizens, consumers, good governance, contestability, globalization, devolution, localism, the public service ethos, multiculturalism, diversity and inequality" as the buzzwords of neoliberal public service reform (Newman & Clarke 2009, 8f.). Depending on political backgrounds these terms have been combined in improbable ways: "for example, when contestability, competition and choice are seen to address diverse needs, remedy inequality and promote social justice." (Newman & Clarke 2009, 8) The Third Way, which New Labour has taken under Tony Blair, has found its own way of recombining these concepts and approaches. As Blair stated "choice must be extended 'from the few to the many' as part of a politics of egalitarianism." (Newman & Clarke 2009, 8f.) What New Labour, in its specific inflection of neoliberal reform, has done was to re-imagine the public as a "diverse public" including "different 'communities', different cultures, and different socio-demographic groups who may have different interests" (Clarke 2004, 39). New Labour's affirmation of difference and its stance on the citizen-as-consumer – a continuation from the Conservative governments – have reshuffled the public's understanding of its interest with an outspoken emphasis on marketisation, consumer choice, and community responsibility.

The 'big society' as envisioned by the coalition of Conservatives and Liberal Democrats that took power in May 2010 can in many ways be seen as an extension of neoliberal reform strategies taken in the public sector since the 1980s. In the very same month in 2010, the BBC reported that Prime Minister Cameron regarded the state as "'often too inhuman and clumsy'" to "tackle the country's social problems." (BBC 2010) In the course of his electoral campaign and upon his accession as Prime Minister, Cameron praised instead the 'big society,' "based around encouraging greater personal and family responsibility and community activism" (BBC 2010). Michael R. Krätke, a German commentator has called the measures instituted in 2010 the "most drastic austerity package in British history"[12] (Krätke 2010, 13). Public investments on the local and community level have been cut by 100 and 74 percent respectively – and while elementary and secondary education seems to be spared from cutbacks (except for the reduction of investments in school buildings), financial state support for higher education has been reduced by 40 percent and the budget for research has been frozen (Krätke 2010, 14).

The following section fleshes out the assumptions underlying these latest developments in education reform in the United Kingdom and looks more precisely at the contexts of outcomes as well as contradictory policy strategies, with a primary focus on New Labour. As in public services in general, continuities and changes of the Third Way vis-à-vis the politics of roll-back neoliberalism under Thatcher can be outlined. In order to understand the particular inflections of policies since New Labour – which we analyse with an emphasis on the two key aspects 'Competition & Choice,' and 'Managerial Re-Organisation' – we need to remind ourselves that education policies and systems are intimately connected to factors such as a given (national and international) economic structure and division of labour, world beliefs and ideology, as well as pedagogical and didactic trends – in other words, their specific historical and logical contexts.

NEOLIBERAL EDUCATION REFORM

In Europe and North America, the role assigned to education has changed quite significantly over the course of the past three centuries – and so has the role of state policies vis-à-vis the education system. From Jean-Jacques Rousseau's Emile – granting age-appropriate education for young boys and viewing children as distinct from adults – to the beginnings of mass education in the 19th century, education always implied a historical world view and was, in this sense, always political. While Rousseau's pupil was supposed to develop into a mature, rational adult, ready to thrive in 'civilisation' and to enter a social contract to provide political stability for society, mass education in public school systems established by the state was a means of achieving social cohesion amidst the societal upheavals of industrial capitalism. As an instrument of discursive power, school book historiography cemented the fragmentary tendencies of modernity and spread the founding myths and 'invented traditions' of the nation-state, while at the same time primary education – literacy and calculus – created a flexible and individualised national labour force, capable of running the industrial machinery (Hobsbawm & Ranger 1983; Gellner 2006).

At the turn of the 20th century, mass education was extended beyond primary schooling in order to enhance the economic productivity of the work force. In Western industrial nations, most notably the United States, Britain and Germany, Claudia Goldin notes, the "novel concern [...] was that post literacy training could make the ordinary office worker, bookkeeper, stenographer, retail clerk, machinist, mechanic, shop-floor worker, and farmer more productive, and that it could make the difference between an economic leader and a laggard." (Goldin 2001, 264) This new emphasis was followed by a geo-political restructuring of societies in the last two decades of the 20th century – commonly referred to as a new wave of 'globalisation,' a partial de-construction of the nation-state and a transition to a 'knowledge-based' economy – which has instigated yet another view of the role and purpose of education.

The crises of the Keynesian model in Western industrialised countries during the 1970s led to the questioning of a political consensus about education policies which had been forged roughly a decade earlier. In 1962, even under a Conservative government, British local authorities were still obliged to pay for full-time students' tuition fees and to financially support their living expenses (Bates 2010). By contrast, in the mid-1980s, the widespread ideal of the "malleable society," the notion that equality of outcomes could be approximated, most notably through the positive impacts of "constructive" mass education, was jettisoned and, particularly in Anglo-Saxon countries, replaced by "more economically oriented educational management theories" (Karsten 1999, 307). From the Keynesian state which assumed the "full responsibility for the protection of national citizens" emerged the neoliberal state where international competitive advantage was matched by internal flexibilisation (Bonal 2003, 162f.).

With regards to primary and secondary education, Sjoerd Karsten has noted a discursive shift that occurred in the mid-1980s in Dutch scholarly and professional debates from an interest in pupils' "equality of opportunity" to their "performances," and, what is more than that, to the performance of schools (Karsten 1999, 307f.). In contrast to the Netherlands, debates in the UK as well as in the United States and Western Germany took an even more decisive neoliberal orientation during that time. There, a new discourse on the implementation of "market-type mechanisms" (e.g. school fees, inter-school competition, shift to private education, school choice), and the reinforcement of traditional values and classroom discipline (especially under Thatcher's national curricula) emerged (Karsten 1999, 309).

In higher education, 'globalisation' urged national governments to re-position their work force through an educational expansion. This happened in the light of a new appreciation of 'knowledge' – the notion that the "most important economic development of our lifetime has been the rise of a new system for creating wealth, based no longer on muscle but on mind" (Toffler 1990, 9). Universities were seen as key drivers in this new type of economy, the 'knowledge economy,' and around the globe higher education expanded even more strongly than primary and secondary education (Olssen & Peters 2005). In industrialised countries, college and university education lost its elitist exclusivity over the course of the 20th century and, at least in theory, it became universally accessible (Altbach 2005, 20). As a consequence of this global expansion of education systems, while in 1900, approximately 500,000 students were profiting from higher education world-wide, in 2011, roughly 1.8 million students were enrolled in higher education in the United Kingdom alone (Schofer & Meyer 2005; British Council 2011). In knowledge-based economies, where, according to the Organisation for Economic Co-operation and Development (OECD), "the production, diffusion and use of technology and information are key to economic activity and sustainable growth" (OECD 1999, 7), education has become an economic product, to be exchanged on the global market place.[13]

Depending on the context of practice, neoliberal reforms of education systems, both in primary/secondary and higher education have centred on a series of core themes. They include the expansion of market elements in the education sector, an emphasis on choice and competition as well as the decentralisation of educational bureaucracies through the devolution of responsibilities to other scales and entities – while at the same time the state has expanded its role of administering and managing education from a distance (Whitty et al. 1998, 3). In our categorisation of neoliberal education reform, which discusses these trends in detail, we conceptually distinguish primary/secondary education and higher education because of their different role in and for society. We also discern a causal, reciprocal relationship between neoliberal policies, as the dominant mode of globalisation since the 1980s, and their results; the interplay of neoliberal principles, policy, and performance.

The common denominator in this development is *efficiency* and the belief that the public interest could be achieved at lower costs by reducing bureaucratic intervention. Two key aspects of neoliberal education reform are highlighted, which characterise – as defining moments or as inevitable and sometimes even contradictory by-products – the pursuit of efficiency by schools and institutions of higher education. The section 'Competition & Choice' examines the logic of increased competition in primary/secondary and higher education and contrasts it to unintended outcomes, namely the potential persistence of stratification, whereas the section 'Managerial Re-Organisation' analyses the retrenchment of the state, the coinciding increase in performance-testing, and the contradictory consequences vis-à-vis New Labour's concept of diversity.

Competition & Choice

Milton Friedman argued for the introduction of more educational choice and competition in order to improve the efficiency of the education system. His idea was that 'producers,' in this case educational institutions, would have an incentive to improve and innovate in order to provide their services at the lowest costs possible and/or the highest quality because 'consumers' would otherwise opt for another 'product.' At the same time, the 'paternalistic' state could be held at bay (Friedman 1962, 103-105). In many education systems, *competition* between educational institutions for 'customers' has hence been introduced by coupling the funding received to the number of pupils/students attracted (*per capita funding*). According to this rationale, educational institutions would become "more responsive to their clients and either [...] more effective or go to the wall." (Whitty & Power 2000, 97f.) In the 1988 Education Reform Act for England and Wales, which took effect in 1989, schools' funding was similarly coupled to the number of 'customers' they attract so that "schools were effectively reconfigured as small businesses [...]." (Gewirtz 2002, x)

In contrast to primary and secondary education, the striving for competitiveness in higher education transcended national borders. In a quasi-market driven by global forces, universities began to compete not only for students from the region or nation, but have attempted to attract more and more foreign students (Arnove, 2003, 2, cited in Denman 2005, 13). This has had quantifiable consequences: While in 1980, 56,003 international students were enrolled at universities in the United Kingdom, the number leaped from 77,800 to 197,188 from 1990 to 1994 and to 213,000 in 1999 (Welch 2001, 479). According to the OECD, this trend continued in the 2000s, when the number of non-citizen students enrolled in the United Kingdom constantly climbed from 364,271 in 2004 to 462,609 in 2008 (OECD 2011).[14]

In this system of increased competition, the question of who was to provide the funds for education has been at the core of numerous debates. Different views on the necessity of public funding have depended largely on the assumed private and social benefits from education. Proponents of a higher degree of private funding have tended to emphasise the private benefits of education. This view was intricately linked to certain expectations of the curriculum: If "employability" and "economic productivity" of competitive, rational actors, was to be the key goal, education would need to shift its focus from "developing the well-rounded liberally educated person" and to be "more concerned with developing the skills required for a person to become an economically productive member of society." (Hursh

2005, 5) Yet, if employability was the main objective, then why not marketise the entire education system, including primary and secondary education?

The reason that even Milton Friedman acknowledged is that education can incur positive externalities which yield social benefits beyond private returns. The relation between private and social benefits from education is usually seen to differ along the distinction between lower and higher education. In primary and secondary education social benefits, such as the promotion of social cohesion, are generally accepted to be of more importance than private ones. As, in higher education, private benefits tend to be seen as relatively more important, a lower level of public funding seems justified from this perspective. Following Milton Friedman, then, the state should play a smaller role in funding higher education, especially with regards to vocational and professional schooling:

> It [vocational and professional schooling] is a form of investment in human capital precisely analogous to investment in machinery, buildings, or other forms of non-human capital. Its function is to raise the economic productivity of the human being. If it does so, the individual is rewarded in a free enterprise society by receiving a higher return for his services than he would otherwise be able to command. (Friedman 1962, 100f.)

In addition to private returns from higher education, proponents of private funding have argued that public funding collected from taxes would redistribute "[...] resources from low income to (future) high income taxpayers and is therefore regressive." (Greenaway & Haynes 2003, 160) This argument is based on the demographic composition of students and the observation that mainly students from high-income families attend universities (Greenaway & Hayes 2003, 155).

Along these lines, the New Labour government introduced means-tested tuition fees for universities in England, Wales and Northern Ireland in 1998.[15] Tuition fees replaced public funding and were initially set at £1,000 per annum. They were not allowed to differ across universities, subjects or students (Greenaway & Hayes 2003, 161). However, it turned out that the resulting amount of funding was not sufficient and that it led to the "[...] steady impoverishment of universities [...]" (Desai 2005, xiii). Therefore, in a second step of privatisation, the Higher Education Bill 2004 replaced the system of *fixed* tuition fees (which in the meantime had augmented to £1,125 per annum) with one of *variable* fees between £0 and £3,000. This system was supplemented by loans provided by the government, which had to be paid back once a student earned more than £15,000 a year (Bates 2010). Even more recently, in December 2010, the maximum fee was increased to £9,000 per annum (Mulholland 2010).

In a nutshell, there is a strong consensus, also in the political reality of the United Kingdom today, that primary and secondary education produces positive externalities, while higher education is a matter of private decision that should consequently be paid out of private pockets. While Milton Friedman agreed that additional schooling was, indeed, "a way of providing better social and political leadership," in other words, while it did have positive externalities (Friedman 1962, 88), he highlighted that "[a]t successively higher levels, there is less and less agreement" about the "appropriate content of an educational program for citizens of a democracy" (Friedman 1962, 98).

If we shift our focus to *choice*, as the necessary correlate of *competition*, we can identify certain unintended outcomes and contradictions in educational reform policies. Parental and student choice, as we have mentioned, was supposed to indicate the quality of a given institution. In addition to furthering competition and quality, however, the emphasis on parental choice was also believed to target inequalities. School choice was perceived by many as a prerogative of richer parents as they could have their children enrolled in private schools. If parents were given vouchers, it was argued, parents could send their children into the schools they best saw fit (Thaler & Sunstein 2009, 201).

The same logic dominated arguments in the United Kingdom during the 1980s. There, open enrolment was reinforced through the Education Reform Act of 1988 which redefined "parents as consumers, who – at least in principle – were given the right to choose a school for their child, rather than be allocated one by local authority bureaucrats." (Gewirtz 2002, x) Prior to 1988 pupils had been placed in schools largely according to the area they lived in. British Conservative politician Kenneth Clarke saw this as an advantage to middle- and higher-income families and called this 'selection by mortgage' because the demand for houses in areas with 'good' schools was mirrored in higher house prices.

However, if we examine this particular case more precisely, we can see that 'open enrolment' after 1988 perpetuated rather than mitigated social injustice – not just despite of the move toward the market, but precisely because of it. Even after 1988, schools retained the right to ultimately select their applicants. As a school's test results have also been based on the performance of its students – perhaps more so than on its management – stratification of pupils by ability has persisted. Put differently, choice has existed more for some than for others. For various reasons, the way choice has been realised has depended largely on pre-existing stratification patterns.

Stephen Ball's qualitative contributions have been particularly influential in examining how different parents responded to the choice offered and are illustrative in this context. Choice, he argues, "[…] is predicated on a consumerist vision that is most likely to be embraced by the middle class." (Ball 2003, cited in Walford 2003, 78) Choosing a school involves numerous far-reaching decisions on the part of the parents. Ball argues that parents' motivation to make an informed choice is based on their interest in education and their knowledge about different possibilities. Consequently, the social and cultural capital of middle class families tend to lead to advantages for these families in the selection process. Robertson and Lauder (2001) as well as Reay and Ball (1997) strengthen this argument when they insist that choices are also based on the attempt to avoid anxiety or failure. They argue that working class families may not choose certain schools because they feel misplaced.

In other words, cream-skimming and the differential exercise of parental choice as possible reactions to the introduction of market elements in primary and secondary education have created and perpetuated new cycles of inequality rather than contained social injustice. A further tradeoff between efficiency and social inclusiveness, which we should also mention at this point, can be seen in the development of school communities. There is evidence that parental choice has undermined school engagement, despite the rhetorical focus on communities and individual agency. Since parents have obtained the option of transferring their child to another school if they were dissatisfied, their interest in the specific school and in the broader, national discourse on education has diminished. This development was reinforced as "children and their parents no longer have shared interests with other students and families and, instead, may become competitors for the available openings." (Hursh 2005, 5)

Managerial Re-Organisation

Increasing efficiency through competition went hand in glove with a restructuring of the state and its role in education policies – which was by no means less contradictory.[16] As discussed above, respective measures have been supposed to diminish government funding of goods and services and to reduce government intervention in their provision (Karsten 1999, 313). Quite paradoxically, as a corollary of increased competition and consumer choice, the decentralisation and dispersal of former state capacities has resulted in the multiplied engagement of "more agencies and agents as the proxies of state power" (Clarke 2004, 36).

In primary and secondary education, New Labour has reinforced the move toward privatisation of the educational sector that had been initiated by the Conservatives since the 1980s by deepening private sector involvement in the schools' administration, as initiatives such as the "Private Finance Initiative, Education Action Zones (EAZs) and City Academies" illustrate (Gewirtz 2002, 158). The idea underlying the increased autonomy of educational institutions has been that schools know best how to manage their organisation, that they are responsible for doing so and that they are more effective in doing so (Karsten 1999, 311). Following this logic, the Thatcher and Major governments passed several Education Acts to re-organise the Local Education Authorities (LEAs) which they deemed to possess a monopoly in public education (Whitty & Power 2000, 97). City Technology Colleges (CTCs) were established in the inner cities which functioned independently from the LEA system and were supported by the private sector, while state schools obtained the choice to "opt out" and receive funding directly from the central government as grant-maintained school (GMS), if enough parents agreed (Whitty & Power 2000, 97; Hursh 2005, 9).[17] Local

Management of Schools (LMS) increased budgetary discretion of schools that stayed under the LEA umbrella and rendered their administration more independent (Whitty & Power 2000, 97f.).

New Labour further reduced the importance of LEAs by having the central government fund schools directly. In this context, compliance with the central government's exigencies has increasingly been maintained through "targeted and time-limited" approaches to school funding in what Sharon Gewirtz has called a "contract model of resource allocation" (Gewirtz 2002, 159). In this scheme, schools can obtain funds in addition to the per-capita funding by the LEAs, if they partake in specific government initiatives such as "'specialist schools', 'early excellence centres', 'family literacy schemes' and 'work-related learning' – all of which are only funded for a limited period." (Gewirtz 2002, 159)

If devolution to lower scales of governance has facilitated the management-by-competition of the education system, it has also been a proficient means to overcome the Keynesian state's legitimation crisis, as some authors have noted. A new epistemological emphasis on terms such as 'personal responsibility' or 'community' has reconstructed individuals as "subjects of duties having to demonstrate that they deserve their rights and entitlements," as opposed to "subjects of rights" who are granted certain benefits qua citizenship (Bonal 2003, 167; also Robertson & Dale 2002). While individuals have arguably benefitted as consumers, then, their capacities as citizens have been reduced[18] in the broader context of marketisation – a development that has not been passive, but that needs to be viewed as the result of conscious political decisions, taken precisely because of the stated lack of legitimation. Bonal notes:

> The state attempts to depoliticise education through discursive and policy strategies that emphasise self-responsibility and self-regulation. Schools and communities are told to act as entrepreneurs that, as such, must pursue their own interest in order to be competitive and more efficient. (Bonal 2003, 168)

Institutional autonomy, community involvement and individual responsibility have hence become the regulatory analogue to the retrenchment of the (Keynesian) provider state. What might *prima facie* sound paradoxical is that, in this process of privatisation and marketisation, the minimal state has become a strong manager and coordinator of services, now provided in a complex re-combination of the public and private sector. The managerial stance – applying to the state as much as to educational institutions at various scales and levels – emphasises quality management and accountability mechanisms while the state, at the same time, has divested "non-core activities" (Olssen & Peters 2005, 323f.). By devolving certain responsibilities to lower scales of governance the state assumes new tasks to 'control at a distance.'

This ambivalent move has to be understood in the light of the re-interpretation of the individual as consumer. For him or her to be able to realise the choices offered in the education market, there has to be some kind of standardisation and evaluation of performances in order to mitigate information asymmetries. Individuals must be able to judge the quality of education before having consumed it. Both choice and responsibility have hence been relegated to the capillary ends of the societal hierarchy, urging the individual, as a rational actor, to demand transparency for an informed choice. Referring to the tax-payer/consumer distinction, John Clarke has noted:

> Where the public as taxpayer legitimates the pursuit of efficiency (and economy), the public as consumer legitimates the pursuit of comparability and permanent improvement in standards of service. (Clarke 2004, 40)

For obvious reasons, the extension of governmental control in quality management creates a contradiction as it clashes with neoliberal demands for small government. Neoliberal proponents would argue against bureaucracy, and yet they "are also the most ardent advocates of higher standards and controls, which would be all the more reason for government intervention." (Karsten 1999, 314) What the state has tended to do in order to dissolve – not resolve – this contradiction was to "pass the ball" by "using contractual strategies that position schools and communities as responsible for school performance" and by intervening only in what it has perceived as emergency situations, i.e. the risks emanating from market failures (Bonal 2003, 167f.).

Standardisation and performance testing have produced oxymoronic effects, not just on the administrative configuration of institutions, but also on the pedagogical contents transmitted through the education system. As we have seen, an increase in *diversity* has been implied as a positive effect of consumer choice; especially in the context of Tony Blair's and New Labour's emphasis on 'difference.' As consumers have different needs, the argument went, products offered on the education market should reflect the plurality of postmodern societies. In reality, however, there has been an inherent tension between the ideal of 'diversity' and the increased necessity of 'standardised' testing. In primary and secondary education, testing has tended to streamline curricula and to foster 'test-driven' learning. Quite understandably so: when a school's funding depends on its performance – or better: the performance of its pupils – it is hardly surprising that teaching will adapt and prepare pupils for the tests. Education is then based on learning 'facts' (often derived from the discursively dominant majority group's politico-cultural heritage) and on proficiency in those core subjects that are tested, rather than on broad and diverse learning objectives.[19]

Criticising the effects of quality control on educational institutions, Karsten has noted that systems organised along the lines of total quality management – an instrument borrowed from the corporate world – tend to "stimulate uniformity, bureaucratic regulations and routine methods of work" while hampering "creative adjustments to new target groups, as well as spontaneous improvements in subject material, instructional equipment or learning situations." (Karsten 1999, 314) In other words, evaluating the health of educational institutions and the success of their students on a quantifiable, test-driven basis has had reverse effects on the plurality of contents transmitted in the classrooms. Uniformity and standardisation in a test-centred approach to education has tended to trump pedagogical ideals such as learner-centred learning which would arguably be more suited to match the objective of reflecting societal diversity.[20]

In higher education, a similar trend can be observed. Students have been increasingly prone to focus more on programmes that offer promising career opportunities, a development that has also led to standardisation. Through the introduction and gradual increase of tuition fees, students are obliged to take a rational choice which will make them ready to enter the labour market and enable them to pay back their student loans – even more so in an environment of 'structural unemployment' and given the uncertainty of flexible employment schemes. Because students are clients of the university, they expect to be procured with what they deem necessary and rational for their professional careers. In its online section on education, The Guardian published an article that sums up this debate on the importance of employability for students' disciplinary choice in higher education. Attempting to answer the question whether 'a master's will get you a job,' Lucy Tobin argues that it is "[...] crucial to ensure you're getting the best value for money – not necessarily the cheapest fees, but a place on the course that is most likely to lead to the job you want, at an institution with good industry links, careers advice and student satisfaction levels." (Tobin 2011)[21]

These arguments show how, not only in the United Kingdom, but in most Western nations, we can witness a drifting away from the historical and etymological idea of *universitas* as an institution that refers to the "whole." The emphasis on vocational aspects has created a strait jacket for students, professors, and administrators alike, narrowing and specialising educational objectives. While, in theory, the market provides diversity, as New Labour was keen on insisting, it tends to streamline education, both in primary/secondary and in higher education. In higher education, where the commodification process has been more pronounced, this tension seems to be even more tangible. Perhaps, the online encyclopaedia Wikipedia's entry on "university" is the most insightful source in this respect because it reflects what seems to have become common knowledge. There, a university is defined as a "*corporation* that *provides* both undergraduate education and postgraduate education." (Wikipedia 2011, our emphasis)

CITIZENSHIP OR HUMAN CAPITAL?

Fiscal austerity and budget cuts prompted by the mid-1970 oil shocks raised questions as to whether the Fordist compromise was still tenable and opened up debates on which culprits were to be held responsible for the concurring decline of British industry. The impact of economic restructuring was recognised as a longer-standing, structural re-alignment that British society had to adapt to if it wanted to keep up with its international competitors. Yet, the soul-searching was also introspective and criticism was targeted to no small extent at the state's instability and its failure to manage these changes. Referring to the Centre for Contemporary Cultural Studies' (CCCS) 1981 book *Unpopular Education*, Sharon Gewirtz identifies "at least three sources of social instability" that were blamed as catalysts for the crises at the time: the failure of universities to produce "bright young managers and technicians of a renovated capitalism," a labour force which "in no way behaved as had been hoped [but rather] as dispossessed wage labourers fighting to maintain or increase their share of the value produced", and finally, the schools that were perceived as unable to reign in "conflicts over discipline, curriculum and the handling of informal school cultures." (CCCS 1981, 174, 174/175, 188; cited in Gewirtz 2002, 11). In other words, crises in "capital accumulation, social control and legitimation" fostered an environment generally critical of state institutions and led to a strong discourse that held these institutions responsible for Britain's ailing competitiveness (Gewirtz 2002, 13).

Embedded in a broader discursive and political shift toward entrepreneurialism and marketisation, the introduction of competition and (consumer) choice into formerly 'decommodified' public services coincided with a restructuring of the state. In education, the selective dispersal of responsibilities from the state and its managerial centralisation of performance and quality control have shifted responsibilities between the public and the private. Educational institutions, communities, and the individual were re-defined so as to accommodate 'consumer sovereignty' and, on the flip side of the coin, were to be held responsible for their choices. In this sense, the state deferred its legitimacy deficit by relegating it to lower scales of governance.

We should not be oblivious to the fact that the emergence of neoliberalism as the hegemonic discourse in public policy debates was influenced by locally specific policy decisions and that outcomes did not necessarily correspond to the stated intentions. As Bell reminds us, and as the other chapters in this book show, individual case studies reveal the panoply of contextually determined processes of policy generation, implementation, and outcomes. As to the present chapter, the best examples for the contradictory nature of intentions and results are the schisms between, on the one hand, inclusive choice and stratification, as well as standardisation and diversity on the other. As we have seen, choice, portrayed particularly by New Labour as mitigating social injustice, has led to the unintended persistence of stratification.

Tensions at the core of this system are left unresolved. Can an orientation toward the market in a 'post-industrial' society where pupils and students are pitted against one another and interpellated as value-maximisers from an early age be expected to provide a fertile ground for a community spirit? Put differently: how are pupils and parents supposed to share a common identity – even if this means just within the boundaries of the school premises – if efficiency redefines them as consumers that are to actively pursue their individual needs? Moreover, while the introduction of market elements into the education system were deemed to reflect the diverse nature of educational demands – reflecting, in other words, the different interests, learning behaviours, and talents of pupils and students – the standardisation that has been necessary to mitigate informational asymmetries has tended to streamline pedagogical contents.

One important point which transcends these contradictions remains to be made. If efficiency is the broadest common denominator of neoliberal education reform and if efficiency is understood as the central advantage of markets, a crucial question needs to be answered: *Which end* is efficiency supposed to serve? For efficiency, no matter if provided through the market mechanism or by the state, cannot be an end in itself. Efficient outcomes are defined as those that cannot be attained with a lower input of efforts. If the marketisation and privatisation of the educational system was legitimised as a response to the perceived inadequacies of state institutions to adapt to economic restructuring toward post-industrialism in the 1970s, as Gewirtz reminds us, the unintended outcomes of these policies seem to be ill-matched to 'efficiently' encounter economic restructuring in the context of a knowledge-based society.

The standardisation through testing in primary and secondary education – noticeable also in higher education – contradicts exigencies of the labour market as latest insights in labour economics and international economics show. Since technological change and international trade increasingly lead to the replacement of routine occupations, the types of skills learned for standardised tests are precisely those that are most vulnerable to offshoring and automatisation. In Alan S. Blinder's words "[...] the nation's school system will not build the creative, flexible, people-oriented workforce we will need in the future by drilling kids incessantly with rote preparation for standardized tests in the vain hope that they will perform as well as memory chips." (Blinder 2006, 7)[22] Similarly, the increase of tuition fees has been based on premises that are no longer valid.[23] The argument in favour of shifting university funding from taxation to fees was based on an increase in the university wage premium that started in the late 1970s. The underlying notion was that graduates earned more – and would continue to earn more – relative to non-graduates. However, this premium has gradually declined since the 1990s, so that the reasons that justified the establishment and gradual increase of private funding in the first place, are based on a world view from the 1980s which no longer mirrors today's realities.

One claim that has been made throughout this chapter about neoliberalism's function as a hegemonic discourse certainly applies also to the creation and contestation of new strong discourses. If neoliberalism that has dominated debates in public policy for three decades emerged from the fringes and gained its momentum as a response to specific crises in the 1970s, a new assessment that takes these new realities into account will have to take a similar path.

NOTES

[2] Criticising state-centred models as too parochial, Stephen Ball has underlined the discursive construction of policy practices. Rather than assuming the one-to-one implementation of state policies, Ball and colleagues suggested that different contexts shaped policies from the emergence of the text to its practical implementation and to the outcomes it creates (Bowe, Ball & Gold 1992; Ball 1994; Lall 2007). This approach allows for an analysis that includes the notions of individual agency, of historical and contextual specificity and of contestation.

[3] In a "sporadic, yet wave-like or 'layered,' non-linear sequence" neoliberalisation processes have gained dominance in Anglo-American countries since the 1980s and spread around the world as the hegemonic paradigm for economic reform (Brenner et al. 2010, 4; Jessop & Sum 2006, 287). Neoliberalism's support in international economic institutions (e.g. OECD, IMF and World Bank), its key role in advanced capitalist economies as well as its dominance in the restructuring of former socialist economies and developing countries have consolidated its hegemonic role (Jessop & Sum 2006, 287/288).

[4] See also Coe et al. 2010 who argue that the externalisation and naturalisation of the economy is inextricably linked with its historical development as a scientific discipline. Emerging in the late 19th century, modern economics has borrowed metaphors from sciences such as biology and physics to underpin its truth claims as universal and natural. The 'cycles,' the 'equilibrium,' and the 'health' of the economy are just some of the examples that reify the economy as an organism or system that functions outside social relations.

[5] The definition based on serving the public interest is different from and broader than the economic notion of pure public goods in contrast to private goods. Public goods are characterised by non-rivalry and non-excludability of consumption and, thus, non-appropriability of adequate revenues (Pelkmans 2006, 58). As a result, the price mechanism fails and their supply by markets will be insufficient – or will not even take place at all. In the case of national defense for instance, the amount consumed by one person does not diminish the quality or reduce the possible consumption available to others. Education is not a pure public good in this sense because each additional child/student raises costs (rival consumption) and people can be excluded easily (Stiglitz 2000, 136f.).

[6] The notion of 'public sector' refers to this distinction. However, if we aim at discussing different organising principles regarding the provision and funding of public goods and services, such a definition changes with the applied organising principles, i.e. due to the increasing privatisation of public service. In the UK National Accounts for instance local authority-controlled schools are classified within the public sector whereas universities are classified within the private sector (Office for National Statistics 2008).

[7] Amenta et al. subsume the most common understanding of the welfare state and social policy as "efforts of states to address economic insecurity and inequality due to risks to regular income" (Amenta et al. 2001, 213), while Gilens concedes that 'welfare', especially in the US context, does have "a fairly clear 'center,'" whereas the concept behind it has "rather fuzzy 'borders'" (Gilens 1999, 12).

[8] The classic example for a negative externality is environmental pollution. The producer does not take these external costs for society into account, although they may be substantial. In the case of positive externalities, leaving the consumption choice to individuals may result in a suboptimal level for society as these individuals are assumed to base their decisions solely on their private benefits (Stiglitz 2000, 80).

[9] For example, before the transaction takes place in a market for used cars the seller knows more about the product than the buyer. Consumers are less willing to pay a high price for a good of unknown quality. As a result, high-quality products will be provided less and the "lemons" in the market drive out the high quality products even though consumers would value them more (Akerlof 1970).

[10] Julien Le Grand gives a lucid account of the two characteristic – if not caricature – stances on the advantages and shortcomings of government bureaucracies. He juxtaposes the perception of functionaries as altruistic "knights" from a left perspective with the perception of self-interested "knaves" held by more conservative observers. (Le Grand 2007, 209)

[11] Moreover, they emphasise the role of order in Thatcher's reform strategies: "'Order' was associated with strong political agencies at the national level and the revival of nationalist identity. Goverment [sic!] may have restricted its direct competence to matters of security and foreign affairs, but its policies in these affairs were assertive and even jingoistic. Strong political government also had a central role in regulating official producers of services so that they best met consumer wishes. As a result, libertarianism toward consumers was combined with authoritarianism toward 'public' producers." (McLean & Voskresenskaya 1992, 77) .

[12] In the original, Krätke writes: "[…] das drastischste Sparpaket in der britischen Geschichte" (Krätke 2010, 13; our translation)

[13] As Elizabeth St. George, researcher at the Australian National University, argues, education was classified as a service in the General Agreement on Trade in Services (GATS) of the Uruguay Round in order to "ensure the gradual reduction of restrictions on educational services such as technology transfer, consultancy, [and] distance education" (St. George 2006, 591).

[14] The equivalent data for non-resident students, more indicative of student mobility was 300,056 in 2004 and 341,791 in 2008 (OECD 2011).

[15] The Scotland Act of 1998 shifted responsibilty for education in Scotland to the Scottish Parliament and university funding has remained largely public (Scottish Parliament 1999)

[16] Movements toward 'marketisation' and 'privatisation' have been more nuanced than these terms suggest, however. While 'privatisation' includes the direct transfer of services to the private sector, Public-Private-Partnerships (PPPs), outsourcing and out-contracting of previously public services as well as the financing of services through fees (as opposed to taxation), the term 'marketization' subsumes the creation of new (adding alternative providers) or internal markets (separation of provider and purchaser, as well as of policy-maker and operator), and the creation of market-friendly conditions (Clarke 2004, 35f.; Whitty & Power 2000, 94).

[17] While the parents' discretion in budgetary negociations and in administrative decisions increased, the national teacher unions lost its collective bargaining rights for "pay and conditions" in 1987 (McLean & Voskresenskaya 1992, 77f.).

[18] For a U.S. version of this broader argument see Robert Reich's book 'Super Capitalism'. Secretary of labor in Bill Clinton's first administration, Reich argues that, since the 1980s, individuals have been empowered as consumers while they were disenfranchised as citizens.

[19] Re-enforcing this trend of curricular standardisation, parents have tended to send their children to schools that teach the core subjects in order to allow them to enter university education upon their graduation.

[20] But, in what goes beyond the desirability of certain methods or contents transmitted in the classroom, test-driven learning has displayed an inherent leniency toward reproducing precisely those skills that are more easily automatised and/or offshored. Put differently, countering economic restructuring with this type of approach seems rather ill-matched, since the skills that are taught contradict the tendencies of the labour market.We discuss this thought in more detail in the concluding section.

[21] This sole focus on employability is underpinned by Tobin's choice to quote a 'career consultant' for her argument:
'If you're serious about investing your time and money in a postgraduate course, ensure you're making an informed decision,' advises Laura Hooke, careers consultant at City University London. 'If you are motivated by the sheer enjoyment of study and a love of the subject, that's great. But if you see further study as a means of getting employment, proceed with caution. A job ... is not guaranteed.' (Tobin 2011)

[22] While Blinder has referred to the United States the same argument holds true in the context of the United Kingdom.

[24] In a lecture given on January 27, 2011 at Berlin's Free University ("The Crisis of the Higher Education System in the United States"), Robert Meister, professor at the University of California in Santa Cruz, has made a similar argument with view to the specific United States context.

REFERENCES

Akerlof, G. (1970). The market for lemons: Qualitative uncertainty and the market mechanism. *Quarterly Journal of Economics, 8,* 488–500.

Altbach, P. G. (2005). Patterns in higher education development. In P. G. Altbach, R. O. Berdahl, & P. J. Gumport (Eds.), *American Higher Education in the Twenty-First Century. Social, Political, and Economic Challenges* (2nd ed., pp. 15–38). Baltimore, Md.: Johns Hopkins Univ. Press.

Altbach, P. G., Berdahl, R. O., & Gumport, P. J. (Eds.). (2005). *American Higher Education in the Twenty-First Century: Social, Political, and Economic Challenges* (2nd ed.). Baltimore, Md.: Johns Hopkins Univ. Press.

Amenta, E., Bonastia, C., & Caren, N. (2001). US social policy in comparative and historical perspective: Concepts, images, arguments, and research strategies. *Annual Reviews, 27,* 213–234.

Ball, S. (1994). Some reflections on policy theory: A brief response to Hatcher and Troyna. *Journal of Education Policy, 9*(2), 171–182.

Ball, S. (2003.). *Class Strategies and the Education Market: The Middle Classes and Social Advantage.* New York: Routledge Falmer.

Barr, N. & Crawford, I. (Eds.). (2005). *Financing Higher Education: Answers from the UK.* London: Routledge.

Bates, S. (2010, October 12). Tuition fees: From 'Free' university education to students Owing thousands. *The Guardian.*

BBC (2010, May 18). Cameron and clegg set out 'big society' policy ideas. BBC, from http://news.bbc.co.uk/2/hi/uk_news/politics/8688860.stm.

Blinder, A. S. (2006). Preparing America's workforce: Are we looking in the rear-view mirror? CEPS Working Paper, (135).

Bonal, X. (2003). The neoliberal educational Agenda and the legitimation crisis: Old and new state strategies. *British Journal of Sociology of Education, 24*(2), 159–175.

Bourdieu, P. (1998, December). The essence of neoliberalism. Le Monde Diplomatique, from http://mondediplo.com/1998/12/08bourdieu.

Bowe, R., Ball, S., & Gold, A. (1992). *Reforming Education and Changing Schools: Case Studies in Policy Sociology.* London: Routledge.

Brenner, N. (Ed.). (2008). *Spaces of Neoliberalism: Urban Restructuring in North America and Western Europe* (1st ed.,[reprint]). Malden, Mass.: Blackwell.

Brenner, N., Peck, J., & Theodore, N. (2010). Variegated neoliberalization: Geographies, modalities, pathways. *Global Networks, 10*(2), 182–222.

Brenner, N., & Theodore, N. (2008). Cities and the geographies of "Actually existing neoliberalism". In N. Brenner (Ed.), *Spaces of Neoliberalism. Urban Restructuring in North America and Western Europe* (1st ed., pp. 2–32). Malden, Mass.: Blackwell.

Brenner, N., & Theodore, N. (2008). Cities and the geographies of "Actually existing neoliberalism". In N. Brenner (Ed.), *Spaces of Neoliberalism. Urban Restructuring in North America and Western Europe* (1st ed., pp. 2–32). Malden, Mass.: Blackwell.

British Council. (2011). *UK Education Systems.* Retrieved January 07, 2011, from http://www.britishcouncil.org/usa-education-uk-system-k-12-education.htm

Cerny, P. G. (1997). Paradoxes of the competition state: The dynamic of political globalisation, government and opposition. *Government and Opposition, 32*(2), 251–271.

Clark, D. (2002). Neoliberalism and public service reform: Canada in comparative perspective. *Canadian Journal of Political Science / Revue canadienne de science politique, 35*(4), 771–793.

Clarke, J. (2004). Dissolving the public realm?: The logics and limits of Neo-Liberalism. *Journal of Social Policy, 33*(1), 27–48.

Coe, N. M., Kelly, P. F., & Yeung, H. W.-C. (2010). *Economic Geography: A Contemporary Introduction* ([Repr.]). Malden, Mass.: Blackwell.

Dale, R. (2000). Globalisation: A new world for comparative education? In J. Schriewer (Ed.), *Komparatistische Bibliothek: Vol. 10. Discourse Formation in Comparative Education* (2nd ed.). Frankfurt am Main: Lang.

Denman, B. D. (2005). What is a university in the 21st century? *Higher Education Management and Policy, 17*(2), 9–28.

Desai, M. (2005). Foreword. In N. Barr & I. Crawford (Eds.), *Financing Higher Education. Answers from the UK* (pp. xi–xiii). London: Routledge.

Eichengreen, B. J. (2007). *The European Economy since 1945. Coordinated Capitalism and Beyond.* Princeton N.J.: Princeton University Press.

Esping-Andersen, G. (1990). *The Three Worlds of Welfare Capitalism.* Cambridge UK: Polity Press.

Esping-Andersen, G. (1990). *The Three Worlds of Welfare Capitalism.* Princeton N.J.: Princeton University Press.

Evans, M., & Cerny, P. G. (2004). "New Labour", globalisierung und sozialpolitik. In S. Lütz & R. Czada (Eds.), *Wohlfahrtsstaat - Transformation und Perspektiven* (1st ed., pp. 207–230). Wiesbaden: VS Verl. für Sozialwiss.

Friedman, M. (1962). *Capitalism and Freedom.* Chicago & London: The University of Chicago Press.

Gamble, A. (1988). *The Free Economy and the Strong State: The Politics of Thatcherism.* Durham: Duke University Press.

Gellner, E. (2006). *Nations and Nationalism* (2nd ed.). New perspectives on the past. Malden MA: Blackwell Pub.

Gewirtz, S. (2002). *The Managerial School: Post-welfarism and Social Justice in Education.* The state of welfare. London & New York: Routledge.

Gilens, M. (1999). *Why Americans Hate Welfare: Race, Media, and the Politics of Antipoverty Policy.* Studies in communication, media, and public opinion. Chicago: Univ. of Chicago Press.

Goldin, C. (2001). The human-capital century and American leadership: Virtues of the past. *The Journal of Economic History, 61*(2), 263–292.

Greenway, D., & Haynes, M. (2003). Funding higher education in the UK: The role of fees and loans. *The Economic Journal, 113*(485), F150–F166.

Harris, R., & Seldon, A. (1979). *Over-ruled on Wefare: The Increasing Desire for Choice in Education and Medicine and its Frustration by Representative Government.* London: Institute of Economic Affairs.

Harvey, D. (2005). *A Brief History of Neoliberalism.* Oxford: Oxford Univ. Press.

Hill, D. (2001, September 26). *The Third Way in Britain: New Labour's Neo-Liberal Education Policy.* Paris.

Hobsbawm, E. J., & Ranger, T. O. (1983). *The Invention of Tradition. Past and present publications.* Cambridge Cambridgeshire New York: Cambridge University Press.

Hoyle, B., Pinder, D., & Husain, S. (Eds.). (1988). *Revitalising the Waterfront. International Dimensions of Dockland Redevelopment.* London, New York: Belhaven Press.

Hursh, D. (2005). Neo-liberalism, markets and accountability: Transforming education and undermining democracy in the United States and England. *Policy Futures in Education. 3*(1), 3–15.

Jessop, B. (2003). *Reflections on Globalization and Its (Il)logic(s).* Retrieved January 14, 2011, from Department of Sociology, Lancaster University: http://www.comp.lancs.ac.uk/sociology/papers/Jessop-Reflections-on-Globalization.pdf.

Jessop, B. (2010). The 'Return' of the national state in the current crisis of the world market. *Capital & Class, 34*(1), 38–43.

Jessop, B., & Sum, N.-L. (2006). *Beyond the Regulation Approach: Putting Capitalist Economies in their Place.* Cheltenham UK Northampton MA: Edward Elgar.

Karsten, S. (1999). Neoliberal education reform in the Netherlands. *Comparative Education. 35*(3), 303–317.

Krätke, M. R. (2010). Thatchers Enkel. *Blätter für Deutsche und Internationale Politik, 55*(12), 12–17.

Kurbjuweit, D. (2010). Der Wutbürger. *Der Spiegel, 41,* 26–27.

Lall, M. (2007). *A Review of Concepts from Policy Studies Relevant for the Analysis of EFA in Developing Countries.* Consortium for Research on Educational Access, Transitions and Equity. Creative Pathways to Access. Research Monograph, (11).

Le Grand, J. (2007). The politics of choice and competition in public services. *The Political Quarterly, 78*(2), 207–213.

Levačić, R. (1995). *Local Management of Schools: Analysis and Practice.* Buckingham England Bristol PA USA: Open University Press.

Lütz, S. & Czada, R. (Eds.). (2004). *Wohlfahrtsstaat - Transformation und Perspektiven* (1. Aufl.). Wiesbaden: VS Verl. für Sozialwiss.

McLean, M. (1995). *Educational Traditions Compared: Content, Teaching, and Learning in Industrialised Countries.* London: D. Fulton.

McLean, M., & Voskresenskaya, N. (1992). Educational revolution from above: Thatcher's Britain and Gorbachev's Soviet Union. *Comparative Education Review, 36*(1), 71–90.

McQuaid, R. W., & Lindsay, C. (2005). The concept of employability. *Urban Studies, 42*(2), 197–219.

Morley, L. (1997). Change and equity in higher education. *British Journal of Sociology of Education, 18*(2), 231–242.

Mulholland, H. (2010, December 09). Tuition fees: Government wins victory as protests continue. *The Guardian.* Retrieved February 23, 2011, from http://www.guardian.co.uk/education/2010/dec/09/tuition-fees-vote-government-wins-narrow-victory.

Newman, J., & Clarke, J. (2009). *Publics, Politics and Power: Remaking the Public in Public Services.* London: Sage.

OECD. (1999). *The Knowledge-Based Economy: A Set of Facts and Figures.* Paris: OECD.

OECD. (2008). *The State of the Public Sector.* Paris: OECD.

OECD. (2011). *Foreign / International Students Enrolled.* Retrieved February 22, 2011, from OECD http://stats.oecd.org/Index.aspx?DatasetCode=RFOREIGN.

Office for National Statistics. (2008). *Public Sector and Private Sector.* Retrieved February 23, 2011, from http://www.ons.gov.uk/about-statistics/user-guidance/lm-guide/concepts/employers/jobs/pub-and-priv/index.html

Olssen, M., & Peters, M. A. (2005). Neoliberalism, higher education and the knowledge economy: From the free market to knowledge capitalism. *Journal of Education Policy, 20*(3), 313–345.

Palley, T. I. (2004). *From Keynesianism to Neoliberalism: Shifting Paradigms in Economics.* Retrieved August 05, 2010, from http://www.thomaspalley.com/docs/articles/macro_policy/keynsianism_to_neoliberalism.pdf.

Peck, J., & Tickell, A. (2008). Neoliberalizing space. In N. Brenner (Ed.), *Spaces of Neoliberalism. Urban Restructuring in North America and Western Europe* (1st ed., pp. 33–57). Malden, Mass.: Blackwell.

Pelkmans, J. (2006). *European Integration: Methods and Economic Analysis.* Edinburgh Gate: Pearson Education.

Phillips, R., & Furlong, J. (Eds.). (2001). *Education Reform and the State: Twenty-five Years of Politics, Policy, and Practice.* New York: Routledge.

Plank, D. N. & Sykes, G. (Eds.). (2003). *Choosing Choice: School Choice in International Perspective.* New York: Teachers College Press.

Power, S., Halpin, D., & Whitty, G. (1997). Managing the state and the market: 'New' education management in five countries. *British Journal of Educational Studies, 45*(4), 342–362.

Reay, D., & Ball, S. (1997). Spoilt for choice: The working classes and educational markets. *Oxford Review of Education, 25*(1), 89–101.

Robertson, R., & Dale, R. (2002). Local states of emergency: The contradictions of neoliberal governance in education in New Zealand. *British Journal of Sociology of Education, 23*(3), 463–482.

Robertson, S., & Lauder, H. (2001). Restructuring the education / social class relation: A class choice? In R. Phillips & J. Furlong (Eds.), *Education Reform and the State: Twenty-five Years of Politics, Policy, and Practice.* New York: Routledge.

Rose, N. (2000). Community, citizenship, and the third way. *American Behavioral Scientist, 43*(9), 1395–1411.

Sassen, S. (2006). *Territory, Authority, Rights: From Medieval to Global Assemblages.* Princeton N.J.: Princeton University Press.

Schofer, E., & Meyer, J. W. (2005). The worldwide expansion of higher education in the twentieth century. *American Sociological Review, 70,* 898–920.

Schokkaert, E. (2001). *Ethics and Social Security Reform* (Foundation for International Studies on Social Security, Ed.). Aldershot Hampshire England Burlington VT USA: Ashgate.

Schriewer, J. (Ed.). (2000). *Komparatistische Bibliothek: Vol. 10. Discourse Formation in Comparative Education* (2nd Rev. ed.). Frankfurt am Main: Lang.

Smith, N. (2008). New globalism, new urbanism: Gentrification as global urban strategy. In N. Brenner (Ed.), *Spaces of Neoliberalism. Urban Restructuring in North America and Western Europe* (1st ed., pp. 80–103). Malden, Mass.: Blackwell.

St. George, E. (2006). Positioning higher education for the knowledge based economy. *Higher Education, 52,* 589–610.

Stiglitz, J. E. (2000). *Economics of the Public Sector* (3rd ed.). New York: Norton.

Thaler, R. H., & Sunstein, C. R. (2009). *Nudge: Improving Decisions about Health, Wealth, and Happiness* (Rev. and expanded ed.). New York: Penguin.

The Scottish Parliament. (1999). *Further and Higher Education in Scotland.* Retrieved February 01, 2011, from http://www.scottish.parliament.uk/business/research/pdf_subj_maps/smda-17a.pdf.

Tickell, A., & Peck, J. (2003). *Making Global Rules: Globalisation or Neoliberalisation?* Retrieved January 27, 2010, from GaWC Research Bulletin 102: http://www.lboro.ac.uk/gawc/rb/rb102.html

Tobin, L. (2011, February 15). Will a master's get you a job? *The Guardian.* Retrieved 23 February, 2011, from http://www.guardian.co.uk/education/2011/feb/15/masters-postgraduate-guide.

Toffler, A. (1990). *Powershift: Knowledge, Wealth and Violence at the Edge of the 21st Century.* New York: Bantam Books.

Walford, G. (2003). School choice and educational change in England and Wales. In D. N. Plank & G. Sykes (Eds.), *Choosing Choice. School Choice in International Perspective*. New York: Teachers College Press.

Welch, A. R. (2001). Globalisation, post-modernity and the state: Comparative education facing the Third Millenium. *Comparative Education, 37*(4), 475–492.

Whitty, G., & Power, S. (2000). Marketization and privatization in mass education systems. *International Journal of Educational Development, 20*, 93–107.

Whitty, G., Power, S., & Halpin, D. (1998). *Devolution and Choice in Education: The School, the State, and the Market*. Buckingham England, Bristol, PA, USA: Open Univ. Press.

Wikipedia. (2011). University. Retrieved February 25, 2011, from http://en.wikipedia.org/wiki/University.

AFFILIATIONS

Julia Püschel
John-F.-Kennedy Institute
Free University Berlin

Boris Vormann
John-F.-Kennedy Institute
Free University Berlin

KATHLEEN EDMONDS

2. YOUNG PEOPLE'S ENGAGEMENT IN SOCIETY, HOW GOVERNMENT POLICY HAS IGNORED THE ROLE OF YOUTH WORK IN CITIZENSHIP EDUCATION:

A Critical Analysis of Britain's future: the citizen and the state, in the Governance of Britain Green paper (2007)

INTRODUCTION

The Governance of Britain Green paper was presented to Parliament by the Secretary of State for Justice and Lord Chancellor, Jack Straw, in July 2007. In Chapter 4 *Britain's future: the citizen and the state*, it talks about Citizenship and national identity. The paper acknowledges in the opening line that

...the concept of Citizenship is a complex one ... (2007:53).

The context that is described is one of legal rights, nationality, democracy and identity; leading to British citizenship. A clearer definition of citizenship would, the Government believes, give individuals a better understanding of their British identity. The "rights and responsibilities" that go with citizenship need to be valued, not only by new arrivals but also by British young people (pt 185, 2007:54).

The paper goes on to state that young people's engagement in society and understanding of what it means to be a "citizen" is the key to having a cohesive society. Reference is made to the achievement that the Government had made during the last decade in citizenship engagement particularly through its Education policy (2002) which introduced Citizenship studies as part of the core School Curriculum. However, concern had been raised about the fall in the number of young people taking part in formal political processes such as voting (Electoral Commission and Hansard Society Research Report, March 2007) and the Governance report states that:

This shows a lack of appreciation of the importance of the democratic process and of the need for active citizenship (pt 189, 2008:55).

M. Lall (ed.), Policy, Discourse and Rhetoric: How New Labour Challenged Social Justice and Democracy, 41–58.

This policy has been chosen for analysis because in a democracy everybody should be given the tools to participate in society and encouraged to have a voice, especially young people. The concern regarding the link between neoliberalism and citizenship is that citizens are educated in order to create individual entrepreneurs who can contribute to a knowledge economy, where education is not seen as a public good improving social needs and challenging social justice but is only about private interest and profit. Citizenship is not a new concept but there is a need to question "active citizenship" as it is promoted by Government particularly as a means of dealing with social problems, harnessing more votes or creating compliant citizens. In particular:

> ...university and college educators should be the most vocal and militant in challenging the corporatization of education by making it clear that at the heart of any form of inclusive democracy is the assumption that learning should be used to expand the public good, create a culture of questioning, and promote democratic social change (Giroux, in Hill & Kumar, 2009:42).

The Government looked at ways to animate young people's understanding of what it means to be a British citizen and to expand their participation in the political arena by launching a Youth Citizenship Commission. The focus of the Youth Citizenship Commission was to find out what support *Schools* needed in order to improve their preparation of young people for adult citizenship. In his review of the Curriculum (DFES, 2007), Sir Keith Ajegbo refers to

> ...all *schools* will teach...the Government wants *schools*...involving all *schools* (pt 190, 2007:56).

It is like Tony Blair's mantra: "Education, Education, Education".

The concern in this chapter is that government policy focussed on the delivery of Citizenship Education only through Schools. If they were serious about enabling young people's engagement in society as "active citizens" and encouraging them to vote, then why was the audience for this education policy only through formal education, namely schools and teachers? Where was the voice of youth work and young people?

This chapter will examine whose voice has been heard and who has influenced the agenda on Citizenship but also identify any gaps and whether as Ball suggests:

> Only certain influences and agendas are recognised as legitimate, only certain voices are heard at any point in time within the commonsense of policy (Ball, 1993:45).

Policy according to Taylor (1997) is more than just words; it is made up of lots of different points of view and is often based on particular ideologies or value bases. Policy is contextual in terms of the social, political and economic climate in which it is created. Policy is created by Government officials on behalf of the state and is more often than not a compromise of differing agendas. The implementation of policy is dependent on a number of complex inter-relationships which are often rooted in an economics and efficiency agenda, rather than one that reflects values such as social justice, equality and democracy. Bowe, Ball and Gold (1992), talk about individuals being:

...marginal to the policy process or they are represented...

often by elite groupings or hand picked individuals. It is often the case that the voices of young people in education policy are ...for the most part strangely silent.... Where advocates for young people are present it is often in a smaller body of academic literature and here voices are heard but as ...theoretically over determined mouth pieces, or even as ...subverters of the status quo (Bowe, Ball and Gold, 1992:6).

There is a contradiction inherent in the relationship between politics and the creation of policy that politicians and policymakers rely on professionals to deliver and implement their policy initiatives. Very few professionals or practitioners get to have a say in the creation of policy, and the cumulative effect of several years of reform in the Education sector has taken its toll on those on the receiving end, both professionals and those that they work with.

This chapter will explore the perceived lack of representation of youth work through using the Policy Cycle (Bowe, Ball and Gold, 1992). Starting with the *Context of Influence*, the chapter looks at where public policy begins, key ideas are established and priorities decided. The role of youth work is considered before an examination of the *Context of Practice*, the arena in which policy is enacted or addressed. The next section looks at different models, a look at the *Context of Outcomes,* and the *Context of Political Strategy* (Ball, 2006). The recommendations of the Youth Citizenship Commission and the government response are reviewed, before an overview of the new Coalition Governments plans for a National Citizen Service and the implications these have for practice.

Context of Influence

The context for the resurgence of interest in citizenship and its priority as a policy issue rests on a number of issues. Research by Macgregor (1990, in Kerr et al, 2009) found that the change of emphasis from individual obligation to a collective responsibility was in part a reaction by the New Labour administration of 1997 to the outgoing Conservative government. This was seen as part of a national educational policy to promote the practice of citizenship as part of a wider regeneration of communities, which along with devolution, sought to renew the debate about national identity and Britishness. The widening of membership of the

European Union from 15 to 25 countries in 2004,and to 27 in 2007,increased pressure in terms of migration and employment. With further countries waiting to join, citizenship education was viewed as crucial as part of a coordinated response to the Global economy (Kerr et al, 2009:253).

Citizenship is regarded as important in modern and fast moving societies because of the need to be able to cope with constant political, social and economic changes which increase the pressure on relationships in society, not least those of young people. Kimberlee (2002) found that research into young people's experience of society today was characterised by longer transitions between childhood and adulthood, the demise of traditional family and community support mechanisms, and less influence from adult role models who had previously encouraged community cohesion. The media translated this as young people displaying signs of alienation and apathy but researchers found that this was not the case rather that young people's engagement with political culture had changed. There is a perception from those in power that there is a link between the lack of active citizenship and a decline in take up of educational opportunities, as well as an increase in crime and poor health, and that more needs to be done to balance individuals' notion of their *rights* along with their *responsibilities*. The concern from Government was that there was a lack of involvement from young people in their communities; that young people do not behave in a morally responsible way; that young people do not understand the changes to the cultural composition of their neighbourhoods and that young people do not participate in formal politics such as voting. So the pressure was for citizenship education to have a more prominent role, not just in education but in the wider society (Crick, 2000, in Lopes et al, 2009:2).

One of the most influential thinkers and writers on citizenship has been Sir Bernard Crick. In his "Essays on Citizenship" he reflects on some fundamental issues, the history of citizenship but also the ideas behind it, its acceptance as part of the political tradition and its implementation.

Crick draws on the work of T.H. Marshall (1950 in Crick, 2000:7), when he describes citizenship as being composed of three elements: Civil, Political and Social. *Civil* is the right to individual freedom; *Political* is the right to participate in the exercise of political power, and *Social* is the right to welfare and security in sharing in the life of a citizen in the making. Active citizenship s achieved when all three elements interact.

Miller (2000, in Brooks, 2007:417) has posited that in contemporary British society there are three understandings of "citizenship". The third understanding which implies a more active, even a collective type of citizenship, was the one that was taken up by the New Labour government and which underpinned a lot of social policy initiatives coming out of Whitehall. Coffey believes that citizenship has been taken up as a key role and:

recast as an active status that carries with it the obligations of social inclusion, mutuality, participation and democracy (2004:43 in Brooks, 2007:418).

Sometimes there is a distinction made between understandings of the concept of "active citizen" made on the right or the left of the political spectrum. In a simplistic analysis those on the right are viewed as promoting active citizenship in order to free people from dependency on the welfare state and those on the left are thought to believe that citizenship is achieved through political involvement and that is best done in the context of community (Deem et al, 1995, in Brooks, 2007:418).Some claim that Labour's longer term aim was to

...re-educate people that the state is an enabler rather than a provider of services (Landrum, 2002, in Brooks, 2007:418).

In this agenda education has a key role. Crick is clear that citizenship is an overarching activity that reflects concepts such as political literacy, political philosophy and should be part of Education but he regards it as

...more than a school educational subject (2000:110).

He regards concepts as the way in which we build a picture of the outside world and that concepts can be expressed in different ways but that it is not necessary:

...to go beyond the language of everyday life to understand and to participate in the politics of everyday life... (2000:77).

He describes political literacy as a combination of Knowledge, Skills and Attitudes, developing alongside each other, each one enforcing the other two. His description of Knowledge includes who has the power and how institutions work, as well as how to be involved. Skills are about acting as an active participant or choosing not to, and being able to communicate. Attitudes are about values such as freedom, tolerance, fairness, and respect for truth and for reasoning; and are all compounds of Democracy. What Crick stresses is that there is a need for a shared understanding and acceptance of what is meant by these concepts before it is possible to secure written criteria for making reliable judgements on any related issues.

Davies (2008) also believes there are reasons why political literacy should be promoted:

Politics has to connect with young people: it must be taught and learned in ways that are congruent with the essential nature of political education... (Davies, 2008:381).

Davies does state that it is difficult for education not to be political but agrees with Harber (1991), that there needs to be a clear distinction between education, socialization and indoctrination.

Crick does not believe that the government focus on being a "good" citizen, through obeying the law, paying your taxes, knowing your place and being grateful to be governed, equates with being an "active citizen". Nor does he view Citizenship as a form of voluntary work but emphasises that education for citizenship must include training for political activity through *acting* together and not just "watching" from the sidelines. Crick regards a state that does not have active citizenship as one in which individuals feel powerless to act, and which results in groups of young people being separated from society, driven to behaving in an anti-social way or displaying a complete absence of interest. He says that:

> ...political activity is too important to be left to politicians. Political activity by citizens is the very essence of a free society (2000:130).

Unfortunately politicians *have* taken charge of citizenship education and the introduction of the Citizenship order in 2000, which led to citizenship education becoming a core subject in the School Curriculum in 2002, has not reflected all of Bernard Crick's concerns even though he was one of the main architects of the policy. It certainly has not taken account of it being more than a "school educational subject".

THE ROLE OF YOUTH WORK

The important role that Informal Education through Youth work can have in working with young people is evident in the characteristics that underpin informal education. These are that informal education makes space for association and deliberation; it enables self directed involvement and action; and it uses a critical perspective to encourage inclusion and participation (Packham, 2008:12).Informal education is usually carried out with young people but can also be used in community learning and active citizenship. Youth workers view the processes and principles of informal education as essential to their work; Banks gives a concise summary of the characteristics as follows;

> ...the process is based on dialogue, it works with cultural forms that are familiar to participants, participation is voluntary, it takes place in a variety of settings, it has educational goals...and makes use of experiential as well as assimilative patterns of learning (1999: p.7).

This does not mean that leaning is unstructured. The framework for youth and community work draws on the work of the Brazilian educator, Paolo Friere (1921-1997). It is about conversational encounters with others; reflection, critical exploration and re-creating knowledge. The youth and community worker works to create space for such interactions to happen. Packham acknowledges that youth and community workers,

...have an important role as informal educators...to enable participants to think critically...and to identify who will benefit and how (2008:40).

This is in contrast to some formal education processes which are didactic, directed and non-experiential. In the Frierian model:

...all participants are recognized as thinking, creative people with the capacity for action... (Stewart, 2008, np, in Packham, 2008:18).

This is not to dismiss all forms of formal education because

...ultimately it is the quality of the relationship which forms out of the engagement, the degree of choice...and other participative practices of the workers... (Ord, 2008, np, in Packham, 2008:18).

However, the informal educational approach is vitally important to improve, contribute to and challenge government policy initiatives, such as the debate on citizenship, because research on the effects of neoliberalism on education has found that:

Capitalism requires increasing numbers of workers, citizens and consumers who willingly do what they are told to do and think what they are told to think. The production of such human capital is the most fundamental role schools play in a capitalist society (Martell, 2005:5, in Kumar and Hill).

Youth work by contrast seeks to be distinctive to other forms of work with young people through its explicit commitment to:

Young people's voluntary participation; seeking to tip the balance of power in their favour... seeing and responding to young people simply as young people, as untouched as possible by pre-set labels; working on and from their territory... respecting and working through their peer networks (Davies, 2005:22 in Young, 2006:2).

CONTEXT OF PRACTICE

The Home Office pilot project, Active Learning for Active Citizenship (ALAC), which ran between 2004 and 2006 reflects the context of the New Labour government's desire for greater participation from communities in government processes, alongside the tension for volunteers of acting in what may have appeared to some as a process of welfare, surveillance and control. This was accompanied by a change in the perception of the role of voluntary work in communities, which previously had been viewed by some as a philanthropic activity and by others as interference. The Governments priorities of seeing voluntary community engagement as contributing to skill development, social cohesion, improved service delivery and a step towards the achievement of full citizenship, culminated in the ALAC pilot programme being set up in seven areas across the UK, involving over one thousand people.

The priority was to encourage different types of citizenship involvement and the influence of youth and community workers in supporting this to happen was vital. Although it was a Home Office directed project, the ALAC programme recognised the role that informal learning could have with the name reflecting,

> ... the importance of action and the learning by doing process (Packham, 2008:8).

The UK government's emphasis on active citizenship had been influenced by the idea of social capital, an idea that derived from the work of Robert Puttnam (2000), which analysed the decline of civic involvement in American communities, seen as the result of a disconnection in the relationships in communities. Adoption of this type of policy has implications for youth and community work practice, which is why it is important for the voice of the profession to be heard and listened to. The paradox is in activities which may benefit some community members but may harm others. What is important here is to question, "For whose benefit?" and to exert influence to enable real and informed choice. The focus on volunteering, particularly amongst young people (DfCSF: 2007), is more about individual capital and an individual responsibility for change, than collective action.

Young people are currently centre stage and are seen as a priority to promote 'active citizenship" to. This is partly due to current moral panics about young people's perceived lack of involvement in anything political (Lister et al, 2005). Young people's perceived lack of engagement in the political process has been highlighted through the recorded decline in turn out of young people in the general elections in the UK in 1997, 2001 and 2005. This lack of participation has been put down to young people not achieving any financial independence by the time they are able to vote; not that young people are not interested (Hall and Williamson 1999).The response from Government has been to increase the management and control of young people, they are seen as a problem to be dealt with. By default so are the professionals that work with them, which is why youth workers are not part of the discussion on citizenship. Young people and youth workers are "objects" of policy, made in response to media panics. Young people are often seen as a homogeneous group because of age and are not regarded as individuals with individual experiences based on class, gender, ethnicity, sexuality or disability.

A top down approach to citizenship identity which is non negotiable, is not the process through which young people gain their own sense of identity, which is usually through interacting with friends and family members and in the post modern world through sites such as Face book and My Space, encouraging contact with global youth cultures (Hall et al, 1998; Coffey, 2004). Schools are a form of social control as it is compulsory to attend (Coffey: 2004), and social citizenship is undermined by the focus on volunteering (2007:420). Brooks believes that the role of citizenship education in schools has serious limitations because the school is acting as facilitator in the role of the state with its "potential" citizens, encouraging young people to contribute to an economic agenda (Aapola et al, 2005). Analysis of the role of teachers in developing workers of the future in texts by Rikowski (2000,2001,2007), demonstrates the fear the capitalist state has of any form of teaching that tries to educate students about the reality of their situation and to raise their awareness of this because of undermining the role of education for social control (Hill & Kumar,2009:20).

Research by Lister et al (2005) found that young people could not identify rights, but could identify responsibilities, with citizenship based on economic respectability and not on a universal status or having a "voice" (Brooks, 2007:422).This approach is not based on the principles of youth work.

A DIFFERENT MODEL

The question Annette (2008:388) asks, is should citizenship education be based on a civic republican model, emphasising individual rights or based on a liberal model which stresses moral and social responsibility? The notion suggested by New Labour was linked to the regeneration of communities and the idea of shared or common ideals rather than an individualistic response. The approach proposed is one that allows for a contemporary perspective of citizenship in British life, based on a shared understanding rather than a traditional republican political stance (Pettit, 1997).

What is proposed is a form of civic republicanism, where rights and responsibilities are reflected in active self governance and participation in a political community (Oldfield, 1990; Pettit, 1997; and Maynor, 2003, in Annette, 2008). It is an idea that is heavily promoted in the United States of America (Barber, 1984; Sandel, 1996; Galston, 2001, in Annette, 2008). Annette talks about the need to know how young people understand the "political" in relation to their own lives and those of their communities, more than the more formal aspects of politics such as voting (2008:390).He believes that now that citizenship education is established as a key part of not only formal education but other forms of learning, that new models are emerging, which need to be built upon. Such as, the use of

...active learning, learning that is by definition *experiential* in nature (2008:393).

This is based on the learning cycle of David Kolb (1998), using "structured learning experience with measurable outcomes", with learning emerging from the structured reflections of the learner. This is used in training youth and community workers and in work between youth workers and young people. Giroux believes that active and critical political agents have to be formed, educated and socialised into a world of politics (Kumar & Hill, 2009:5). This is what is missing from government policy on citizenship education and formal education.

What is important here is the experience of developing and using skills, which is what Crick was proposing (Hart et al, 2007, in Annette, 2008:395; Crick, 2000). This is done on a daily basis in youth work, where young people can become politically aware through projects that encourage their involvement with the local community and with a wider national/international audience. Shaw and McCulloch (2009) define citizenship as:

the practices through which subjects engage in democracy (p9).

Democracy itself can be viewed either as a set of political institutions which are managed by the state to achieve conformity or as an ongoing process of negotiation through which disagreement and dissent is seen as an asset to be harnessed for the benefit of the community and individuals. This latter definition of Democracy reflects the difficulty of competing points of view and the struggle from the powerless to challenge the powerful.

Fyfe (2003) believes that democracy as a process must allow people to form their own identity as well as to express it (Shaw and McCulloch, 2009:9), and should enable them to say "no" when they need to. This is very important in work with young people because their identities are still being formed and if policy formulation is based on a "deficit" model rather than a "potentiality" model (Davies,1992) ,then young people who do not feel they have the power to challenge negative images may become disillusioned and alienated from the political arena. In his study, "Disconnected Youth" , Barham(2004) found evidence that young people are engaged in political issues but often ones that are single issues ,which can be reacted against in the short term, rather than proactively trying to change things in the longer term. Young people need to be enabled to see a broader picture and to be able to understand how power can be used to maintain inequality. To assist them to develop skills to participate and to think critically, "we need research into how young people understand the "political" as it relates to *their* everyday concerns in *their* communities, to the more formal political sphere of voting, political parties and holding public office" (Annette,2009 :390).

CONTEXT OF OUTCOMES

Policy is not just implemented it is subject to interpretation and re-creation, as well as "interpretations of interpretations"(Rizvi and Kemmi, in Bowe et al, 1992:23) based on practitioners experience , history, purpose and values. The idea that the arena of change is only made up of policy makers on one side and practitioners on the other is naïve and only serves to reinforce the idea that policy comes from the top down, implying that theory and practice are not linked and that policy is more important than practice (Bowe, Ball and Gold, 1992:10). Ball (1994:51) talks about the need to counter the effects of the Policy Cycle through the *Context of Outcomes*, where the relationship between changes to practice and the impact of those changes on access and participation are identified. By including youth workers and young people in the discussion about policy on citizenship education, society's relationship with young people today could be improved. Dialogue and discussion are seen as a vital part of democratic education (Parker, Hess and Avery, 2008:506). Research has shown that young people's participation in discussion and debate impacts on what young people learn and that there is a positive link between knowledge acquisition and political engagement:

> Active involvement in decisions that affect individuals and the places with which they associate can give greater depth to citizenship (OPDM, 2005:11).

There is a need to take account of citizenship learning outside of school (McDevitt and Kiousis, 2007; Ostler and Starkey, 2003, in Lopes et al, 2009:4). In their research, Lopes et al propose that young people's,

> ...experience of empowering activities ...may foster efficacy (2009:9).

Discussions are also regarded as a way of supporting and validating equality, because through discussion, decisions are made and all participating should be regarded as equal in contributing to any decision (Dahl, 1998:65, in Hess and Avery, 2008:506).

Lopes et al (2009) researched two models: one that concentrates on the processes and agency through which individuals chose to join in and one that concentrates on the structures, both social and institutional that can influence participation. The first one, the *Rational Actor theory* (Downs, 1957, Whiteley and Seyd, 2002, in Lopes, 2009:4) looks at what people get out of participating, a cost/benefit analysis. This is looked at alongside *Cognitive engagement*, the impact that being politically literate can have on an interest in politics. The second model looks at where political knowledge gained through citizenship education is seen as a *resource*; here education and socio-economic status can contribute to understanding *how* to join in. This is examined alongside *equity fairness models* of participation (Runiciman, 1966, Gurr, 1970, Muller, 1979, in Lopes, 2009:5) where individuals have a conception of how society should treat them. If people feel that they are being treated unfairly then they may be motivated to vote for a different political party, or not join in at all. The role of citizenship education here is to provide impartial information on the balance of power and relative inequality within society. The *Context of Political Strategy* identifies strategies which may be political or social but which seek to tackle "...inequalities and forms of injustice" (1994:51).

CONTEXT OF POLITICAL STRATEGY

Research findings from the Youth engagement summary report (2008) found that young people are interested in issues but new ways need to be found to engage them. There is a need to change the structures and institutions of Government not just change some of the procedures:

> ...no matter what formal structures are in place, it is how individuals approach, make sense of and use them that finally count (Skidmore and Bound, 2008, in Lopes, 2009:16).

The Youth Citizenship Commission research findings were published in June 2009 and were organised into themes:
1.   Empowered Citizenship
2.   Connecting with young people
3.   Changing the way decision makers and institutions work.

The research found that citizenship learning needs to be embedded from a young age and citizenship education should focus more on political literacy and include practical opportunities, which echo findings by Annette (2008) and Davies (2009). It also found that young people are not engaged because they do not have enough information, do not feel empowered and do not feel that they can make a difference. The findings also state that different ways to communicate with young people need to be found as formal language and processes put them off (Participation Works partnership report, June 2009).

Research by 2CV for the Youth Citizenship Commission in 2009 found that all the ideas for citizenship engagement were based on two fundamental conditions for engaging young people: building young people's confidence for engaging, and fostering cross-generational trust (p.11).The research supports the argument that youth workers have an essential role in working with young people who are the most difficult to engage. Workers were able to create a dialogue where most other adults had failed. However, in order to be effective, youth workers needed information, as well as practical and financial resources which were part of a longer term strategy not just one off initiatives.

The governments' responses to the recommendations of the YCC report were published in February 2010. The Minister for Young Citizens and Youth Engagement, Dawn Butler, MP wrote in her introduction that

> It is up to young people to decide how engaged they want to be as citizens, through activities such as politics, public service, volunteering and participation (2009:4).

The government in its report, "*An Agenda for Engagement*", was in general agreement with the issues raised by the YCC research, promising to review its interactions with young people at a local and at a national level, and offering support for electoral registration in schools; the use of schools as polling stations on election day; and providing sustainable funding for the UK youth parliament. However a number of findings were ignored, for example, the finding that 82% of young Britons didn't think politicians could represent them fairly was sidestepped with the government apportioning responsibility to the complexity of politics and its lack of appeal , not the fact that research by a Children's society survey showed that politicians were more interested in older voters.

The Minister's response that "… it's time for young people to grab the initiative and be vocal" does not address the lack of joined up coordination across local and national government regarding young people's involvement and the need for more universal representation of young people on youth councils in order to influence decision making. The cuts to local authority budgets and the lack of youth provision in some areas are also ignored, at a time when the numbers of young people unemployed is twice that of the adult population. The report is based on actions taken in England and does not represent the devolved administrations with no UK wide policy in place to measure the effect of policy decisions on young people as part of an equality impact assessment.

The issue of lowering the voting age to 16 was not supported by the majority of young people interviewed and so not endorsed in the YCC recommendations. The researchers found that the role of citizenship education and political literacy within the school curriculum needed more resources, as well as training for staff and suitable environments to deliver in.

A report by the National Federation for Educational Research, a mapping study on connecting with citizenship education, published in July 2010; states in its key recommendations that there is a gap in the range of resources available to support citizenship education in the curriculum and that the Department for Constitutional Affairs needs to raise its profile as a department with a role in promoting education, information and advice in the key areas of justice, rights and democracy. It also states that it needs to be flexible in its delivery, as there is no one model of effective delivery. The focus needs to be clear as to who the target audience is; young people, other groups in society, stakeholders, or practitioners. Finally, the authors question where the main focus should be, in schools and colleges, or whether other areas have a role to play.

A NATIONAL CITIZEN SERVICE

The issue of a National Civic service was not raised during the year long YCC campaign and is an initiative that the Conservatives attribute to David Cameron from 2005, with the other two main parties at the time keen to support such a programme, as part of an induction for young people into the responsibilities of citizenship.

At his first press conference for the 2010 General Election campaign, David Cameron announced that the Conservative party had developed plans for a National Citizen Service for all 16 year olds. It was described as a scheme that would help young people in the transition to adulthood, promoting social mixing and community engagement. It would be delivered by social enterprises,

independent charities and businesses. David Cameron said: "This is about sowing the seeds of the Big Society, and seeing them thrive in the years to come" (Conservatives.Com April 2010). In other coverage of his speech, Cameron describes the proposal for a voluntary "citizen service" programme, as a "21st century version of "National Service", although non-military. However it would not be a compulsory scheme, but would be universal, bringing together youngsters from all backgrounds' – "north or south, rich or poor, black or white" (www.bbc.co.uk).

The National Citizens Service was piloted in 12 sites in the summer of 2011 and involved up to 11,000 young people aged 16 undertaking a 7-8 week programme of voluntary work in different communities. The idea is to make this available to all 16 year olds in the UK; although the Commons Education Select committee feels that the money would be better being diverted to existing youth service provision (Guardian Politics). The aim of the service is to create young social entrepreneurs who can set up and run projects in the community (www.actionforchildren.co.uk/policy).

Speaking at the Conservative party conference in Birmingham in October last year; for the first time as Prime Minister, Cameron said:

> Citizenship isn't a transaction in which you put your taxes in and get your services out. It is a relationship – you're part of something bigger than you, and it matters what you think, and feel and do (The Telegraph, October 6th 2010).

However the scheme has a number of flaws. It is unequal in its involvement of young people, being aimed primarily at those not in education, employment or training (NEET), and tied to welfare benefits. Its focus on payment sees citizenship needing to be rewarded with financial incentives which goes against the philanthropic idea of volunteering. A resource currently dedicated to a variety of youth programmes and to the delivery of citizenship education in schools is likely to be diverted, with it being compulsory for some and not others. Following the general election in May 2010 citizenship education is under threat because the view of the new Minister for Education, Michael Gove, is that it is "state sponsored political indoctrination".

IMPLICATIONS FOR FUTURE PRACTICE

The Conservative/Liberal Democrat coalition government are sending a set of very mixed messages here: a programme which is voluntary not compulsory; universal but considered a failure if not all young people participate; and what Crick (2000) did not advocate, citizenship as a form of voluntary work. There is a clear commitment to diversity but the programme is only being piloted in England, not in other parts of the devolved UK administration, ignoring an equality impact assessment. It aims to encourage aspiration and offer responsibility to young people but is also about saving money by cutting crime and anti-social behaviour. The coalition government is in danger of focusing on an economic agenda which appears to be punitive and about conformity rather than about fostering efficacy.

Youth work is about social education not social control, it is about informed choice. What I would argue is that we should reflect:

> practice based not on the need to address current social problems and political priorities but on a commitment to developing the truly life long goals of rational judgement and authentic human experience (Young, 1999:122).

Young people have very few opportunities for expressing themselves or of contributing their perception of what citizenship is to them. Without the opportunity to express their view of the world in a way that is listened to, then they may turn to destructive or harmful behaviour. There is a need to harness what John Dewey (1958) called "impulsions", a kind of creative energy derived from their experience of the world. If we are serious as a society about being inclusive then we need to work where those with the least power congregate, which may be on the streets with gangs, or in isolated communities: "What is disastrous for young people and for democracy is when the potential rebels are turned into real hooligans" (Shaw and McCulloch, 2009:13).

CONCLUSION

Kerr, Smith and Twine (2009:260) believe that the successful development of citizenship education has some way to go but that work needs to be undertaken in the areas of theory, policy, research and practice. First there needs to be agreement about what citizenship education is and what it is for, so that a working definition can become policy. For policy to be effective, it needs to be coherent and determined as an overall educational policy for the UK, not something that is decided ad hoc and at a local level. In order to translate policy into practice it needs to include all the key players, this means beyond formal education and outside of schools. Training and resources need to be available to make citizenship education a central feature not just an "add on" or option. There is a role for Youth work in ongoing research, not only evaluating existing programmes of participation but looking beyond schools and teachers, to evaluate and compare new ways of working. The Youth Citizenship Commissions findings suggested that to create a strong society investment was needed in youth citizenship (YCC, 2009: pt 197).

Davies (2008) research talked about the idea of "interrupted democracy", where practices that promote or create injustice are challenged. Young people need access to public space, as well as the opportunity to protest and to speak freely. As a society we should be providing a quality education that develops the knowledge and skills young people need to become autonomous citizens who are disposed to challenge (Giroux, 2011).

Young people are not encouraged within formal education to challenge the system or its rules. If this is not done here then it will not be done in other arenas. If individuals feel that their actions have an impact, however small then they become engaged and are more likely to connect with others, creating a shared sense of identity and belonging. This can lead to reflecting and acting on more possibilities for effecting change. An example of this is the Arab Spring, with teenagers on the streets in cities in the Middle East challenging governments and demanding change. Neoliberal policies put profit above democracy and pitch individual against individual rather than working towards the collective good. The idea of the "Big society" is not a new one , the recent report on "Children and the Big Society" states that youth groups can provide opportunities for young people to contribute to their communities but that building social capital in this way requires innovation, trust and a long term professional input (Action for Children,2011).

Youth workers are most effective in practice when they are providing role models for young people, when they are encouraging creative interpretations of policy, and when they are acting collectively and making their challenges public. Youth workers need to continue using their distinctive informal educational approach to assist young people to develop the knowledge and skills to become active citizens and governments need to take account of this in their policy creation and implementation or face the consequences of a disenfranchised alienated generation of young people and adults.

BIBLIOGRAPHY

Anderton, A., & Abbott, R. (2009). *Youth Engagement-Deliberative Research.* 2CV for Youth Citizenship Commission.

Annette, J. (2008). Community involvement, civic engagement and service learning. In J. Arthur, I. Davies, & C. Hahn (Eds.), *The Sage Handbook of Education for Citizenship and Democracy* (pp. 388–397). London: Sage.

Apple, M. W. (2006). *Education, the Right Way. Markets, Standards, God and Inequality* (2nd ed.). New York and London: Routledge Falmer.

Arthur, J., Davies, I., & Hahn, C. (2008). *The Sage Handbook of Education for Citizenship and Democracy.* London: Sage.

Ball, S. (2008). *The Education Debate.* Bristol: Policy Press.

Ball, S. (2006). *Education Policy and Social Class, The Selected Works of Stephen J.Ball.* Abingdon: Routledge.

Banks, S. (1999). *Ethical Issues in Youth Work.* London: Routledge.

Barham, N. (2006). *Disconnected Youth, Why our Kids Turned their Backs on Everything We Knew.* London: Ebury Press.

BBC. (2010). *Cameron Proposes Citizen Service.* Available at: www.bbc.co.uk.

Bowe, R., Ball, S. J., & Gold, A. (1992). *Reforming Education and Changing Schools: Studies in Policy Sociology.* London: Routledge.

Brooks, R. (2007). Young people's extra-curricular activities: Critical social engagement –Or "Something for the CV"? *Journal of Social Policy, 36*(3), 417–434. Cambridge University Press.

Cabinet Office. (2010). *National Citizen Service.* Available at: http://www.cabinetoffice.gov.uk.

Crick, B. (2000). *Essays in Citizenship.* London: Continuum.

Conservatives.com. (2010). *David Cameron Launches Plans for a National Citizen Service.* Available at www.conservatives.com.

Davies, I. (2008). Political literacy. In J. Arthur, I. Davies, & C. Hahn (Ed.), *The Sage Handbook of Education for Citizenship and Democracy* (pp. 377–387). London: Sage.

Davies, L. (2008). Education for positive conflict and interruptive democracy. In J. Arthur, I. Davies, & C. Hahn (Ed.), *The Sage Handbook of Education for Citizenship and Democracy* (pp. 1029–1039). London: Sage.

DfCSF. (2007). *Aiming High.* London: DfCSF /H.M. Treasury.

Ferri, E., Bynner, J., & Wadsworth, M. (2003). *Changing Britain, Changing Lives: Three Generations at the Turn of the Century.* Bedford way papers: University of London.

Fisher, D., & Guesu, S. (2011). *Children and the Big Society, Building Communities to Keep the Next Generation Safe and Happy.* Action for Children /Respublica Available at: www.actionforchildren.co.uk/policy.

Fitz, J., Davies, B., & Evans, J. (2006). *Educational Policy and Social Reproduction.* London: Routledge.

Giroux, H. (2011). *Neo-Liberal Politics as Failed Sociality: Youth and the Crisis of Higher Education.* Available at: http://logosjournal.com/2011/neoliberal-politics-as-failed-sociality-and-the-crisi-of-higher-education.

Goldsmith, Lord QC. (2008). *Citizenship Review, Citizenship; Our Common Bond.* London: Ministry of Justice.

Guardian Politics. *Youth Volunteer Scheme Criticised over £355m Cost.* Available at: www.guardian.co.uk/politics.

Hall, T., & Williamson. (1999). *Citizenship and Community.* Leicester: Youth Work Press.

Hess, D., & Avery, P. G. (2008). Discussion of controversial issues as a form and goal of democratic education. In J. Arthur, I. Davies, & C. Hahn (Eds.), *The Sage Handbook of Education for Citizenship and Democracy* (pp. 506–517). London: Sage.

Hill, D., & Kumar, R. (2009). *Global Neo-Liberalism and Education, and Its Consequences.* New York: Routledge.

H M Government. (2009). *An Agenda for Youth Engagement, Government Responses to the Recommendations of the Youth Citizenship Commission*. London: TSO.

Jochum, V., Pratten, B., & Wilding. (2005). *Civil Renewal and Active Citizenship: A Guide to the Debate, a Report from the National Council for Voluntary Organisations*. London: Home Office.

Jones, G., & Wallace. (1992). *Youth, Family and Citizenship*. Milton Keynes: Open University Press.

Kerr, D., Cleaver, E., White, G., & Judkins, M. (2010). *Department Constitutional Affairs-Connecting with Citizenship Education- a Mapping Study*. Slough: NFER.

Kerr, D., Smith, A., & Twine, C. (2008). Citizenship education in the United Kingdom. In *The Sage Handbook of Education for Citizenship and Democracy* (pp. 252–261). London: Sage.

Kimberlee, R. (2002). Why don't British young people vote at general elections? *Journal of Youth Studies, 5*(1), 85–98.

Kolb, D. (1988). *Experiential Learning*. Eaglewood Cliffs, NJ: Prentice Hall.

Lauder, H., Brown, P., Dillaborough, J. A., & Halsey, A. H. (2006). *Education, Globalization and Social Change*. Oxford: Oxford University Press.

Lopes, J., Benton, B., & Cleaver, E. (2009). Young people's intended civic and political participation: Does education matter? *Journal of Youth Studies, 12*(1), February, 1–20. Abingdon: Routledge.

Ministry of Justice. (2007). *The Governance of Britain*. London: TSO.

Mycock, A. (2010). *An Opportunity Missed? The Government Response to the Youth Citizenship Commission*. Available at www.opendemocracy.net.

Packham, C. (2008). *Active Citizenship and Community Learning*. Exeter: Learning Matters Ltd.

Phillips, R. & Furlong, J. (Eds.). (2001). *Education, Reform and the State: Twenty Five Years of Politics, Policy and Practice*. London: Routledge.

Shaw, M., & McCulloch, K. (2009). Hooligans or rebels? Thinking more critically about citizenship and young people. *Youth and Policy*, (101) Winter 2009.

Smith, M. K. (1996). *Local Education, Community, Conversation, Praxis*. Buckingham: Open University Press.

Taylor, S., et al. (1997). *Educational Policy and the Politics of Change*. London: Routledge.

Telegraph. (2010). *Conservative Party Conference 2010: A Prime Minister Who Relishes the Challenge*. Available at: www.telegraph.co.uk.

Young, K. (2006). *The Art of Youth Work* (2nd ed.). Dorset: Russell House Publishing.

Young, K. (1999). *The Art of Youth Work*. Dorset: Russell House Publishing.

Youth Citizenship Commission. (2009). *Making the Connection, Building Youth Citizenship in the UK, Final report of the Youth Citizenship Commission*.

AFFILIATIONS

Kathleen Edmonds
Institute of Health, Medical Science and Society
Glyndwr University Wrexham,
North Wales, UK

THEOPHILUS MOMA TAMBI

3. THE SPECIAL EDUCATIONAL NEEDS AND DISABILITY ACT (SENDA) 2001:

A Neoliberal Appraisal.

BACKGROUND

On either side of the Atlantic, neoliberalism is engulfing schools with a tsunamic magnitude. In the United States under certain provisions of the 2001 No Child Left Behind there is a pernicious government disinvestment in public schools on the one hand, and an insurgency of capitalist private take overs, on the other. In the United Kingdom, under provisions of the largely controversial Academies Act 2010, the coalition government is continuing with New Labour's structural transformation of schools. It should be noted that this brutish transformation is backed by certain legislation and that other previous legislation while still active will need to be interpreted in a way that is responsive to current trends. In terms of policy and practice, special/inclusive education has been left basking in the bashing climate of neoliberalism.

Policy making in special education goes back more than a hundred years today and some of the problems that necessitated those early policies are still recurrent today. For example, in 1870 there was the Elementary Education Act that sought to make education accessible to all especially through paying fees for the poorest children. Within the last hundred years special educational needs theory and practice have seen significant developments particularly in terms of shifts from segregation to integration and more recently into inclusion. Such developments have also been matched by swings in ideological perspectives between the individual and the social models of disabilities and between different theorized categories within special education (Clark, Dyson, & Millward eds., 1998). These developments could be seen in the context of a 'transformation in the organising principles of social provision right across the public sector' (Ball, 1997: 258). Over the same period there has been numerous policies on the provision of education for learners experiencing difficulties and disabilities (1902 Education Act, 1918 Education Act, 1944 Education Act, 1981 Education Act, 1993 Education Act, 1994 Special Needs Code of Conduct, 1995 Disability and Discrimination Act, 1996 Education Act, 2001 SENDA, 2004 Children Act, etc). Most of the earlier legislation was substantially influenced by a sense of equality, social progress and

M. Lall (ed.), Policy, Discourse and Rhetoric: How New Labour Challenged Social Justice and Democracy, 59–78.

the need for developing the learner's innate altruism – all these being, arguably, the underlying values of good education. The last few years of the previous conservative government encouraged dislodgement from legislation based upon such values to new legislation underpinned by a market-place and 'the law of profit maximization' philosophy with impetus from principles of academic excellence, choice and competition.

It is important to note that a change in government from the Conservatives to New Labour did not represent any significant change in policy directions as New Labour especially under the rhetoric of 'the third way' forged on with policies underpinned by neoliberal philosophies. This was typified in 2000 when the door was opened to a network of city academies which even though were partly paid for by the government, were governed by market accountability.

Almost as if taking over a relay race baton, the current Conservative-Liberal coalition government has, in significant ways, sought to pursue such neoliberal policies. This is seen in the re-introduction of free schools and academies and the drastic shrinking of central and local government intervention in education. As Exley and Ball (2010) maintain, 'New Labour took the [previous] Conservative infrastructure and gave it meat and teeth .... In a sense New Labour 'did' many of the [previous] Conservative policies but 'did' them differently' (p. 11). Similarly, 'New' Conservatives have taken steps in the same direction albeit more drastically and faster. For example, New Labour adopted the 'Third Way' which is essentially a dual-governance of the state and market, while the New Conservatives extended it to 'poly-governance' (Ball, 2009) which entails mixed governance by the state, the market, and stakeholders or customers of educational services.

The implications of this shift are not that hidden especially as some voices have rightly given it a priority. Fifteen years ago, Potts et al. (1995, eds.) asserted that issues of equality and diversity plagued the education system and that the struggle for an inclusive agenda remained rife. Two years later Rouse and Florian (1998) warned that '... in a climate in which educational reforms are based upon the principles of the market, students with disabilities and or special educational needs are particularly vulnerable. For schools, the task of becoming inclusive is to swim against the tide of educational reform (p. 324). Similarly, Bines (2000,: 22) alerts that within a market based system, the impact of policy on learners and their families is under-researched. In the light of these observations one ponders whether there is any real lasting impact of policy on practice. This chapter is aimed at offering a better understanding some of the implications of a particular policy within a neoliberal era.

The struggle for inclusive education, be it a matter of human rights, social justice or moral obligation (Armstrong & Barton 1999), has given rise to the articulation of varied values and expectations from some people affected by educational matters and these values have substantially informed developments in policy. Rix et al (2005, eds) have examined what these values are, how they are represented in policies and how the policies are in turn translated into practice. They conclude that, despite changing values and the developments in policy, education today is still not sufficiently inclusive.

Current developments in policy for special educational needs in England and Wales have been discussed by Bines (2000). Beginning with policy legacies, then current policies, she also looks at some outcomes of current policies. Bines (ibid.: 28) highlight three areas of policy outcome that need to be considered:

'The first involves the likelihood of achieving certain short-term policy intentions such as the reduction of statements of SEN. The second concerns longer-term objectives, such as developing inclusion and increasing school's capability to provide for SEN. The third is more general and is related to strategic approaches to continuing educational reform, including implications for SEN in particular.'

While the first outcome identified above has nearly been achieved, measures started by the previous government to reduce by forty thousand the number of learning and teaching assistants in schools will diminish possibilities of achieving the second and third.

The current state of special educational needs policy and practice have not only been a preoccupation of some scholars and researchers but also that of others including politicians. Fairly recently, Ofsted (2010) claimed that schools are exaggerating special needs to hide poor teaching. Burkard (2010) also claims that the 'special needs industry is a gigantic con [and that] what pupils really need is to be taught properly'. Warnock (2005) in a retrospective overview of the Warnock Report 1978, also asserts that 'inclusion has been carried too far' ... [and now needs] 'a new look'. Regardless of whether these positions are anti or pro full inclusion, the reader needs to approach them with a cautious inquisitiveness into their validity. As Barton (2005) exemplifies in an appreciation of Warnock 2005, 'the document is a mixture of important historical insights, but also a reflection of naivety, arrogance and ignorance on the part of the author'. I also find Burkard's stance of having pupils 'taught properly' as being overly positivist and top-down. It is espoused here that what pupils, especially those experiencing difficulties and disabilities, require is the creation of appropriate and accessible circumstances and environments for their learning. Good 'teaching' can be part of such frameworks.

The importance of critical studies to the development of policy cannot be overstated. Campoverde ('no date') identifies three forms of policy analysis, prospective, retrospective, and integrative. While the first and second forms are respectively concerned with getting information before and after policy action, the third form is continuous and gets information before and after thereby benefiting from the previous two forms. In analyzing the Special Educational Needs and Disability Act (SENDA) 2001, this chapter uses the integrative form of analysis.

As this study centres on policy analysis, an exercise in which values and theories inform and inhere in one's work, it is necessary to point out some related ethical issues. As Ozga and Gewirtz (1994:122) explain, '... what we do when we set out to understand education policy must, of its nature, be 'theorized' as we are seeking to make statements about how things connect, about how things come to happen as they do and, simply put, theories are statements about such matters.' The problem here is therefore that these values and theories we use are potentially subjective. Ozga and Gewirtz however provide a solution which is relevant to this study. According to them we 'need to look at our research activity in a self-conscious, theorized way, interrogating our theoretical 'hunches' and their associated sensitizing concepts while looking at policy at the macro, meso, or micro levels, or all three.' (p.122). In order to derive an objective analysis, one bears in mind Ozga's foregoing suggestion but, more importantly, to apply neoliberalism as a backdrop from which the SENDA is conceived, conceptualised, produced and practiced.

The DDA 1995 was criticised for not sufficiently and specifically addressing special educational needs and was thus reviewed in 2001. SENDA 2001, which as a result formed Chapter IV of the DDA 1995, was introduced in order to address, more comprehensively, the educational needs of learners who have disabilities. SENDA 2001 introduces the right for disabled students not to be discriminated against by Local Education Authorities, maintained schools, early education settings and others when carrying out their statutory duties to identify, assess and make provision for children's special educational needs. Compliance to this legislation was meant to take effect through a graduated approach whereby its provisions came into force on 1st September 2002, with two exceptions. The provision of auxiliary aids and services came into effect from September 2003 and alterations to physical features from September 2005.

To date, the SENDA 2001 is arguably one of the most single important pieces of legislation underpinning the provision of services for learners experiencing disabilities and difficulties. This high level of importance, as we shall later discuss, is also matched by the level of controversies and, sometimes, contradictions associated with this legislation.

One of the trends in special education studies today is the growing gap between policy and practice or between rhetoric and reality. This implies that the introduction of SENDA in 2001 does not exactly mean all the policy objectives have been accomplished. The policy therefore needs to be subjected to analyses that would lead to better understandings and hopefully might help to address such a growing gap.

It is ten years today since the SENDA 2001 was introduced and that renders it pertinent to revisit and analyse it to see what implications a decade of practice has unveiled. Also, as we shall see below, the policy has some key terms that can potentially cause inconsistencies and incompatibilities. It would be necessary to analyse this policy and give it meaning especially within a framework of service provision 'governed' by neoliberalism.

The reason for choosing to analyse this amendment is partly due to the dramatic reaction it provoked from educational providers and policy researchers. Since it promulgation, SENDA 2001 has formed a core reference point in policy processes within local education authorities, schools and other responsible bodies providing education both for learners experiencing difficulties/disabilities and otherwise.

CONTEXT OF INFLUENCE

In order to aid the discussion and analysis of the context of influence for SENDA 2001, the diagram below has been devised (figure 1) to give a quick overview of the various agencies that potentially influenced the SENDA 2001. Where the overall practice of policy making could be seen as 'a profusion of entangled events' (Ball, 1994), the context of influence is where we see a juxtaposition of competing interests projected by different agencies that might even be in opposition to each other. Regardless of their relationship to each other, these proliferated interests converge to form what is referred here as a 'confluence of influence' which essentially becomes the final substantive core of policy. While not all of the identified agencies have been discussed in details, the following account exemplifies how some of these factors impacted on SENDA 2001.

Either directly or indirectly and to differing extents, most previous legislation would have had an influencing effect on the SENDA 2001. However, only some of those considered to have a distinct and significant influence are discussed here. For example, under the 1902 Education Act school boards were abolished and in their place Local Educational Authorities (LEAs) were created to organize funding, employ teachers and allocate school places. The role of the LEAs as we now have it expressed in the SENDA 2001 therefore had its origins from this Act. Also under the 1918 Education Act the provision of additional services in schools, such as medical inspections, nurseries and provision for pupils with special needs was made statutory. It is from this that the SENDA 2001 was later built to demand the provision of auxiliary services with effect from September 2003. With SENDA 2001 not having defined auxiliary services specifically, this chapter refers to the same, to mean all reasonable adjustments and designated aids which when provided will facilitate disabled learners to gain better access to educational provisions.

The foregoing legislation notwithstanding, it was the 1926 Hadow Report that, among other things, prioritized activity and experience, rather than rote learning and discussed most directly, for the first time, the specific needs of children with learning difficulties. The sheer courage and clarity to address these issues has probably had an effect on the SENDA 2001.

With other legislation in between, the next big influence on SENDA 2001 was the 1978 Warnock Report. The recommendations of this report were reflected in the 1981 Education Act and later inspired the Butler (Education for All Handicapped Children) Act of 1985. While the Butler Act (1944) pointed out that there existed significant disparities and inequalities in the provision of services for handicapped children', the Warnock Report emphasized the need to 'integrate' all learners within mainstream institutions as much as possible. All of these influenced the SENDA 2001 as we can see its main contents restating these same key points.

A major development from the above was the Disability and Discrimination Act (DDA) 1995 that made 'it unlawful to discriminate against disabled persons in connection with employment, the provision of goods, facilities and services or the disposal or management of premises; to make provision about the employment of disabled persons; and to establish a National Disability Council' (DDA 1995). However, because this act did not directly address the needs of learners experiencing disabilities and difficulties, it became an extension/addition of Part IV, which became known as the SENDA 2001.

From an international perspective and by virtue of its content, the Human Rights Act (through its universal and European conventions and its domestication into UK laws through the Human Rights Act 1998) has also had a tremendous influence on the SENDA 2001.

As the forces of neoliberalism gain a stronger hold on educational practices, learners are increasingly being seen as 'consumers' of educational services. In return for their purchasing power, they bargain for better 'value for money'. This kind of educational topography is validated where increasingly over the years, stronger learner advocacy and empowerment has resulted in the desire for educational services providers to listen more to learners. Competition and marketisation are factors which are prompting further the need to listen to learners. This desire has now become an intention on the part of the providers and the state to enhance the influence of learners. As Shevlin and Rose (2008: 424) point out:

> This intention was strengthened when, in 2001, the SEN Code of Practice was revised and a whole chapter of the new document was used to emphasise the importance of pupil participation. Within this chapter it was recognised that children and young people with special educational needs have a unique knowledge of their own needs and this should be taken into consideration when influential decisions concerning an individual are made.

SENDA 2001 Context of influence

Constituents within SENDA's context of influence

Explanation of diagram: The items in the bubbles refer to the factors that potentially influenced the SENDA. The arrows point to the object of such an influence. For instance, 'globalisation' influences not only the SENDA but also researchers, practitioners, schools, colleges and other institutions. Also, each constituent can dialectically influence and impact on each other without necessarily going through the linear connections as exemplified in the diagram. For instance, pressure groups can influence the international community even without having influenced learners and families.

Here one needs to be reminded that the revised SEN Code of Practice was a promise under the SENDA 2001. This also helps to point out the level of success associated with this kind of influence.

Even though institutions are made up of individuals who work under institutional and organisational canopies, some individuals have burst through such canopies and got into positions where they have made individual contributions in the development of special educational policy and practice. Shaw (1987) discusses how some individual professionals manage to prevail over institutional tendencies that are not pro-learner. Their contributions have in turn had significant influence on SENDA 2001. Examples of individuals whose contributions have had a remarkable influence include Professor John Tomlinson. In 1996 Tomlinson chaired the Further Education Funding Council Learning Difficulties and/or Disabilities Committee that defined inclusion as 'the greatest degree of match or fit between a learner's needs and existing provision.' This is by far the most realistic definition of inclusion, the one adopted by the Centre for Studies in Inclusive Education and the one recommended in SENDA 2001. It has to be pointed out here that the inclusive nature of this definition has made it vulnerable in the hands of market-oriented 'businesses' operating in the guise of educational establishments, to determine 'existing provisions' in terms of profit maximisation principles – mostly at the expense what is best for the learner. Another individual whose contributions have helped shaped the SENDA 2001 is Professor Mike Oliver. Oliver is Emeritus Professor of disability studies with much of his work centred on advocating the social model of disability. The social model of disability is one of the strongest influences on current ideological trends. One of the most significant shifts that have had a substantial influence on SENDA 2001 is society's glide from the individual into the social model of disability. As clearly explained by Oliver (1990: 2)

> [the individual model] locates the 'problem' of disability within the individual and it sees the causes of this problem as stemming from the functional limitations or psychological losses which are assumed to arise from disability. These two points are underpinned by what might be called 'the personal tragedy theory of disability' which suggests that disability is some terrible chance event which occurs at random to unfortunate individuals.

It should also be noted that a significant feature of this model, also known as the deficit model, is the recourse to medical treatment of what was seen as the 'problem' within the individual. On the other hand, the social model of disability locates the problem within the society. 'It is not individual limitations, of whatever kind, which are the cause of the problem but society's failure to provide appropriate services and adequately ensure the needs of disabled people are fully taken into account in its social organisation.' (ibid).

This shift in social ideology is strongly evidenced in the SENDA as this legislation places the onus of responsibility towards meeting disabled learners' needs on education providers and the society as a whole. The fact that SENDA 2001 has been so informed by socially oriented values whereas more and more educational institutions are today 'forced' into 'marketisation', means that the policy might be of little benefit in the struggle for inclusive education.

Economic and political globalisation has also constituted an influence on SENDA 2001. The global market for skills is driving up competition among many countries. As Kelly (2009: 51) points out, 'The growing international pressures of globalisation affect practitioners in unpredictable and different ways, so the development of national policy is tied to the process of translating global trends to local contexts'. One of these trends is that of the 'knowledge economy' or 'knowledge capitalism' (Mark and Michael, 2005) where governments have to continuously update their skills capacities in respect to skills type, level and quality. For example, the UK has to increase its workforce in order to meet the demands of this global competition. Within a neoliberalised economic atmosphere that calls for maximisation of individual and national skills capacities, it is impossible to turn a blind eye to substantial skills gaps amongst a majority of individuals experiencing learning difficulties and disabilities, whose potential for the sustainability of their individual and social wellbeing has for long been undermined by the effects of the vicious cycle of non-inclusive education. The realisation that to successfully compete in the global skills economy meant improving on the propensity for all individuals to sustain economic wellbeing became an influential factor for SENDA 2001. The influence of the same realisation is evident in a later policy, Every Child Matters 2003, where one of its core objectives is to enhance the economic wellbeing of the child. Even though governments need to protect national interests, it is logical to see that underneath the government professed drive for inclusive education, there is a hidden agenda which is to maintain its place within global market-liberalism. Maintaining its place in a competitive economy is not problematic in itself. The problem is that it is done under the guise of inclusive education. More so, inclusive education ceases to be about addressing and meeting the needs of individual learners. It is more about serving a national economic interest.

With all the above agencies attempting to influence the legislation, it is more than likely that some of their ideals would be in opposition to each other's. In such a situation the government or the state would try to establish hegemony. According to Fraser (1992: 53) hegemony:

'is the power to establish the common sense of a society, the fund of self-evident descriptions of social reality that normally go without saying. This includes the power to establish authoritative definitions of social situations and social needs, the power to define the universe of legitimate disagreement and the power to shape the political agenda.'

The government is thus seen as a mediator. In such a mediating role, Colebatch (2005:14) 'presents the government as a process of authoritative problem solving [and that the government] confront problems and make choices, which are then enforced with the coercive power of the state'. It is this type of intervention that determines and shapes some of the discourses that dominate the rest of the policy formation process. This kind of model where the state intervenes to rationalise policy discourses, impartially or otherwise, can be seen as a top-down approach. This way of influencing policy could therefore be in contrast to the bottom-up approach where weaker agencies influence policy from an inferior power position. The tension between these two models of influencing policy is more conspicuous where the government is a 'player and arbitrator' at the same time. Instead of the hegemony established by the government being a rational consensus it quickly degenerates into the ideology and antics of just another 'merchant' in the neoliberal economy.

CONTEXT OF PRACTICE

Even though we have chosen to leave out a full discussion of the context of text production, from time to time we shall still make reference to it because what happens in the context of practice is partly due to the way the text was written in the first place. As much as services try their utmost to meet the needs of learners, the context of practice is sometimes fraught with 'troubles and contests' (Barton, 2003), challenges, tensions, contradictions, and controversies. Below is a critical understanding of these issues and how they are informed by neoliberalism.

From September 2002 it was a requirement of the SENDA 2001 for 'responsible bodies' (SENDA 2001: 8) to take 'anticipatory action' in the provision of services for learners with special needs. Theoretically the expression, 'anticipatory action' meant that institutions were obliged to be proactive and pre-emptive in the provision of services. In practice, this aspect still remains a challenge for some institutions as the extent of anticipation is not clearly defined. The extent to which schools, for example, should speculate and provide services in advance of the learners actually indicating the need for such services remains a contentious one and tends to vary from one institution to another. For example, personal experience of working with different schools brings to life some schools that engage in rigorous assessment of learners several months before the start of the school year and others that carry out the same assessment only when the academic year has already started. Schools like the former tend to be more proactive and generally more effective than others in responding to learners' needs. However, the more education is left to struggle within the market economy, more and more schools are transferring emphasis from academic effectiveness onto economic viability. While economic viability is very important, it should not be sustained at the expense of effectively not meeting the needs of mostly learners experiencing difficulties and disabilities.

SENDA 2001 makes use of the terms 'reasonable' and 'reasonably' in several places. Where a need is identified, a responsible body is required under SENDA 2001 to make 'reasonable adjustments' to services in order to accommodate the learner and address their needs. In the context of practice, this poses a challenge as the expression 'reasonable adjustment' is also not clearly defined. What some practitioners might interpret as reasonable might not be the interpretation of others. This variation in interpretation leads to differing levels of provision to the extent that dissatisfied stakeholders launch legal proceedings against institutions. This type of litigation is usually heard in the first instance in a Special Educational Needs Tribunal (SENDIST). The SENDIST is also a provision set up as part of the promises of the SENDA 2001.

Another key term of the SENDA 2001 that has great implications for practice is 'substantial 'disadvantage'. According to SENDA 2001,

The responsible body for a school must take such steps as it is reasonable for it to have to take to ensure that—

(a) in relation to the arrangements it makes for determining the admission of pupils to the school, disabled persons are not placed at a substantial disadvantage in comparison with persons who are not disabled; and

(b) in relation to education and associated services provided for, or offered to, pupils at the school by it, disabled pupils are not placed at a substantial disadvantage in comparison with pupils who are not disabled. (SENDA 2001(1) 28c)

Again, circumstances that could be interpreted as causing a 'substantial disadvantage' by some providers might not be interpreted in the same way by others.

Another key term of the SENDA 2001 that has sparked controversy and contradiction in the context of practice is 'less favourably'. In defining discrimination SENDA 2001 states that

a responsible body discriminates against a disabled person if—

(a) for a reason which relates to his disability, it treats him less favourably than it treats or would treat others to whom that reason does not or would not apply; and

(b) it cannot show that the treatment in question is justified.'

(SENDA 2001(1) 28b)

Again, the interpretation of this term varies from one provider to the other and so too the expectations of stakeholders. Consequently, a specific way of delivering educational services could be deemed inclusive in one context, yet discriminatory in another. Within a fierce market economy, learners experiencing difficulties are therefore potentially left at the discretionary mercy of service providers rather than being adequately protected by the law.

However, an understanding of the cause and effect relationship between these two expressions can help with their clarification and interpretation. For example, for a treatment to be considered as 'less favourable' it must lead to a 'substantial disadvantage', and the latter needs to be a function of the former. Any disadvantage that results from a less favourable action and that is observable, measurable and has implications for a learner needs to be interpreted as 'substantial'.

This kind of practical problem stemming from the definition of terms has unfortunately been long standing. Nearly four decades ago, the Karmel Committee (1973) identified that even the definition of special educational needs was 'an arbitrary one', a crucial consideration which the Warnock Report 1978 seemingly ignored.

Another important feature that characterises the context of practice as far as SENDA 2001 is concerned is the challenge of limited funds for institutions. Due to limited funds some institutions find it difficult to match, in practice, what is prescribed within the policy text. Limited funding puts a constraint on the provision of specialist resources, specially trained teachers and other auxiliary workers. This constraint is made worse in contexts where the needs of learners with disabilities are not the priority. Since its promulgation, there is hardly a time one would think schools have not been pointing a finger of blame at limited funds. The general lack of adequate funding notwithstanding, Whittaker (2001) argues that unnecessary reliance on segregated special schools had exacerbated the situation:

> Sending a child away from their own home and local community to a residential segregated special school can cost on average £40,000 per year, with costs of over £100,000 not unusual for extra "special" segregated schools. For a child to go to their local school with the necessary support, would be a fraction of the cost. Whilst I would argue that cost should not be the issue for effective and meaningful support it is bizarre for education authorities and head teachers to deny disabled children the right to attend their local school on the grounds of insufficient funding (p. 4).

In these times of phenomenal austerity the above statement should be given the greater consideration it perhaps deserves.

Under SENDA 2001 and with effect from September 2005, institutions are meant to have extended reasonable adjustments to cover physical resources like buildings. In the context of practice, this is a problem for some providers whose built environments are classified as listed. This means that they would find it difficult to make physical alterations to a building where access might be a problem for some learners.

As seen from the above examples cited from SENDA 2001, not all policy intentions are usually so easily translated into practice, let alone into the desired outcome. Tee (2008) examines this tendency and explains that this gap between policy and reality is due to three main 'issues with policy rhetoric, issues with the implementation process, [and] issues with the examining reality' (p. 596). This gap is usually wider with policies like the SENDA 2001 that, with a lot of cited controversial demands, presents more like a 'writerly' than 'readerly' (Hall, op cit) policy text.

In writing about the gap between theory and policy, Nye draws from Lepgold and Nincic (2001) who argue that 'the professional gap between academics and practitioners has widened in recent years. Many scholars no longer try to reach beyond the Ivory Tower, and officials seem increasingly content to ignore it' (Lepgold & Nincic 2001 in Nye 2008: 594).

Within educational practices there is interplay between professional values and the demands for accountability that drive a performance culture, all within an era when education has been taken to the market place. Within this jungle of competing interests, policy is being tossed about to find a justification for differing approaches. Fundamental elements of inclusion like access and equity inscribed in SENDA 2001 are all now being redefined in practice.

It is recognized that one of the main factors that has put a strain on teachers' professionalism and consequently on learners' achievement is performativity. Performativity, as Ball (2002: 215) explains, is '... a new mode of state regulation which makes possible to govern in an 'advanced liberal' way. It requires individual practitioners to organize themselves as a response to targets, indicators and evaluations. To set aside personal beliefs and commitments and live an existence of calculation. The new performative worker is a promiscuous self, an enterprising self, with a passion for excellence.' Responding to targets and indicators in itself is not a problem. What makes for a problem here is the fact that the value of such targets and indicators is not necessarily shared by stakeholders. The targets and indicators are mostly there to serve the interest of the dominant stakeholders, eg the government, schools and colleges, at the expense of the dominated and mostly oppressed ones eg, learners and parents. Even though in a marketised educational provision where the learner is the consumer of services, they still lack the bargaining power to negotiate targets with institutions as most of the time the institutions get paid not directly by the learners. Learners are forced to succumb to certain irrational practices because it is never so easy for them to transfer their custom to other providers.

Some professionals exploit the performative culture for selfish designs where as for others the same culture breeds inner conflicts, inauthenticity and resistance. It is not uncommon to notice how the terrors of performativity (Ball, 2003) and marketisation have caused critical incidents for some teachers in respect of them downscaling responsibilities, changing jobs, or even resigning. Where a professional has no other means to interrupt educational injustices it is still a positive action for them to resign as no 'true teacher' should stay around only to perpetrate the marginalization of the oppressed.

CONTEXT OF OUTCOME

The context of outcome is where we see the impact of policy on existing social inequalities or what could be referred to as the 'policy problem'. This context is therefore the total of the zero-situation and the interpreted policy – the zero-situation being what prevailed before the policy was introduced. While it is almost impossible to 'measure' changes in educational practices and ascribe those to specific policies, it however goes without saying that SENDA 2001 has had a significant impact with regards to individual and institutional dispositions relating to issues of equality and diversity. As Ball (1994:26) reiterates, 'the analytical concern [here] is with the issues of justice, equality, and individual freedom. Policies are analysed in terms of their impact upon and interactions with existing inequalities and forms of justice.' The impact of policy cannot therefore be discussed in isolation of the zero-situation, stasis, or policy problem – all of which are imbedded and discussed in the context of influence. As emphasised by Hanberger (2001: 46) 'if the evaluation should do justice to the real conditions under which a policy is made and [interpreted], it must take into account different stakeholders' views and arguments, including those who fail to influence the definition of the policy problem'. In evaluating the outcome of policy it is therefore important to account for the views of learners (especially those experiencing difficulties and disabilities) particularly given that while policy is made for them, their voices are hardly ever included in the definition of the policy problem.

To further analyse the context of outcome in relation to SENDA 2001, a Policy Outcome Window has been devised (see figure below) which is a diagrammatic conceptualisation of policy outcomes. As illustrated, four main types of policy outcomes and the terms 'planned outcome', 'unplanned outcome', 'zero outcome' and 'hidden outcome' have been suggested in this study to explain these various outcomes.

In terms of the planned outcome, the introduction of SENDA 2001 has led to some improved service for learners with difficulties and disabilities. For instance, before its introduction, it was not entirely illegal for institutions not to ask of the disability status of students at point to admission. With its introduction now, these institutions are obliged to request this information and to make pre-emptive reasonable adjustments where necessary. Here is an example of a situation before the SENDA 2001:

Policy Outcome Window (POW)

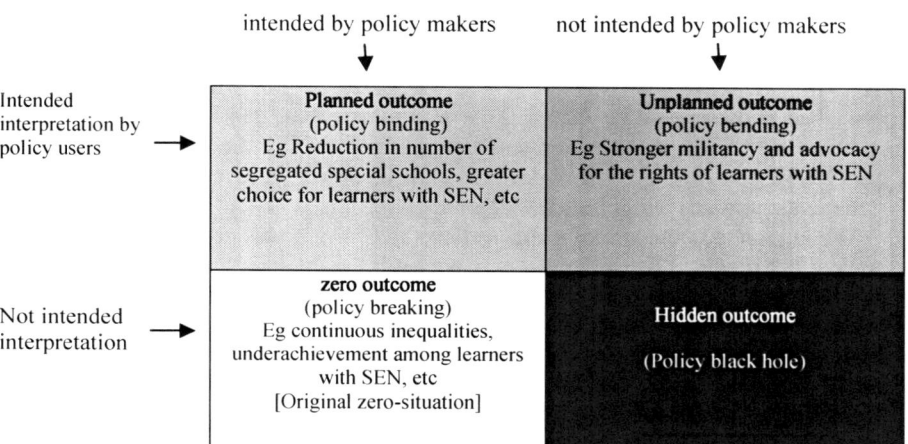

	intended by policy makers	not intended by policy makers
Intended interpretation by policy users	**Planned outcome** (policy binding) Eg Reduction in number of segregated special schools, greater choice for learners with SEN, etc	**Unplanned outcome** (policy bending) Eg Stronger militancy and advocacy for the rights of learners with SEN
Not intended interpretation	zero outcome (policy breaking) Eg continuous inequalities, underachievement among learners with SEN, etc [Original zero-situation]	Hidden outcome (Policy black hole)

Key and explanation of diagram

	Planned outcome: Here there is mutual concession between policy makers and policy users. The outcome was intended by both policy makers and users and policy is being interpreted in the intended fashion. Here, there is no disparity between policy intention and policy outcome - policy binding.
	Zero outcome: This is a situation where policy makers intended a certain outcome but had a response of indifference from policy users. This can happen as a result of people ignoring policy or not being aware of its existence. There is no impact and therefore a reversion to the zero-situation – policy breaking.
	Unplanned outcome: Here, due to interpretation of policy, there is a change in practice but not that which policy makers had intended. The difference between this situation and the one above is the fact that there is an actual change in practice in this latter case – policy bending.
	Hidden outcome: This situation arises when both policy users and makers feel that policy might have some unintended consequences which they are not aware of. This area is therefore open to research that might help unveil the unnoticed impact of policy - policy black hole.

On Peter's arrival at university in 1998 staff were not aware of his visual impairment because the form that would have alerted staff asked only whether the applicant had a 'registered disability' (which Peter didn't!). Consequently, his needs were not assessed until a few weeks later after a friend told him of the

Disabled Students Allowance (DSA) and the university's Assistive Technology Centre (ATC) which provides advice on assistive technology and supports disabled students in their studies whilst at the university. (Anonymous, 2002: 6)

Upon the introduction of the SENDA 2001 where institutions must ask about disability, regardless of whether it was registered or not, situations like the one described above would be illegal. This also means that, due to the SENDA 2001 students must not have to have a statement of needs before they are supported. This has consequently let to the desired and intended outcome of reduction of statements of needs being issued to learners.

The unplanned outcome of policy reflects that which was not intended by policy makers but intended by policy users. Here policy users have interpreted the policy in a way that supports their interest but defeats the initiatives of policy makers. In terms of the SENDA 2001, some policy users have used its success as a platform from which to demand more related legislation from the government. For instance, partly building upon the success of this legislation, MENCAP (a charity organisation for disabled people) has since been campaigning for legislation to force responsible bodies to compulsorily introduce 'Changing Places Toilets' in their premises. By encouraging their sympathizers, supporters and members to forward petitions to their Members of Parliament, MENCAP is building a forceful current of influence for such policy. This kind of precedence set partly by the SENDA 2001 is not what policy makers would have generously signed up for. In a neoliberal era, for marginalised groups to achieve unplanned policy outcomes that are beneficial for them, they need the power of their own coercion and a substantial amount of counter-hegemony against dominant and domineering agencies.

The zero-outcome of policy accounts for what results when policy makers are intent on a certain outcome but policy users do not take any interpretive action to make that happen. Here, policy has a zero impact. Based on this, the status quo or stasis is unbroken. In terms of SENDA 2001, the zero impact effect can be related to the situation that some people's attitudes and perceptions towards learning disabilities and difficulties have and would not change simply because of the introduction of SENDA 2001. In his study of ethnic minorities in the Netherlands, Driessen (2000) further stresses such discrepancy between educational policy and practice. This partly explains the fact that neoliberalism, like the capitalism of Gramscian era, partly relies on an ideological consensus and consent from the marginalised groups to achieve its aims.

Sometimes both policy makers and policy users are blind to the hidden outcome of policy. As shown in the POW above, such outcomes are not usually intended by either of the two parties. It is possible that these outcomes are hardly realised even with the most rigorous of policy evaluation practice. Same for the SENDA 2001, it is difficult to determine what its hidden outcomes are. This should therefore constitute an incentive for constant reviews and evaluations of policies. What might not be discovered at the current time might be subsequently unveiled in the future. It is arguable that modern civilisation today has been greatly shaped by capitalism that emerged far back in the 1700s. The current systemic neoliberalisation of educational services presented as a policy response to current crises could land future societies into ditches too deep for anyone to estimate the depth.

THE CONTEXT OF POLITICAL STRATEGY

As Lall and Vickers (2009) remind us, education is a 'political tool'. Where this is largely true of developing countries it is also the case in more advanced economies. The state therefore has a major stake in educational practices. In most instances, 'the role of the State has always been central in delivering education and the prime role of the state education system is to underpin the fulfilment of broader societal development goals. These goals could predominantly be economic, political, social or cultural, determined by the national, regional and international contexts.' (Lall 2009: 127). The shift in educational reform (Ball, 1997; Rouse and Florian, 1998; and Ball, 2007) notwithstanding, the government continues to politically strategise in education albeit 'underdriven' and constrained by market forces.

Due to the outcome of policy, governments tend to engage in political explanations, justifications and, eventually, strategies to contain existing situations and influence new ones. Even with its dramatic influence on practice, the Labour Party government (through local education authorities) was still under immense scrutiny by other agencies as to its ability to justify some of the outcomes of SENDA 2001. For instance, SENDA 2001 led to an increased number of learners with SEN in mainstream schools. This in turn led to the need to assess more students which also let to more statements of needs being issued. To curb this outcome and amidst rising criticism, the government encouraged the introduction of 'school action' and 'school action' plus' whereby schools will have to address the need of learners without necessarily issuing statements of needs or relying on statutory procedures. While some parts of the society welcomed the encouragement to reduce statutory statements of needs, others did not and consequently staged an outcry for a reversal of that aspect of the policy. It has hardly been clear whether the drive to reduce statements of needs was underpinned by a hidden agenda for the government to reduce SEN funding or whether it was due to the published intention of driving inclusion forward. This controversial outcome of policy has so far been left to nearly a-political means of resolving where practitioners have to implore their professional discretion. It should be understood here that the intention of the government to rely on professionals in this way is not compatible with enhancing autonomous professionalism. It is rather part of a wider scheme to of setting the scene for deep rooted marketisation of education. At institutional level this government move is tantamount to the current coalition's ideology of a 'big society' where social and educational communities are left to their own device and demise.

The underlying political strategy as seen in the above example is to make the world of educational practices 'flatter and flatter' (Friedman, 2006). The world is becoming flatter not in terms of a plain level field that breeds equality but one that launches a norm for survival of the fittest. How often do we see individuals engaging in 'Do It Yourself' ventures? How often do we see more and more people sitting in the privacy of their homes, searching for holidays, booking their flights and doing self-check-in at airports? All these are global resonations of the above mentioned 'big society' ideology. This ideology has implications with multiplier effects in the context of the UK, especially when the path is paved for the mushrooming of 'free schools' and academies. The big question remains as to what will happen if individual practitioners like doctors and teachers took to the same speed in encouraging patients and students to do more for themselves.

CONCLUSIONS

Using the Policy Cycle, this chapter has analysed SENDA 2001 highlighting its implications for inclusive education within an era of neoliberalism. As per its context of influence, the role of some of the key individuals and groups that influenced the legislation has been discussed. Even though some of the priorities of these individuals and groups have sometimes been different and even conflicting, they conglomerated into forming the context of influence that now represent the substantive core of the legislation.

The context of practice was also analysed resulting in further revelations of how policy rhetoric is often not successfully matched by practice. As seen in the case of SENDA, this discrepancy between policy and practice has been partly due to inadequate clarity and precision in the wording of the policy. Especially where this lack of clarity has resulted in different interpretations it could be argued that such lack of precision is a deliberate strategy by policy writers to permit manipulation opportunities in policy interpretation. It could be beneficial for further research to investigate the link between the way policy texts are written and the outcome of those policies.

This study has also analysed the context of outcomes. In identifying and suggesting four possible types of outcomes, this study indicates that SENDA 2001 has both intended and unintended outcomes. With the discussion of 'hidden outcomes' it also shows that some of the impacts of the SENDA are still not known and can hardly be fully estimated. This is particularly so because since the introduction of SENDA in 2001, there has not been any other legislation with such far reaching impact on special education. It would be interesting for further research to analyse more recent policies like Every Child Matters (2003), Children Act 2004 and Education Act 2005 for their implications for learners with SEN. It is necessary to warn that some of the effects of neoliberalism on educational services could sink into a 'black hole' and remain 'hidden' and possibly unexpectedly manifested in more extended domains of people's lives. An unchecked continuous decentralisation of government administration into capitalist hands in the name of autonomy and civic responsibility might tilt the balance of power to such a detrimental proportion that it will need more than an ideological shift to re-establish equality and diversity in essential services.

The successful use of the Policy Cycle in this study indicates that this framework remains a good tool in the analysis of policy within changing times.

Where this chapter began with the substantiated claim that education is not fully inclusive despite many decades of policy making, it seeks to somehow indicate that it is through studies of this nature – studies that enhance the understanding of the different contexts of policy – that the struggle for a more inclusive agenda can remain alive. For inclusive education to take a giant step towards reality, I feel it is appropriate to end this chapter by restating Apple (1999: 6) who in honour of Paulo Freire encourages that sympathisers of justice in education must not stop at 'mourning' but must 'organise' and interrupt such injustices.

BIBLIOGRAPHY

Anonymous. (2002). Have you seen this? SENDA 2001 and DDA 1995 legislation checklist: implications for higher education. *MSOR Connections*, *2*(4), 1–8.

Apple, M. (1999). Freire, neoliberalism and education. *Discourse: Studies in the Cultural Politics of Education*, *20*(1), 5–20.

Armstrong, F. & Barton, L. (Eds.). (1999) *Disability, Human Rights and Education: Cross-Cultural Perspectives*. Buckingham: Open University Press.

Ball, S. (1994). *Education Reform: A Critical and Poststructural Approach*. Buckingham: Open University Press.

Ball, S. (1997). Policy sociology and the critical social research: A personal review of recent education policy and policy research. *British Educational Research Journal*, *23*(3), 257–274.

Ball, S. (2003). The teacher's soul and the terrors of performativity. *Journal of Education Policy*, *18*(2), 215–228.

Ball, S. (2007). *Education PLC*. London: Routledge.

Barton, L., & Armstrong, F. (2003). Engaging with disabling policies: Troubles and contests in a local education authority in England. *Research in Education*, *70*, 37–49.

Bines, H. (2000). Inclusive standards? Current developments in policy for special educational needs in England and Wales. *Oxford Review of Education*, *26*(1), 21–33.

Campoverde, C. Frameworks for Policy Analysis, FAU, 297–324. Retrieved June 01, 2009, from www.fau.edu/~campover/framework.doc.

Clark, C., Dyson, A., & Millward, A. (Eds.). (1998). *Theorising Special Education*. London: Routledge.

Colebatch, H. (2005). Policy analysis, policy practice and political science. *Research and Evaluation*, *64*(3), 14–23.

Driessen, G. (2000). The limits of educational policy and practice? The case of ethnic minorities in the Netherlands. *Comparative Education*, *36*(1), 55–72.

Fraser, N. (1992). Rethinking the public sphere: A contribution to the critique of actually existing democracy. In C. Calhoun (Ed.), *Habermas and the Public Sphere* (pp. 109–142). MIT Press.

Friedman, T. (2006). *The World is Flat: The Globalised World in the Twenty-First Century*. London: Penguin Books.

Hall, K. (2001). An analysis of primary literacy policy in England using Barthe's Notion of 'Readerly' and 'Writerly' Texts'. *Journal of Early Childhood Literacy*, *1*(2), 153–165.

Hanberger, A. (2001). What is the policy problem?: Methodological challenges in policy evaluation. *Evaluation*, (7), 45–62.

Howard, C. (2005). The Policy Cycle: A model of post-Machiavellian policy making. *Australian Journal of Public Administration, 64*(3), 3–13.

Karmel Committee, Report. (1973, May). *Schools in Australia: Report of the Interim Committee for the Australian Schools Commission.* Canberra: Australian Government Publishing Service.

Kelly, A. (2009). Globalisation and education: A review of conflicting perspectives and their effect on policy and professional practice in the UK. *Globalisation, Societies and Education, 7*(1), 51–68.

Lall, M. & Vickers, E. (Eds.). (2009). *Education as a Political Tool in Asia.* London: Routledge.

Lall, M. (2009). Education in Myanmar – the interplay of state, civil society and business. In M. Skidmore & T. Wilson (Eds.), *Dictatorship, Disorder and Decline in Myanmar.* Canberra: ANU E-Press.

Mark, O., & Michael, P. (2005). Neoliberalism, higher education and the knowledge economy: From the free market to knowledge capitalism. *Journal of Education Policy, 20*(3), 313–345.

Nye, J., Jr. (2008). Bridging the gap between theory and policy. *Political Psychology, 29*(4), 593–603.

Oliver, M. (1990, July). *The Individual and Social Models of Disability.* Paper presented at joint workshop of the living options and the research unit of the Royal College of Physicians, Thames Polytechnic.

Ozga, J., & Gewirtz, S. (1994). Sex, lies and audiotape: Interviewing the education policy elite. In D. Haplin & B. Troyna (Eds.), *Researching Education Policy: Ethical and Methodological Issues.* London: Falmer Press.

Potts, P., Armstrong, F., & Marsterton, M. (Eds.). (1995). *Equality and Diversity in Education: National and International Contexts.* London: Routledge.

Rix, J., Simmons, K., Nind, M., & Sheehy, K. (Eds.). (2005). *Policy and Power in Inclusive Education: Values into Practice.* Oxon: RoutledgeFalmer.

Rouse, M., & Florian, L. (1998). Inclusive education in the market-place. *International Journal of Inclusive Education, 1*(4), 323–336.

SENDA. (2001). Retrieved May 17, 2009, from www.opsi.gov.uk/acts2001/ukpga_20010010.

Shaw, K. (1987). The Politics of higher education. In L. Robins (Ed.), *Politics and Policy-Making in Britain.* England: Longman Group UK Ltd.

Shevlin, M., & Rose, R. (2008). Pupils as partners in education decision-making: Responding to the legislation in England and Ireland. *European Journal of Special Needs Education, 23*(4), 423–430.

Tee, N. (2008). Education policy rhetoric and reality gap: A reflection. *International Journal of Educational Management, 22*(6), 595–602.

Whittaker, J. (2001). Segregated special schools must close. In *Greater Manchester of Disabled People's Magazine, Coalition* (pp. 12–16).

Theophilus Moma Tambi
Institute of Public Policy and Management,
Keele University
Staffordshire, UK.

IRENE BREW-RIVERSON

4. WIDENING PARTICIPATION AND SOCIAL CLASS-
THE MYSTERY OF UNCHANGING LEVELS
OF ENGAGEMENT:

*A Critique of the 5th Chapter of The Future of Higher Education
White Paper (2003)*

INTRODUCTION

When the Secretary of State for Education and Skills (Charles Clarke) presented this White Paper to Parliament in January 2003, one important tenet of the Labour Government's strategy was that of expansion that improved university access for those from less advantaged backgrounds. This chapter subjects the part of the Department for Education and Skills (DfES) 2003 White Paper that deals with the expansion of Higher Education to meet the needs of the United Kingdom (UK), to a level of scrutiny facilitated by the application of Stephen Ball's (1992) Policy Cycle.

This section of the DfES White Paper appears, (as has been the case in numerous policies of governments past and present,) to have been born from diverse and intricate interactions between stakeholders with varying degrees of power from a variety of sources. It was chosen in the light of its crucial role in establishing the dominant discourse in higher education particularly with regards to the role of foundation degrees in higher education and society at large. Its way of constructing the topic is a good illustration of how policy and ideological shifts can be enhanced at a macro-level in order to impact upon micro-sociological experiences (Jensen and Walker, 2003). The White Paper demonstrates the struggles and contests between empowered parties and those who often legitimate this power. Unfortunately, it gives credence to the neoliberal view that education has become a market commodity (Lynch, 2006) – market forces are highlighted as the ultimate determinant of successful higher education policy and a legitimate form of natural selection. No longer is higher education revered as serving the public good for although the need to be competitive as a nation is discussed, the responsibility is placed at the feet of the individual who has a number of choices open to them. It legitimises the metamorphosis of higher education establishments

*M. Lall (ed.), Policy, Discourse and Rhetoric: How New Labour Challenged
Social Justice and Democracy, 79–97.*

into corporate networks that are unlikely to advance social mobility. The reaction of the Russell Group universities to the fact that education participation has not widened, especially in professions such as law, medicine and dentistry goes unchallenged, as the paper subtly suggests that certain courses with lower status are more suited to particular groups of people.

The key policy discourse of widening access is presented as one that resulted in the increased participation of students from professional backgrounds - eighty percent study for a degree (Galindo-Rueda cited in Reay, David and Ball, 2005) whilst only fifteen percent of people from unskilled backgrounds are so engaged. The issue of a more appropriate 'habitus' (Bourdieu cited in Bowl, 2003) for middle and upper class families is cited as one of the reasons for the continuing improvements in engagement amongst the privileged, to the disadvantage of those less privileged. Habitus is used in this context to refer to the established cultural order that dominates a system and is imposed by those with the power to do so. It refers to norms adopted as though they were the natural state of affairs to the extent that it is thus not clear that the organisational practices, educational status accorded and the expressive order exist because,

> ...the ruling ideas in every age are the ideas of the ruling class and serve to reinforce the rule of the dominant class by establishing themselves as legitimate. There is thus a denial of the fact that the power that establishes the norm results from the economic and political power that the ruling classes wield (Bourdieu and Passeron, 1990: 31).

Policy is viewed as both text and discourse (Ball, 1994) that seeks to steer the manner in which higher educational establishments conduct their affairs. There is a clear demarcation between the extent to which elite establishments influence policy making and are influenced by the same and the extent to which less prestigious universities and colleges have policy 'done to them' (Ball, 1994).

The positioning of students as consumers in the higher education market place with the responsibility for their own success (Burke, 2008) is explored in the light of the fundamental lack of a level playing field because of the complexities that characterise the lives of many non-traditional entrants into the higher education sphere. The recent Labour Government's neoliberal stance is presented as the abdication of responsibility from a social -justice perspective as issues such as the payment of tuition fees and the kinds of institutions available to those from more non-traditional backgrounds are all cast as a result of choice and the appropriateness of different courses to suit different skills, interests and abilities. Students from non-traditional backgrounds in this context denotes those from working class backgrounds, ethnic minority groups, immigrants, students aged over 21, and others with unconventional educational biographies (Schuetze & Slowey, 2002).

The Policy Cycle permits the deconstruction of the neoliberal hegemonic discourses in place and highlights the rhetorical nature of the commitment New Labour appeared to have made to widening access. The Policy Cycle permits the exploration of shifts in the loci of power, something that illuminates the very nature and composition of the paper. The promotion of Foundation Degrees as viable and supposedly valuable alternative higher education qualifications in this document is the focus in the interrogation of this policy.

WIDENING ACCESS

Widening participation (WP) became recognised as a key policy discourse when New Labour came into power in 1997. In 2000, the Government announced a target to increase participation in Higher Education towards 50 per cent of all 18 to 30 year-olds by the year 2010 (HEFCE, 2006: 14).

When the 2003 White Paper was published, forty-three percent of eighteen to thirty year olds were reported to be participating in Higher Education (DfES, 2003), compared to only six percent of under twenty ones in the early 1960s. Whilst this appears to be a marked improvement in participation, a closer examination of statistics relating to social class paints a different picture. Reay, David and Ball (2005) highlight the fact that whilst there has been recognisable expansion and an improvement in the situation as regards gender inequality, there has been no reduction in relative social class inequality.

Watson, (2008) in commenting on progress made by New Labour since the Dearing Report of 1997, suggests that the last government's obsessive pursuit of 'world-class' status for a few institutions resulted in inertia where widening participation is concerned. It is clear that whilst New Labour was unflinching in its rhetorical devotion to WP, policies put forward did not result in notable changes. Blair's term of office from 1997 till 2007, appears to have resulted in a widening of the class gap and the accentuation of divisions in society. We now appear to be more inure to the disadvantaged amongst us. Statistics explored by Reay et al. (2005) suggest that policy changes have increased the difficulties non-traditional students face in seeking to attend university – New Labour rhetoric suggested otherwise as it resonated with practitioners involved in the delivery of such programmes, to the extent that they did not critically assess the various discourses that exist in the widening participation arena (Burke, 2002).

In 2004, Blanden and Machin (cited in Kelly and Cook, 2007) indicated that children whose parental incomes were in the highest twenty per cent were around five times more likely to acquire a degree by the age of twenty three compared to children in the lowest twenty per cent category. The lack of economic and cultural capital contributes to this situation. Economic capital denotes financial wealth and cultural capital refers to the possession of the dominant cultural values that are often translated into a state of being more likely to fit into the higher education sphere. A number of working class students are automatically deemed to have lower aspirations as the situations they sometimes find themselves in, limit the options available when choice of institution (for example) is considered. Working class students face greater economic, social and personal risks. Participation is also more costly for such students. Whilst people like Martin Harris (Director of the Office for Fair Access in 2010) may suggest that no students are deterred on financial grounds, research by Bowl, (2003), Reay (2005) and Thompson, (2009) point to the fact that a number of students are seriously affected by the lack of financial support.

Whilst there are complex reasons for the existence of the situation Britain finds itself in, the middle classes most certainly seem to feel most at ease in the 'habitus' of the more prestigious higher education establishments in the United Kingdom (Bourdieu 1984,cited in Reay et al. 2005). The previous government's attempts to change that situation through policy interventions appear to have failed to the extent where it was effectively peddling a second-class higher education to particular groups in society.

The last government's view of the primary purpose of higher education appeared to have shifted markedly from societal transformation to the economic and vocational uses of education (Taylor et al. 1997) - this is clearly demonstrated in the White Paper. As Bourdieu and Passeron (1979 cited in Reay et al. 2005) noted in the university sector in France, there continues to be an over-representation of middle class students in higher education in the United Kingdom (UK).

EDUCATION POLICY

Policy is hereby viewed as both text and discourse as described by Ball (1994). This policy was crafted by a government department (The DfES) with a view to steering the manner in which certain educational establishments conducted their affairs (Taylor, S., Rizui, F., Lingard, R., Henry, M., 1997). It would have been assumed in the recent past that education policy was designed to ensure that what education was provided took place in the public interest but the neoliberal ideology that dominates the policy making sphere in education today has resulted in a democracy that can at best be described as 'shallow' (Apple, 2006). Students are positioned as consumers in the free market of higher education. The student is now referred to as a learner and is expected to take responsibility for their own learning as a self-directed individual. There appears to be a contradictory claim- on one hand, it is advocated that class no longer exists but on the other, as for example Aim Higher programmes were put together to encourage young people from deprived areas to sample and engage in higher education, class is powerfully invoked.

Admittedly, the extremely diverse issues that need to be taken on board in policy making have rendered the process particularly complex but the fact still remains that New Labour's adoption of a neoliberal stance served to derail the possibility of education playing an emancipatory and empowering role in the lives of working class people. Education was primarily perceived to be a means of ensuring improved economic efficiency in the knowledge oriented and complex economy we operate within. New Labour appears to have fed practitioners with a stream of policies that sought to displace educational theory from its central guiding role in the professional lives of practitioners. The unfortunate state of affairs was the dominance of managerialism (Boston, 1991) – in embracing the neoliberal agenda, it is difficult to isolate the divide between capitalism and social movements; we seem engulfed in what appears to be a situation in which 'the erotic dream of the right came true as its policies were put into place by the left' (Apple, 2009).

The State was effectively absolved of the responsibility to educate its citizens so that our right to education became more and more contingent upon the ability to pay (Lynch, 2006).

WIDENING PARTICIPATION

Although widening participation was promoted as central to New Labour's higher education policy, Brooks (2004 cited in Reay et al. 2005) refers to the negligible impact policy has had in terms of class equity. Key groups that would be able to promote the cause of working class students were not involved in policy formulation (Greenbank, 2006). People from non-traditional backgrounds often view themselves as outsiders in higher education and even in the supposedly new climate created by New Labour's countless WP initiatives and policies, the situation was not truly improved 'on the ground'. Leathwood quotes Webb in referring to the homogenization of the masses; she describes how working class students and those from other minority groups are;

> ...pathologised and marked as 'Other' compared with existing students who are perceived to be there 'as of right, representing the norm against which the others are judged and may be found wanting (Webb 1997: 68, cited in Leathwood: 2003: 600).

There appears to be a paradoxical situation in the WP field. The value placed on the new qualifications as explored below in reference to the White Paper is lower than is the case with traditional degrees; that situation coupled with the kinds of institutions non-traditional students access, makes the WP mantra vacuous. The support needs of groups such as single parents are not appropriately catered for as higher education levels four and five students in colleges for example, do not have access to the child care facilities provided for Level three students. Some students have had to withdraw from part time evening programmes of study when they are unable to find someone to look after their children. McNay (2009) and Thompson (2009) make reference to the fact that an inflexible core exists in higher education that is untouched by the rhetoric of widening participation. The structural make up of institutions and their practices appear to favour the middle classes and are not on the 'negotiating table' of widening access. The impervious nature of these structures is exemplified in situations where for example, a student from a poor background with excellent grades at A Level is turned down for the ostensible reason that they are unlikely to benefit from an Oxbridge education. The most obvious issue relates to the funding of higher education. Pledging a devotion to widening participation whilst charging fees and offering loans made it difficult for non-traditional students. Unlike many middle class students they have very little support from family and as such, the government's true commitment to WP was called into question. Students from non-traditional backgrounds supposedly have the opportunity to access higher education but the worsening financial position they find themselves in militates against the uptake of these opportunities. The introduction of fees and loans has served to exacerbate the conundrum faced by those unfamiliar with the complicated arena of higher education provision and the options available to them. Such prevailing inequalities make the transition into and survival within higher education, especially in the pre-1992 sector, particularly challenging.

THE WHITE PAPER

The expansion of higher education made the economic case pivotal to the process and accentuated the intention to ensure that quality was not compromised.

The main points of the chapter (DfES, 2003) were as follows:

The increasingly knowledge-based nature of society had made it very necessary for the country to have a more highly skilled workforce, something that would be facilitated by a responsive education and training system, acknowledged to be an effective vehicle for increasing productivity.

The government sought to emphasise two-year work-focused foundation degrees as the kind of qualification that could be tailored to the needs of students and of the economy. Support for employers that developed foundation degrees and students that joined such programmes of study highlighted the desire to move away from the single template of the traditional three year honours degree.

Further Education colleges were proposed to be the main type of institution via which foundation degrees would be delivered – students would also benefit from attempts to strengthen links between further and higher education that would provide progression routes.

Foundation Degree Forward was to be established as an organisation charged with validating degrees offered in further education and as a catalyst for the further development of foundation degrees.

THE CONTEXT OF INFLUENCE

Bowe, Ball and Gold (1992), make reference to the arena or context in which policy is initiated – stakeholders engage in a struggle as they seek to influence how education is defined and what its social purposes should be.

In terms of this White Paper, the influence of previous policies can be identified. The Robbins Report and to a more significant extent, the Dearing Report of 1997 as well as proposals such as the Partnership for Progression (HEFCE 2001 cited in Bowl, 2003) had an impact upon this section of the White Paper. The history of significant events influencing policy can be traced to the expansion that had already begun (Blackburn and Jarman, 1993 cited in Greenbank, 2006) and was recognised in the Robbins Report. That report's endorsement of the principle advocating the provision of higher education for all those with the ability and qualifications to benefit set the scene from a policy standpoint for the rapid expansion of higher education. In the Dearing Report, further expansion was advocated. Additionally, the situation in the remainder of Europe where higher education is not perceived to be the preserve of the elite had clearly made the government recognise the need to address and improve levels of participation in the UK as countries such as Finland, Sweden and Norway (DfES 2003: 60) had a better educated populace and were consequently more competitive. The need to be much more competitive internationally is recognised in the rationale presented in the paper. The level of economic development in China and the remainder of Asia where labour costs are much lower also pointed to a need to facilitate the expansion that would make a knowledge-based economy more of a reality in the UK.

The concept of stakeholder analysis using the dimensions of power and interest can be applied in assessing the context of influence in this policy document – it illustrates the manner in which private and public arenas of influence impact upon the discourses at play in the drawing up of policy.

The model, developed by Mendelow (1991 cited in Johnson, Scholes and Whittington, 2006) depicts the political context within which a particular strategy is followed.

Stakeholders are put into categories on the basis of the power they wield in the situation at hand and the extent to which they are likely to demonstrate an interest in opposing or supporting a particular strategic option. An understanding of stakeholder power and interest in a situation enables those championing a particular strategy to employ tactics that will ensure that their strategy is followed successfully. The most important stakeholders are the 'Key Players' that occupy the 'high interest/high power' quadrant.

THE POWER/INTEREST MATRIX

	Low	Interest	High
Low Power	Minimal effort		Keep informed
High	Keep satisfied		Key Players

(Mendelow, 1991 cited in Johnson et al, 2006)

Power in the context of the higher education policy arena can be described in social class terms as the collective levels of economic, social, symbolic and cultural capital that individuals and particular socio-economic groups possess (Social capital denotes the benefits that accrue in the light of collective and socially negotiated relationships and links; symbolic capital arises from prestige and personal qualities possessed by an individual).

The various stakeholders affected by this particular policy proposal are highlighted below. An assessment of the level of power they wielded at the time the policy was being developed and the level of interest they had in the composition of the policy explains what the final policy became in terms of what it appeared to be seeking to achieve, how it was worded and to some extent how it was subsequently interpreted and applied. This use of a matrix acknowledges the political complexities ubiquitous in policy making.

People in lower socio-economic groups are situated in the quadrant requiring minimal effort from the proponents of the policy - they do not have the same level of cultural, economic and social capital that the middle classes possess (Bowe et al, 1992). Consequently they would not normally be sufficiently organised to obtain the information that will create a significant awareness of the impact of policies on their chances in higher education and as such, they are unlikely to seek to engage in the political processes involved in effecting the changes that will make a meaningful difference to their prospects in higher education. Should they wish to impact upon the process, they are not likely to be members of the social networks in and around political parties, Government and the legislative process (Bowe et al, 1992). When the government acknowledges that Further education colleges already play an important role in delivering higher education and proposes that

...we need to help individuals to make sensible and appropriate choices (DfES, 2003:62),

it is unclear the extent to which the views of such members of society have been solicited.

The category appeased by the provision of information, is occupied by students and lecturers in post-1992 institutions, Further Education colleges that provide Higher Education programmes and interest groups that are effectively on the margins as their voices are not sought nor particularly influential in the din created by the neoliberal ideology of today's education sphere. A large number of students in lower tier institutions are often on vocational programmes of study and it is also likely that the deficit perspective that is expressed in relation to their standing as post-1992 university students does not improve their confidence in their ability to make a difference (Apple, 2006). As expressed in the White Paper

'...work-focused higher education courses focused on this skill (associate professional) level have suffered from social and cultural prejudice against vocational education (2003: 61).

Students in these institutions are often engaged in working to support their studies and are not likely to have the time to engage in activities within societies or groups that can improve their awareness of issues relating to policy and its ultimate impact upon their lives.

The information policy makers provide is often to do with what expectations are with regards to fees and retention targets and not an invitation to engage in the crafting of policies per se.

In terms of the industrial relations situation amongst Further Education Colleges and Higher Education Institutions, the requirements resulting from performativity driven cultures (Ball, 2008) that require colleges to ensure that they are enterprising and taking responsibility for their performance in league tables has made engaging in industrial action (for example) more difficult – lecturers with targets to meet who additionally loose a portion of their salaries for each day they strike has been a deterrent for many who are already struggling to make ends meet.

The electorate is categorised as needing to be kept satisfied because, as a collective, they wield power through their votes to effect changes in government periodically. Their level of interest is not normally high outside of periods within which elections are held. The working classes are not effectively represented because they struggle for survival in an increasingly complex social and economic environment.

The key players highlighted demonstrate the concept of hegemony; they effectively ensure that their agenda remains in the foreground and by so doing; other interests are effectively sidelined or ignored (Apple, 1996). As a result of the devotion to the maintenance of 'world-class status' by the last government, Russell Group universities are denoted as key players. They are the ones that possess expert, economic, social, symbolic and especially cultural capital. Their possession of cultural capital and a sense of entitlement enable them to influence what occurs in the field of education (Reay et al, 2005). The Higher Education Funding Council (HEFCE) and the Policy writers are highlighted as key players also. They have the greatest ability to influence the policy process because they are ultimately responsible for crafting policy. HEFCE also provides a level of interpretation to institutions. The power of the media is especially potent during periods preceding election campaigns. By highlighting issues such as 'the dumbing down' of educational standards, they pander to neoliberal and neoconservative views and einforce the discourse propounded by other key players.

STAKEHOLDER MAP FOR CHAPTER 5 OF DFES WHITE PAPER

	• Low Interest High	
Low	(Minimal effort) SEGs not aware of policy making implications	(Keep informed) Students in lower tier institutions, Interest Groups Lecturers (unions; fragmented) Lower tier HEIs & Colleges
Power		
High	(Keep satisfied) Electorate	(Key Players) HEFCE, Mass Media Elite Institutions (Staff & students), Higher SEGs Policy writers

(SEG – Socio-Economic Grouping)

(Model adapted from Johnson, Scholes & Whittington, 2007)

It is on the basis of the above categories that the contents of this section of the White Paper are appraised below:

References to safeguarding the standards of traditional honours degrees (DfES, 2003:64) for example, imply the willingness of the government to ensure that key players are not unduly perturbed by the proposed expansion of higher education – their concerns are listened to and as dominant groups they do not have to give up their position of leadership (Apple, 1996). A policy settlement is alluded to in the assurances given about the new foundation degree qualification and its impact upon the education field.

The implication in the statements made about the monitoring of such programmes of study by universities and the acceptance of the Government's inability to alter the status quo where higher value is accorded to honours degrees indicates a settlement with the Right that whilst widening participation will be sought, it will be effectively limited to a second tier and will not intrude upon the space occupied by the elite.

> ...Our overriding priority is to ensure that as we expand higher education places, we ensure that the expansion is of an appropriate quality and type ...we will maintain the quality and standards required for access to university, both safeguarding the standards of traditional honours degrees and promoting a step-change in the quality and reputation of work-focused courses (DfES, 2003:60).

The WP policy discourse, masks issues of structural inequality (Burke, 2008). The adoption of a neoliberal ideology as previously noted makes it possible for policy makers to ignore issues of social inequality. This discourse reflects a denial of the role played by institutional habitus (Reay, 2005) – students from non-traditional backgrounds are not necessarily on the 'same footing' as the middle-class, white British student for whom university is a natural step in their progression, not as a result of a difference in ability but as a result of varied (amongst others), educational and social experiences that have resulted in different levels of cultural, economic, social and symbolic capital.

The dominance of the economic argument in this White Paper, to the exclusion of real social inequalities in the current system of higher education (Apple, 1996; Reay, 2005), effectively makes it possible for the government to present its position as a common sense position that should not be subjected to further debate.

This White Paper appears to tacitly acknowledge the fact that the expansion of higher education is not going to result in equity. It does not make explicit reference to the fact that the mass system of higher education is racialised, gendered and classed. It acknowledges limitations it has come to accept by proposing success only if employers value the qualification, institutional support is gained and students attracted. This panders to the idea of a 'natural inequality' that is not founded on prejudicial norms and values in the education sphere. The neoliberal and neoconservative stance that inequality is a good thing, symbolised by an acceptance of the notion that the poor get richer only when everyone including the rich get richer (Apple, 1996) is at play in this situation.

An assessment of the policy text suggests a customer –oriented ethos in line with neoliberalism. The customer is put at the centre of the policy and made an offer with incentives (DfES, 2003: 61) in order for the policy to have any hope of being successful:

> …But in order to get over the barrier of unfamiliarity and suspicion with which new courses are often regarded …we also intend to incentivise both the supply of and demand for foundation degrees.

Statements relating to lower status organisations and especially further education colleges (DfES, 2003: 61) serve to limit students to achieving a qualification primarily for work. The pursuit of education for other purposes is depicted as unnecessary. There is the unspoken assumption that those from lower social classes are primarily interested in education for economic capital gain. In a similar manner to which middle class students see higher education as their right and what is expected of them, (Bourdieu, 1990 cited in Reay et al. 2005), policy writers expect working class participants to embrace work-focussed degrees - the ability to earn a living is assumed to have pride of place amongst such groups.

This section of the White Paper suggests an attempt to match a certain kind of student to a certain kind of institution and course similar to the class matching described by Reay et al (2005) that takes place as students go to universities that mimic the environment they are comfortable within.

The White Paper's reference to the lower status afforded vocational courses, acknowledges the devaluation of higher education that comprises sub-degrees and as per Bourdieu (1993 cited in Reay et al, 2005), the widespread nature of the qualification reflects the fact that it is seen to have lower value because of the place in society occupied by the majority of people who join such courses.

THE CONTEXT OF PRACTICE

Ball's (1992) context of practice refers to what practitioners do as a result of their unique interpretation of the policy that is addressed to them. The uniqueness of this interpretation acknowledges the fact that practitioners interpret policies in the light of their own experiences, histories values and purposes. This results in the recreation of policy, a dynamic that cannot to a large extent be controlled by policy writers (Ball, 1992, Greenbank, 2007).

In terms of the first tier of interpretation, the dialectical nature of education policy means that unless the State, non-State organisations and individuals cooperate, policy outcomes are not likely to resemble the primary intentions of the authors of a policy (Skilling,1988 cited in Bowe et al, 1992:15).

The power various organisations can exercise determines how successful the policy is from the point of view of what the initial policy goals were. What would have appeared contradictory in this chapter is no longer so in the light of the fact that the key players in the WP arena wield power that makes it well nigh impossible for the government to make incursions into practices that reinforce inequalities.

Taylor et al. (1997) highlight the situation in which the official agenda of policy makers is often different from local interests.

In this light, the three ways Jones and Thomas, (2005) outline for the enactment of WP policy can be understood: The academic strand refers to what can be witnessed in elite (pre-1992) institutions – WP is on the fringes and does not play a part in the hegemonic discourses. Such institutions continue largely as per normal except in situations where decreases in demand may force them to consider more inclusive practices (Greenbank, 2007, Lyons, 2006). Normally they relate to non-traditional students by limiting themselves to 'cherry picking' the gifted and talented amongst working class students (Burke, 2008).

It appears as though the elite institutions and the policy writers expect (as is the case when habitus encounters an unfamiliar field) that the disjunctures that take place when students from non-traditional backgrounds join elite establishments to result in alterations to the students' behaviour and not the institutions themselves (Reay et al. 2005). The resulting disquiet, ambivalence, insecurity and uncertainty are assumed to be something that the WP staff on the fringes of the organisation can deal with – these issues resulting from a lack of cultural economic and (often) social capital may result in an assumption that working class students belong elsewhere even though they have the academic ability to succeed in such institutions. Post-1992 institutions are often perceived to adopt the 'double deficit stance' or the Utilitarian approach (Jones and Thomas, 2005) in which they embrace students with lower aspirations and non-traditional qualifications as a result of WP policy, seeing themselves as well placed to support such students (Greenbank, 2007). What is rare (Jones and Thomas, 2005) is a Transformational approach in which the institutions realise that change should not be the sole responsibility of the student and should be considered by the institution as structural change could facilitate improvements without jeopardising standards.

THE CONTEXT OF OUTCOMES

This context highlights the manner in which policies impact upon existing social inequalities (Bowe et al, 1992). In terms of this WP policy, the result has been the entrenchment and legitimisation of a differentiated field that results in poorer job prospects and lower economic returns from higher education for students who join programmes of study such as foundation degrees (Reay et al, 2005). Meritocratic equalisation is at best political rhetoric. The policy writers effectively acknowledge and more or less accept the government's apparent powerlessness to effect meaningful change:

> ...We believe that these stimuli are necessary to break the traditional pattern of demand...But we know that we will only succeed in changing the pattern of provision if foundation degrees are valuable to employers, attractive to students, and supported by institutions. We cannot impose this change...
> (DfES, 2003:62)

Presenting the 'others' in higher education with two year work-focussed degrees whilst assuring the elite that their turf is sacrosanct is the concept of 'half a loaf being better than none' – a true lack of political will in the face of too many common-sense arguments for this state of affairs to continue (Apple, 2006).

The proposals put forward serve to embody a devotion to creating a society that is more acceptably unequal rather than one in which there is a more just social order.

Whilst the government proposed to encourage diversity through this policy, it did nothing to stop the hierarchical ordering of institutions on the basis of activities like research and results (Whitty, 2002).

THE CONTEXT OF POLITICAL STRATEGY

A continued apathy in view of the perception that post-1992 universities and further education colleges cannot influence policy making in a meaningful way, especially now that a conservative-liberal coalition government has taken over the reigns of government, will equate to positioning such institutions in the 'low power/low interest' category, content to have the title university or the letters FDA (Foundation Degree in Arts) after their names. The reality of the fact that there is a need to seek ways of influencing the political processes that influence non-traditional learners will have to be continuously acknowledged and challenged by every means at the disposal of such institutions. As practitioners working with students from diverse backgrounds, there is a need to struggle for a commitment to widening participation in institutions so that policy makers consider how structural change in institutions will help resolve some of the problems non-traditional learners face (Burke, 2002).

Meaningful change, similar to that facilitated by the civil rights movement, the women's movement and more recently the Citizen School Project in Port Alegre, Brazil (Gandin, 2009) will be facilitated after a long political struggle. In this situation, the need to expose the deep inequalities that still continue such as the average spend on students in the provision of academic services being £1,418 for the top ten universities as per the Good University Guide (2008 cited in Leathwood, 2009) and £673.6 for the bottom ten universities (Leathwood, 2009) will take sustained action against the seemingly common sense and meritocratic ideology of change that is the hegemonic discourse in education today. A commitment to seeking meaningful alterations in social values that will usher in a policy regime with social welfare at its heart is necessary. There needs to be an acknowledgement of the fact that no one model fits all contexts (Gandin, 2009) as the issues non-traditional learners face are varied and complex.

The student demonstration that took place on the 10th of November 2010, appears to be one of the ways in which those with a social conscience must seek to raise the consciousness of others who are taken in by the common sense arguments put forward by the coalition. Whilst violence cannot be condoned, the collective expression of unhappiness with this state of affairs must continue. When 50,000 people gather, they are certainly sending a message to the coalition about an awareness that they have of their collective position as key players in the education field. Cameron's statement of bringing the full force of the law to bear on those who turned violent in some way skirts around the issue that is really at stake – how can we not bring our conscience as a nation to bear on the issues that confront us today?

POST NEW LABOUR – WHAT FUTURE FOR WP?

The new coalition government, in setting out its stall in May (Guardian, 20/5/10), has indicated that it intends to attract a higher proportion of students from disadvantaged backgrounds into higher education. It also states a commitment to increasing social mobility. These two goals sound positive but against the backdrop of a £1.5 billion cut in education funding and the removal of the cap on student fees proposed by Browne, this may be as Sally Hunt of the Universities and Colleges Union puts it, the beginning of 'ignorance policy' making. Foundation Degrees do not seem to be popular with the coalition – Foundation Degree Forward was abolished in July 2011.

Whilst Browne's review cites increased participation as an aim and increased competition between Higher Education Institutions as a benefit, it is still very difficult to see how there can be any fairness in the competition when there certainly will not be a level playing field. Coughlan's (http://www.bbc.co.uk/news/education) assessment of winners and losers post Browne's report summed it up well – the Russell Group wins as it is empowered to protect its world class status whilst some new universities face what was hitherto unthinkable - the possibility of closure as they fail to attract cost conscious students (customers) in the future. It is possible to concur with Browne's judgement that the public purse can no longer fund the tuition fees of the growing number of people who wish to enter higher education but if so many generations have benefited from free higher education, would it not be much more equitable for the burden to be distributed amongst the population through taxation so that the burden is shared? It does not appear to be just that thousands who have gained from a free system only to stand back and watch whilst this generation shoulders the burden of past excesses and difficult economic times.

Lord Browne (2010:1) has made references to the great advances made into ensuring that those from disadvantaged schools or backgrounds could access Higher education – such head line statements hide the truth of the matter indeed.

The admission that:

> The most advantaged twenty per cent of young people are around seven times more likely than the most disadvantaged twenty per cent to enter the most selective one third of institutions (Browne, 2010: 34)

gives a more accurate picture of the stratification that continues to exist. Regrettably, what lies ahead appears to suggest a more elitist education system than one that will provide more opportunities to those from non-traditional backgrounds. (http://www.bbc.co.uk/news/education)

Lord Browne's assertion that the increase in maintenance grants to help the poorest people does not give due regard to the fact that students will still leave university with huge debts and no guarantee of employment post degree courses. One in eleven graduates are currently unemployed, six months after leaving university (The Guardian Newspaper, 1/11/10). The aversion to risk previously referred to is likely to influence the decision making of students who do not have the support of family and friends who are not already acquainted with the education sphere.

However, one positive outcome of the Browne review is the opportunity for those wishing to study part time to finance their studies via the loan system. Whilst students will still be expected to pay back the money they owe, more of those already in employment are likely to be encouraged to study, providing the programmes available are designed with a more diligent consideration of the needs of working people.

CONCLUSION

> ...part of a conscious collective attempt to *name the world differently,* to positively refuse to accept dominant meanings, and to positively assert the possibility that it could be different...
> (Apple, 1996: 21)

A close examination of this widening participation policy has demonstrated the dominance of the ideologies of neoliberalism and neoconservatism in the field of higher education. What policy has sought to achieve is the normalisation of the premise that the market and not the democratic state is the natural producer of cultural logic and value – the student of higher education is an economic maximiser, primarily motivated by self-interest (Lynch, 2006). It is clear that the Labour government resigned itself to the existence of a two tier system of Higher Education , acknowledging the fact that it would rather have 'world-class' institutions than pursue a more equitable state of affairs for all those who could benefit from higher education. The imbalances in the power wielded by various stakeholders reinforces this stance and it will be imperative for the voices that have become marginalised to do everything possible to disrupt the neoliberal and neoconservative agenda that appears to have a firm hold on the higher education field today. Unless that occurs, unchanging levels of engagement will continue to characterise the working classes – inequalities will be produced ad infinitum. The key players in policy development in the higher education field will continue to be those who will not necessarily advance the cause of all those who regardless of background can benefit from higher education.

As Apple (1996) highlights, having our educational institutions respond to the needs of those who are not so powerful is a long but essential struggle – much must be done so that regardless of background, students are not seen as inferior because they do not fit a particular mould.

By so doing, the work in higher education with people from non-traditional backgrounds should facilitate an increase in economic and social capital that will improve their potential cultural and symbolic capital. As educators, it is time to question the commercial normalisation of higher education and provoke a greater consciousness of our collective responsibility to all those seeking to educate themselves.

BIBLIOGRAPHY

Apple, M. W. (1996). *Cultural Politics & Education*. Buckingham: Open University Press.
Apple, M. W. (2006). *Education The 'Right' Way: Markets, Standards, God and Inequality*. New York and London: Routledge.
Apple, M. W. (2009). *Understanding and Interrupting the Right*. Institute of Education, 26/6/09.
Ball, S. J. (1994). Some reflections on policy theory: A brief response to Hatcher and Troyna. *Journal of Education Policy*, *9*(2), 171–182.
Ball, S. J. (1994). *Education Reform*. Buckingham: Open University Press.
Ball, S. J. (2007). *Education Plc*. Oxon: Routledge.
Ball, S. J. (2008). Performativity, privatisation, professionals and the state. In B. Cunningham (Ed.), *Exploring Professionalism*. London: Institute of Education.
Ball, S. J. (2007). Private lives: Middle-class practices, class insulations and four-wheel drives. In M. Reiss, R. DePalma, & E. Atkinson (Eds.), *Marginality and Difference in Education and Beyond*. Stoke on Trent: Trentham Books.
Bowe, R., Ball, S. J., & Gold, A. (1992). *Reforming Education & Changing Schools*. London: Routledge.
Bowers-Brown, T. (2006). Widening participation in higher education amongst students from disadvantage socio-economic groups. *Tertiary Education and Management*, *12*(1), 59–64.
Bowl, M. (2003). *Non-Traditional Entrants To Higher Education 'They Talk about People Like Me'*. Stoke on Trent: Trentham.

Browne, J. (2010). Securing a sustainable future for higher education. In *An Independent Review of Higher Education Funding and Student Finance*. Retrieved October 27, 2010, from http://www.bis.gov.uk/assets/biscore/corporate/docs/s/10-1208-securing-sustainable-higher-education-browne-report.pdf

Burke, P. J. (2008). The challenges of widening participation for professional identities and practices. In B. Cunningham (Ed.), *Exploring Professionalism*. London: Institute of Education.

Burke, P. J. (2002). *Accessing Education: Effectively Widening Participation*. Stoke on Trent: Trentham Books.

Coughlan, S. (2010). *University Fees-Winners and Losers*. Retrieved October 27, 2010, from http://www.bbc.co.uk/news/education-11522593

Dearing, Sir R. (1997). *Higher Education in the Learning Society*. London: National Committee of Inquiry into Higher Education.

DFES. (2003). *The Future of Higher Education*. London: DFES.

Gale, T. (1999). Policy trajectories: Treading the discursive path of policy analysis. *Discourse*, 20(3), 393–407.

Gale, T. (2001). Critical policy sociology: Historiography, archaeology and genealogy as methods of policy analysis. *Journal of Education Policy*, 16(5), 379–393.

Gandin, L. A., & Apple, M. W. (2003). Educating the state, democratising knowledge: The citizen school project in Porto Alegre, Brazil. In M. W. Apple, et al. *The State and the Politics of Knowledge*. New York and London: Routledge Falmer.

Greenbank, P. (2006). The evolution of government policy on widening participation. *Higher Education Quaterly*, 60(2), 141–166.

Hatcher, R., & Troyna, B. (1994). 'The Policy Cycle': A ball by ball account. *Journal of Educational Policy*, 9(2), 155–170.

Johnson, G., Scholes, K., & Whittington, R. (2007). *Exploring Corporate Strategy*. London: Prentice Hall.

Jones, R., & Thomas, L. (2005). The 2003 UK government higher education white paper: A critical assessment of its implications for the access and widening participation agenda. *Journal of Education Policy*, 20(5), 615–630.

Kelly & Cook. (2007). DFES Report –Full-time Young Participation by Socio-economic class

Lall, M. (2009). *Contemporary Education Policy Presentation Feedback*. Institute of Education, 27/6/09.

Leathwood, C., & O'Connell, P. (2003). 'It's a struggle': The construction of the 'new student' in higher education. *Journal of Education Policy*, 18(6), 597–615.

Leathwood, C. (2009). *Researching Post-Compulsory Education; Policy, Practice and Social Justice*. London South Bank University, 3/6/09.

Lewis, B. (2002). Widening participation in higher education: The HEFCE perspective on policy and progress. *Higher Education Quaterly*, 56(2), 204–219.

Lightfoot, E. (2009). *Michelle Obama: First Lady of Hope United States*. Lyons Press.

Lynch, K. (2006). Neo-liberalism and marketisation: the implications for higher education. *European Educational Research Journal*, 5(1), 1–17.

Lyons, J. (2006). An exploration into factors that impact upon the learning of students from Non-Traditional backgrounds. *Accounting Education: an International Journal*, 15(3), 325–334.

McGivney, V. (1990). *Education's for Other People*. Leicester: National Institute of Adult Continuing Education.

Minter, C. (2001). Some flaws in the common theory of widening participation. *Research in Post Compulsory Education*, 6(3), 246–258.

Morley, L. (2008). The micropolitics of professionalism: Power and collective identities in higher education. In B. Cunningham (Ed.), *Exploring Professionalism*. London: Institute of Education.

Nicoll, K. (2006). *Flexibility and Lifelong Learning: Policy, Discourse and Politics*. Oxon: Routledge.

Ranson, S. (1995). Theorising education policy. *Journal of Education Policy*, 10(4), 427–448.

Reay, D., David, M., & Ball, S. J. (2005). *Degrees of Choice: Social Class, Race and Gender in Higher Education*. Stoke on Trent: Trentham Books.

Schuetze, H. G., & Slowey, M. (2002). Participation and exclusion: A comparative analysis of non-traditional students and lifelong learners in higher education. *Higher Education, 44,* 309–327.

Shepherd, J. (2010). Graduate unemployment at highest level for 17 years. *Guardian Newspaper.* Retrieved November 12, 2010, from http:www.guardian.co.uk/business/2010/nov/01/graduate-unemployment-highest for 17 years

Stuart, M. & Thomson, A. (Eds.). *Engaging with Difference: The 'Other' in Adult Education.* Leicester: National Institute for Adult Continuing Education.

Taylor, R. (2007). Social class and widening participation. In A. Tuckett (Ed.), *Participation and the Pursuit of Equality.* Leicester: National Institute for Adult Continuing Education.

Taylor, S., Rizui, F., Lingard, B., & Henry, M. (1997). *Educational Policy and the Politics of Change.* London: Routledge.

Thompson, D. W. (2008). Widening participation and higher education: Students, systems and other paradoxes. *London Review of Education, 6*(2), 99–181.

Watson, D. (2008). *Whatever Happened to the Dearing Report? UK Higher Education 1997–2007.* London: Institute of Education.

Whitty, G. (2002). Consumer rights versus citizen rights in contemporary education policy. In *Making Sense of Education Policy.* London: Paul Chapman.

Irene Brew-Riverson
Department of Higher Education
Westminster Kingsway College

STEPHEN COLWELL

5. THE DOCTRINE OF CREATIVITY AND THE COMMODIFICATION OF IDENTITY:

The consequence of the Cox Review of Creativity in Business for education in communication media

INTRODUCTION

The Cox Review of Creativity in Business (2005a) attempts to promote the importance of creativity, innovation and design to UK business in its entirety, as vital to our national prosperity within a framework of global competition. It describes the arena of intervention and the mechanisms by which solutions may be implemented; changing business attitudes towards creativity and creative people and the critical role of education in changing attitudes of creative people towards business and also improving the effectiveness of public procurement in encouraging creativity and innovation.

This critique employs the 'The Policy Cycle' as a framework for analysis. The method of text production effectively excludes all but the author and commissioner. Their framing, I argue, places Schumpeter's (1943) analysis of the decline of capitalism and Popper's (1943) reading of Hegelian Historicism at the heart of the text of the Review. Analysis of influence identifies the ideological elevation of the 'global competition narrative' and the promotion of business as the primary source of policy wisdom and direction and management of creativity which represents a rationale that legitimises contingent and, by extension, de-legitimises absolute individual creative autonomy. The chapter then focuses on the practice implications for educational institutions and professional educators and addresses outcomes in the light of recent policy developments following the election of May 2010. Within this framework the analysis seeks to show that by 2005 New Labour had moved decisively from its initial approach of embracing creativity as a social good to fully endorse a neoliberal hegemonic rationality expressed in an exploitation model of power relationships between Business and 'Creative's' articulated by the Cox Review.

Cox does not acknowledge discrete fields of endeavour or the diversity and complexity of our social, cultural and economic environment, however, its implications for teachers and learners, particularly those concerned with

M. Lall (ed.), Policy, Discourse and Rhetoric: How New Labour Challenged Social Justice and Democracy, 99–120.

communication media and its social, cultural and political function are explored in this analysis. The intrinsic tension between autonomous agency in communication media, particularly in journalism, and elites exercising power within the 'Public Sphere' is a fundamental socio-political theme. The rise of bourgeois power and pluralist democracy in the UK (Perkin 1989; Habermas 1992; Held 2006) marches in time with the development of mass media. Critical analysis of the relationship between economic and political elites and media encompasses critical political economists such as Herman and Chomsky (1994) McChesney (McChesney 2004) Croteau and Hoynes (2006) and Murdoch and Golding (2006) and liberal theorists such as Curran (1981; 2002; 2005) and Schudson (1995; 1999; 2003) but all agree on the centrality of agency and contested space for autonomy in media in debates.

While the role of the State in media differs between political cultures (Hallin and Mancini 2004) the supposed openness and pluralism of British Media is of concern here. The 'mixed economy' of unfettered and politically committed press and broadcasting regulated by a statutory duty to promote pluralism, fairness and ethical professional practice had, until the mid-eighties represented a media which was, to a large degree, still rooted in a public service ethos borne out of the post-war consensus. There was space for many distinct voices, despite a primary focus on the voice of elites, competing or otherwise. Since then the activity of the State has focused on de-regulation, encouraging the growth of giant media conglomerates and the destabilization of state regulated media dedicated to public service. As Thompson (1995) observes;

> Left to itself the market does not necessarily cultivate diversity and pluralism in the sphere of communication. (Thompson 1995: 240)

The Cox Review does have one thing to say about media; it extols the use of the "...broadcast media to encourage creativity and innovation..." but in the context of getting "... a stronger sense of enterprise across to young people." (Cox 205: 21) This propagandist position rather makes Thompson's point and highlights the tenor of the review. Its importance lies, I suggest, in its relation to the dramatic policy changes wrought in Higher Education in the aftermath of the election of 2010; its significance is situated in its simplicity. The Review is a digest of neoliberal economic and social nostrums prepared for education and business senior management, a powerful, easy to understand propagandist directive which encapsulates the ideological basis of and motivation for Managerialism. I suggest that it is not a text that invites scepticism but then it is not written for the sceptic but the believer.

THE PRODUCTION OF TEXT: FRAMING THE PROBLEM.

The Cox Review is notable for its speedy production; announced by Gordon Brown in the budget speech of February 23rd 2005, with a questionnaire response deadline of August 31st, published on December 2nd 2005. Its purpose was outlined in its questionnaire sent to businesses;

> ...how best to strengthen the relationship between businesses – particularly SMEs - and creative professionals and secondly strengthening the links across university departments and with industry, proposing specific action in both of these areas, for Government, businesses and other institutions, with the objective of raising UK productivity. (Cox 2005b)

The Review is strategic; it claims to "... address a question that is vital to UK's long term success – namely, how to exploit the nation's creative skills more effectively..." (Cox 2005a: 1) Sir George Cox, Chairman of the Design Council, formerly Director General of the Institute of Directors, states that "...the basic approach has been to consult widely, tapping into the best available thinking that has already been given to the problem, rather than undertaking time consuming research." (Cox 2005a: 3) This assertion invites critical examination of the way in which the problem is framed, in this case, by two narratives, Risk and Nation, set within the context of economic globalisation, deregulated financial markets, flexible labour markets, privatisation and transnational corporatism that have reduced the capacity of national governments to exercise control over their economies.

The stated aim is to persuade leaders in business and education that "Creativity" is central to national economic success in a competitive global market. To achieve this required outcome those involved must first be made aware of the jeopardy which should persuade them to make common cause:

> The Review was triggered by concerns about how UK businesses can face up to the challenge of a world that is becoming vastly more competitive. ...the competitive threat from emerging economies notably India and China... ... this Review supports the reality of the threat... ... it is hard to think of any sector that will remain unaffected... [Emerging economies] are investing massively in education, technical skills and creative capabilities. (Cox 2005a: 5-8)

The significance of creativity and innovation is articulated in terms of competitive advantage and national character. Emerging economies are constrained by lack of marketing and customer insight which is evident in free market economies:

> ...they have fantastic factories but don't know what to make ...the ability to innovate depends on the availability and exploitation of creative skills. In a real enterprise culture these needs create a virtuous circle: companies need to draw on the talents of a flourishing creative community which needs

to respond to the demands of a dynamic and ambitious business. That ought to be good news for the UK. It plays to one of our national strengths. (Cox 2005a: 10)

Cox attempts to organize the reader's perspective through division. An opposition of national denigration and nationalist hubris fixes the globalisation perspective of competing nation states rather than international collaboration; classification continues with distinguishing a 'Creative Community' from 'Business', to whose demands it needs to respond. These are simplistic dichotomies justified by contested narrative frames. The concept of "Nation" used here needs to be examined; are we speaking of the romantic notion of Nation as an embodiment of values drawn from shared histories or, I would argue is the case here, the identification of the welfare of the Nation with purely commercial values.

The concept of 'State' articulated in terms of competition is paramount here, but the exploitation of the creative capabilities at its disposal in response to that risk is a Historicist model revealed in Popper's (1943) critique of Hegel's writing when in the service of Frederick William 3rd of Prussia in the reactionary and repressive years after the turmoil of the French Revolution and the Napoleonic Wars:

> ...'the State is the actual, existing, moral life... ...to the complete State belongs, essentially, consciousness and thought ...shows [Hegel's] insistence on the absolute moral authority of the State, which overrules all personal morality, all conscience. (Popper 1943: 35)

Hegel's philosophy, according to Popper, links to modern totalitarianism:

> Hegel's success was the beginning of the age of dishonesty and the age of irresponsibility; first intellectual and later moral irresponsibility; a new age controlled by the magic of high sounding words and by the power of jargon. (Popper 1943: 31)

Echoes of Hegelian Historicism, I suggest, can be discerned in Cox's nationalist framing and its ideology of division and subordination to the requirements of the nation.

The language of Risk is significant as is the particular concept of Nation. Beck (1992) describes the concept as the Risk Society, "...where the social production of wealth is systematically accompanied by the social production of risks," (Beck 1992: 19) and explores various categories and social implications of risk but questions of political and economic management of technologies are central and globalised. The risk frame that Cox selects is one of diminished creative capacity in UK's businesses but one could equally apply Becks catastrophe theory, for example, where risk is exported to poorer populations. Competitors like India and China are also burdened with ecological disasters like Bhopal (Burke 2010) and the chemical plant catastrophe on the Songhua River (Lorenz 2005) and countless others, not to mention staggering levels of pollution and industrial devastation.

Hazardous industries have been transferred to the low wage countries of the third-world. This is no coincidence. There is a systematic 'attraction' between extreme poverty and extreme risk. (Beck 1992: 41)

However alternative, more complex discourses are excluded from the Review. The UK must be solely dependent on neoliberal solutions to a problem of neoliberal values; simplistic dichotomies and dubious narratives provide the rationale for the thrust of Cox's argument and intended outcomes. Thus, the ideological parameters of text production are set as tightly as possible.

THE PRODUCTION OF TEXT: ...DEFINING THE SOLUTION.

Cox goes further, however, by identifying the solution to the problem as "Creativity", an absolute human quality. But Cox's "Creativity" is as ideologically contingent as his frame to the problem, narrowly defined as a commodity to be exploited for national strategic purposes, exclusively in an entrepreneurial context. 'Entrepreneur' is the salient term contained in the Review and embodies the ideology that drives the whole. I suggest that the theoretical basis of this position derives from the decline of capitalism described by Schumpeter (1943). He states that the success of capitalism inevitably leads to the elimination of competitors and an increasing desire to protect capital value through the creation of giant enterprises;

> The perfectly bureaucratized giant industrial unit not only ousts the small and medium sized firm and 'expropriates' its owners, but in the end it also ousts the entrepreneur and expropriates the bourgeoisie as a class. (Schumpeter 1943: 119)

This process not only progressively diminishes the effect of creative destruction but also leads to the detachment of the mass of people from the fundamentals of capitalist institutions, individual ownership of property and freedom of contract. The inevitable emergence of giant enterprises;

> ...by substituting a mere parcel of shares for the walls and machines in a factory takes the life out of the idea of property... ...this evaporation of the material substance of property affects not only the attitudes of holders but that of the workmen and public in general. Dematerialized, de-functionalized and absentee ownership does not impress and call forth moral allegiance..." (Schumpeter 1943: 127)

We live in an age of the Giant Enterprise or Corporation which, as Schumpeter predicted, distort national economies and polities. Schumpeter argues that the corporatism of late stage capitalism will inevitably drive out "Unternehmergeist", or entrepreneur-spirit, embodied in those special individuals who make things work in an economy, whose function is to develop or transform patterns of production by exploiting an invention or an untried technology. Schumpeter attempts to distinguish exceptional people, a classification apart from the mass population, who have an innate capacity to get things done, to overcome resistance to new ideas and ways of doing things. There are, unsurprisingly, few of these exceptional individuals who exemplify the entrepreneurial type and fulfil the entrepreneurial function. The fantastic leap that Schumpeter made when he associated entrepreneurialism with a quasi-mythical type rather than with physical and mental processes involving many individuals in multiple activity contexts and socially interactive situations, even viewed from this distance, is extremely questionable. The grotesque rewards claimed by those fulfilling leading corporate roles in an era of spectacular corporate failure might be viewed as compelling evidence of Schumpeter's error and why, despite its manifest flaws, this doctrine appeals so much to corporate elites.

It is, perhaps, understandable that Schumpeter's analysis and his emphasis on property and ownership should have led him to his concept of entrepreneurship as "Unternehmergeist". One must recognize the period of writing, a time when eugenics was still respectable in some quarters and concepts of class, race and gender superiority were for the most part unchallenged. However, Schumpeter's theories were contested by many contemporary social economists, in particular the concept of the entrepreneur as a type associated solely with capitalism. This was challenged by von Mises (1946), hardly a bleeding heart liberal, who recognised that agency stems from uncertainty inherent in every action and is not confined to the economic sphere. He bluntly stated that the "...entrepreneur is not a social type but a social role attributable to all participants." (von Mises 1946: 253).

Despite these challenges and the fact that his writing was contextualised by genuine totalitarian threat Schumpeter's theories have clearly influenced those who influence the Cox Review such as Hayek, (1944) Freidman (1962) and other Chicago School economists. Contemporary devotees tend, however, to substitute the Keynesian Welfare State both for 'Socialism' and as the culprit in the "death of the entrepreneur". For example, the current, reduction in the public sector budget will, in theory, allow the Private Sector to flourish. In his first budget speech Chancellor Osborne (2010) promised "...an economy where the state does not take almost half of all our national income, crowding out private endeavour..." And, with apparent lack of irony, representatives of corporate interest insist that the State take responsibility for 'creating' entrepreneurs through the education system. This is an essential component of the strategy of concealment of contradiction which lies at the heart of neoliberal ideology.

THE CONTEXT OF INFLUENCE: OVERWHELMING THE ALTERNATIVE DISCOURSE.

Schumpeter's theories are complex and point directly to the dangers of Corporations which must be subject to restriction and regulation if Capitalism is to successfully contest the drift towards Socialism. The problem was that if Corporatism was inevitable and would extinguish that which made it possible a mechanism must be devised to justify the corporatisation of capitalism. The solution was found in an almost exclusive focus on one of many factors identified by Schumpeter, the Entrepreneur as 'Type' and the function of 'Entrepreneurism' as exclusively commercial. This allowed the development of a powerful, simple idea of how the world should be if the contradictions made clear by Schumpeter were to be concealed, their eradication being demonstrably impossible. The success of this ideology is manifested both in the elevation of business leaders to dominant positions in policy formation and the drive to establish "Homo-econimus" as the idealised and required "type" of individual through education.

This is the wellspring of policy influence flowing from Corporations and their ideological Satraps, trade associations and policy think tanks. The European Round Table is an organisation representing executives and chairmen of major multinational companies of European origin. ERT is the source of a succession of reports promoting neoliberal values and policies. Its report "Job Creation and Competitiveness through Innovation," (1998) under the Chairmanship of Baron Daniel Janssen, states:

> Education systems need to be receptive to innovative ideas coming from an ever-widening range of disciplines. But Europe's education leaders also need to embrace innovation. All too often the education process itself is entrusted to people who appear to have no dialogue with, nor understanding of, industry and the path of progress. This goes some way to explaining the persistent mismatch between the skills required by employers for new vacancies and those offered by entrants into the labour market. Greater emphasis must be placed on entrepreneurship at all levels of education." (Janssen 1998: 17-18)

The invocation of "...the path of progress" and the condemnation of those who obstruct it provides an insight into the Hegelian historicist subtext of the catechism which is repeated in innumerable policy papers echoing the line from the ERT and organisations such The Cato Institute in America, The Adam Smith Institute, the Confederation of British Industry and the Institute of Directors, once chaired by Sir George Cox. The CBI is particularly active and has published several reports including "In Search of Quality in Schools" (Thompson, Mitterbauer et al. 2000) which bemoans the skills schools equip their students with, calling for a focus on skills to strengthen the competitiveness of our economy. The language used in promoting the market in education gives an indication of the ideological belligerence inherent in the policy position. The CBI policy document, "The business of Education Improvement" (Jones 2005) is explicit in its aims and criticism:

> We want to challenge any ideological opposition to private sector involvement in public services... The failure to develop the market beyond the initial intervention process stemmed, in part, from the apparent stigma associated with public-private partnerships. (Jones 2005: 4)

The paper is explicit in targeting perceived cultural and political resistance from local authorities and advocating a change in their role from direct providers to commissioners of services This aggressive stance is underpinned by the report 'Innovation and Public Procurement" (Bradshaw 2006) which advances both the entrepreneur and innovation agenda with investment from the public purse.

The Corporate position is endorsed by a flood of policy documents published by a variety of government departments and Quango's since 1997 which endorse or build on the central neoliberal discourse or provide detail on the tactics and mechanics of how aims might be achieved. It was preceded by "The Innovation Report" (Sainsbury 2003), accompanied by "Creativity, Design and Business Performance" (Pryce 2005) and followed by "Prosperity for all in the Global Economy – world class skills". (Leitch 2006) The "Lambert Review of Business – University Collaboration" (2003) suggests giving the lead to business in research and development and intellectual property rights in the university sector. One of the most alarming is "Nurturing Creativity in Young People" (Roberts 2006) commissioned by the D.f.E.S. and D.C.M.S. which incorporates an agenda for education and creativity of young children contingent on the demands of the economy. Together with policy papers that have flowed from organisations and institutions such as N.E.S.T.A (Wayman and Brown 2007), N.C.G.E. (Gibb 2005; Herrmann, Hannon et al. 2008) and H.E.A – E.S.E.C.T. (Moreland 2006; Yorke and Knight 2006), the quantity of policy texts, of which this represents a small sample, the Cox Review being one example, each repeating and supporting the other, excluding different or contesting perspectives and analyses, arguably amounts to an ideological and doctrinaire assault on political and institutional deliberation. This raises questions for educational institutions where 'outcome' and 'performance' dominates while social interaction as the basis of creativity remains a "black box" where the magic happens, a paradigm exacerbated by government policy that elevates education for work and employer requirements over pedagogy and andragogy.

THE CONTEXT OF INFLUENCE: NEW LABOUR AND THE DOCTRINE OF CREATIVITY.

How did a Labour government arrive at this point and why did they pursue this ideological agenda so ruthlessly? The Author, Sir George Cox, acting alone, without benefit of research or competing perspectives arguably guaranteed complete control over the content of the review to the commissioner, the then Chancellor, which invites an examination of the intent of New Labour's senior policymakers. Tackling unemployment through education and training and acquisition of skills was a key New Labour Objective examined by Dolowitz (2004) who argued that by

> ...adopting an endogenous growth strategy the government will be able to reinstitute an activist policy regime capable of promoting the party's traditional values of equality, justice and fairness within a socio-economic policy designed to ensure long-term growth and prosperity." (Dolowitz 2004: 213)

The critique is that New Labour abandoned the political, particularly in economic policy, and in effect accepted neoliberalism by default. By de-politicising economic policy, accepting the premise that markets are natural and impartial, regulated by effort and merit, it abrogated democratic responsibility of the State to assert the primacy of the political over the economic sphere.

In domestic policy New Labour abandoned its constituency in pursuit of policies like 'Workfare', the acceptance of a de-regulated labour market and the introduction of market practices in Public Services. (Kenny and Smith 1997; Smith 2003; Wring 2005; Hay 2006; Jessop 2007; McAnulla 2007) The last of these was laid out by Jessop (1993) who observed the hollowing out of the National State in Western Europe and North America and the replacement of the "Keynesian Welfare State" with the

> ...Schumpeterian Workfare State... Its distinctive economic and social objectives can be summarized in abstract terms as: the promotion of product, process, organizational, and market innovation; the enhancement of the structural competitiveness of open economies mainly through supply-side intervention; and the subordination of social policy to the demands of labour market flexibility and structural competitiveness." (Jessop 1993: 9)

Jessop's definition neatly illustrates the ideological dominance of Corporatism cunningly embodied in the myth of the Entrepreneur as "Ubermensch", possessor of aptitudes that can be present in only a small fraction of the population, who are concerned with innovation in production, processes, organizations and markets, which necessarily excludes the mass of people and denies the historic pre-eminence of collective action, communities of practice and social interaction. The people's function in this system is to serve; in the case articulated by Cox as 'Creative's'.

From the beginning New Labour's policy on employment and social exclusion sought to utilise the cultural sphere though not as part of an economic strategy promoting neoliberal values. A key text from this period is 'All Our Futures: Creativity, Culture and Education' (1999) the Robinson Report, commissioned by the Secretary of State for Culture, Media and Sport, Chris Smith. Its focus is on creativity and creative practice as a general benefit to individual and wider society though encouraging the development of confidence and self esteem in those that participate thereby encouraging personal growth, social cohesion and providing skills needed for employment. The report devised a value free definition of creativity; "We therefore define creativity as: Imaginative activity fashioned so as to produce outcomes that are both original and of value..." clearly choosing not to make value contingent, and stated that "...creativity is possible in all areas of human activity and that everyone has creative capacities". Robinson is clear about the importance of creative practice and that it is not the sole province of the arts or supposed gifted elites but for all and in all areas of endeavour, including business and industry. The report acknowledges other discourses and purposes, particularly those inherent in individual development as an absolute.

However, New Labour Policy in government rapidly developed from the Robinson Report to a policy which linked 'Creativity' to Britain's economic success and employability. It shifted to a concept that is contingent, an essential requirement for adaptation to new social and economic complexities that depends less upon the capacity for expressiveness than on an ability to respond effectively - creatively – to new challenges, a position articulated by the Cox review. This is 'Creativity' as 'Fairy Dust', a doctrine that promotes its transformational qualities as a vital component for economic success in a globalised world but detached from practice and activity, from social interaction and context, divorced from imagination and culture. The theoretical underpinning, as we have seen, comes from a variety of sources, but at the beginning of the journey think-tanks such as Demos provided the intellectual muscle. According to Bentley and Seltzer (1999), for Demos, creativity is not only a set of skills, but a modality:

> It is about equipping people with the skills they need to live full lives; the ability to respond creatively and confidently to changing situations and unfamiliar demands, to solve the problems and challenges they face at home, in education, at work, to make a positive contribution to the life of their communities.' (Bentley and Selzer 1999: 9)

The stress now is on a different sort of creativity; not only is the politics of culture disregarded but individual creativity becomes contingent rather than absolute. Bentley and Selzer separate 'creativity' from artistic discourses, processes of interaction and reification and imagination; it becomes instead "...the application of knowledge and skills in new ways to reach a valued goal." (Bentley and Selzer 1999: 9) The value free definition of creativity in Robinson is progressively abandoned and, as we see in the Cox Review, creativity has become a means to serve industry and commerce and individual autonomy is proscribed.

Even though the case presented by Cox is based on selective and contested narrative frames he asserts that "Creativity, properly employed, carefully evaluated, skilfully managed and soundly implemented, is a key to future business success – and to national prosperity." (Cox 2005a: 3) He is saying that business managers need not to be afraid of the creative individual because their 'talent' can be constrained and harnessed for national strategic ends and profit. This argument is most clearly evidenced in Chapter 6; Preparing future generations of creative specialists and business leaders:

> The requirement is simple. We need business people who understand creativity, when and how to use to use the specialist and who can handle innovation; creative specialists who understand the environment in which their talents will be used and who can talk the same language as their clients and business colleagues;" (Cox 2005a: 28)

The duty of the 'specialist' is to accept the exploitation paradigm; their position is subordinate, a relationship where business exercises control and insists on 'Creative's' adopting the language of their superiors. The definition of 'Creativity' in the Review reinforces the power imbalance; 'Creativity' is the generation of new ideas – either new ways of looking at existing problems, or of seeing new opportunities, perhaps by exploiting emerging technologies or changes in markets." The outcome of creativity is innovation; '...the successful exploitation of new ideas. It is the process that carries them through to new products, new services, and new ways of running the business or even new ways of doing business. (Cox 2005a: 2) Cox has recommendations for achieving the aims contextualised by his definitions; "...stronger links need to be formed between Universities and SME's Universities will benefit from access to and connection with entrepreneurship which is to be found in SME's, particularly when a business agenda is being promoted in Higher Education." (Cox 2005: 29) Embedding entrepreneurship in education leads to a recommendation that students are taught to work with and understand other specialists, a seemingly laudable ambition but given the tenor of the Review the implications are clear. Another strand of the argument is the development of entrepreneurs; "The skills agenda figures highly in this, as does the nurturing of the creative industries themselves, and the general climate for encouraging enterprise and entrepreneurship." (Cox 2005a: 5) Here the relationship between creativity and "Unternehmergeist", or entrepreneur-spirit is articulated in an argument for training for the development of the entrepreneur located in concepts of 'type' linked to S.M.E's.

Schumpeter's influence is apparent however the case plainly neglects Schumpeter's explicit warning against the anti-competitive character of corporatism, that unregulated market mechanisms are not benign, neutral or efficient but rigged and unfair, denying genuine opportunity to succeed to most of those who take on the role of entrepreneur when setting up a small business. The pattern, envisaged by Schumpeter, that the corporation "...not only ousts the small and medium sized firm and 'expropriates' its owners..." is a familiar story of rewards to a few and excludes the rest who contributed to the enterprise. The sale of the Huffington Post to AOL (Harris 2011), a 'New Media' enterprise and exemplar of the Cox Review's approach to 'Creative's', is an object lesson in this tendency. This cycle, enthusiastically promoted by Cox, uses theory developed by Schumpeter to entrench the exploitation model that he warned against, a cycle of continual enrichment and expansion of a tiny oligarchy and the impoverishment of the rest, not only economically but culturally and socially.

The political and social implications of ceding ever greater control to corporate interests and the concomitant constraint of opposition to neoliberal and neo-conservative hegemony, particularly prevalent in communication media, and the intrusion on the creative, social, cultural and political integrity of the individual is excluded from the Review. Responsibility for this lies in the coalescence of New Labour policy on employment, social exclusion and creativity framed by neoliberal proscription of legitimate and illegitimate actions both for individuals and the State, to the exclusion of any competing narrative. Given the extent of government control over text production the Cox Review establishes that by 2005 New Labour had moved decisively from its initial approach of encouraging creativity as a social good to fully embrace neoliberal hegemonic rationality.

IMPLICATIONS FOR PRACTICE: AGENCY, AUTONOMY, INTERWOVEN NARRATIVES AND VOICE.

The Review throws up significant ethical and practical problems for teaching, learning and curriculum development and must be considered in the light of wider neoliberal and neo-conservative agendas for education. Imposing private enterprise management practices in public institutions, particularly education, is widely documented and critiqued as an advancement of a neoliberal agenda. (Jessop 1993; Whitfield 1999; Hirtt 2000; Newman 2000; Ball 2001; Hatcher 2001; Ball 2007; 2008) The second strand is neo-conservative prescription regarding curricula and is also well documented (Apple 1995; Olssen 1996; Apple 2006; Buras 2006; McCarthy, Pitton et al. 2009; Robertson and Dale 2009; Saltman 2009; Santome 2009) It represents a melange of ideas associated with an idealised version of the past in which 'real knowledge' based on 'facts' was unchallenged, where people were deferential and where communities guided by respect for class disparity ensured stability and security.

The Cox Review represents the link which provides the self referential circularity of policy providing the neoliberal equivalent of neo-conservative education thinking. Legitimate knowledge is combined with legitimate behaviour which is entrepreneurial exercised within a market context. Neoliberalism requires the political regulation of human behaviour as opposed to the political regulation of corporate behaviour. Classical liberalism, derived from the period of the establishment of bourgeois political power (Perkin 1989; Habermas 1992) represents a negative conception of state power. The individual is characterised as having an autonomous human nature and can practice freedom in a struggle against governmental constraint while simultaneously supporting those institutions that support the development and expansion of the bourgeoisie. But the triumph of the bourgeoisie has been translated into a neoliberal corporate hegemony which offers only a devalued and degraded view of individual autonomy. As the democratic state withers it is replaced by the Corporate State which offers an illusion of autonomy, an autonomy that is contingent on accepting neoliberal values and the repudiation of all others. It is severe constraint masquerading as freedom.

This critique is articulated well by writers like Olssen (1996) and Frank (2000) who focus on neoliberal modification of human behaviour. Classical liberalism, rooted in the commercial and political rise of the bourgeoisies and the challenge to existing elites, represents an idea of state power as detrimental to the individual who is conceived as an autonomous agent. There is more than an echo of this philosophy in anti-State propaganda peddled by politicians such as Blair and Cameron, however, as Olssen points out their position is disingenuous because "...in neoliberalism the State seeks to create an individual who is an enterprising and competitive entrepreneur ...homo-econimus." (Olssen 1996: 340) This echo of Schumpeter's early debate with von Mises over 'Role' or 'Type' reveals its significance as the elevation of 'Type' requires modification of those who do not live up to this ideal. This conception of the social world must imagine people as fully sensible economic actors, qualified to make their needs known in the open market and of acting in their own interests. Frank observes that any opposition to this ideology is met with extreme hostility; "This image of homo-econimus evaporates when people refuse to act within the constraints of the market or in accordance with neoliberal values." (Frank 2000: preface) Recall the hostility of the CBI to perceived resistance in local government, relentless attacks on professionals in education from a neoliberal and neo-conservative policy groups and most particularly from committed political elites.

When hitherto respected professionals, particularly in publicly funded services like health and education, respond citing an alternative rationale they are subjected to a profound and aggressive intellectual denigration. They cannot possibly understand the democratic perfection and auto-regulation of the market in all its quasi-mechanical, quasi-mystical complexity. Merely by questioning what appear to be fundamental contradictions and failings they commit acts of vanity and arrogance, unpardonable offenses against "The Nation". Their endorsement of "The State" as a complex web of institutions with resources and power is condemned as anti-democratic because democratic "choice" can only be situated in individual freedom purely expressed in commercial transaction. The Corporate State is progressively excluding even other bourgeois professional elite groups which have historically constituted the Bourgeois Public Sphere through an attack on public service masquerading as a critique of elitism. Legal, medical, scientific, academic and other elite professional classes find their authority undermined and their voice of significantly diminished consequence as the apparent complete ascendancy of ideology over pragmatism in policy making, a trend begun by

Thatcher and Howe, continued by Blair and Brown, reaches its apotheosis under Cameron and Osborne.

This denial of voice spreads far beyond privileged bourgeois professionals. Governmental responses to the financial collapse of 2008 which exclusively favour 'Corporate' interests and reflect neoliberal values have resulted in protests across Western Europe which has had little or no impact, so far, on policies. The crisis of voice is identified by Couldry in "Why Voice Matters" (2010) who observes that

> ...above all voice is undermined when societies become organised on the basis that individual, collective and distributed voice need not be taken into account, because a higher value or rationality trumps them." (Couldry 2010: 10)

Couldry draws attention to a discourse that acknowledges the importance of individual narratives that are interwoven in infinitely complex ways with the narratives of others and the threat posed to that society by an ideology that only recognises interaction expressed in market terms as valid.

This has grave ethical and practical implications for teaching and learning. In communication media it undermines concepts of individual and collective autonomy, ensuring that creative practice is subject to neoliberal ideological direction. 'Creative's' must embrace business ideologically, to understand their role and function and 'Creativity' as conceived by Cox is merely utilitarian; "...the majority of students studying creative arts will never have the opportunity to practice as professionals... If we could channel some of this interest in creativity into other jobs that would benefit from creative thinking then we could fully harness the education investment." (Cox 2005a: 32) The casual detachment of 'creativity' from individual identity and meaning and the articulation of its value as merely commercially contingent could not be more explicit. Appropriation of education investment that fails to acknowledge students dedication of human and material resources does not simply echo Hegel's totalitarianism.

The creative process is rooted in social interaction. A media artefact, a TV documentary for example, is made from ideas about a world which is subject to differing and competing social constructions of reality. Dramatic imagery and sound, dialogue, performance, the content that comprises the narrative becomes the artefact. It is the physical outcome of a process of making where interaction between members of the group tasked with making, forms a milieu constructed from investigation, argument and deliberation from which an ethos, represented by a narrative, is created. The outcome is dependent on competence, understanding of and expertise in deployment of a wide range of technical skill and tacit knowledge which is both individual and collective. The multi-contextual complexity and emotional intensity of collaborative creative processes create a dynamic setting where new knowledge and significant meaning for the individual is created. In fact the significance of the process for the individual is intrinsic and essential to the outcome.

The context of the activity and the activity itself appear to have decisive significance as an arena for social interaction and individual ethical positioning within that interactive context. Rogers (1961) developed an eminently serviceable definition of how the mechanics of a creative process work for the individual who

> ...constructs a relationship with reality that has meaning. Extensionality and internalised evaluation are essential. Two other factors are required; feelings of having ventured into unknown territory and the need to communicate, the necessity of sharing the newly created knowledge of self in relation to the environment with others." (Rogers 1961: 354)

Strauss (1997) observes that in adult life we are invariably engaged in multiple roles, the nature of the task or problem differs, emphases within the multi-contextual environment shift but our perception remains uniquely our own, the cognitive, attentive and physical activity we undertake, the new knowledge we construct and the meaning we take from it is intrinsic to the formation of self.

> ...it is perfectly clear that conceptual change – hence transformation – marks the course of adult careers. ...the transformation of perception is irreversible, there is no going back." (Strauss 1997: 94)

Social interaction and individual exploration within that context is Creativity; new ways of thinking and looking at the world, of social construction within multiple contexts. In education, learning and creativity is the province of individuals and communities of practice, freely entered into, contextually complex and ethically rooted, where relations of power, agency and structure are explored not imposed.

The Cox Review's simplistic view of 'Creativity' has serious implications for educators. When Cox says, "...We need business people who understand creativity, when and how to use to use the specialist..." and recommends that business introduce "...greater understanding of creativity into the boardroom by recruiting people with creative experience," (Cox 2005: 27) his detachment of creativity from interaction and identity is explicit. Higher Education is exhorted by Government and neoliberal think-tanks to conform to market driven practices and embed the demands of 'Business' in the curriculum. Since the publication of the Cox review the emphasis on utilitarian approaches to 'Creativity' appears to have strengthened, however, neoliberal values cannot be attributed to every enterprise. In fact the imposition of neoliberal or any other ideological values represent political constraint on what should be learned and how, denying that which is acknowledged as most valuable; the genuinely creative process. Employer's labour needs are complex and their simplification, in the cause of imposing neoliberal values, does not aid commerce or industry.

The idea that simplistic definitions of creativity can be applied across all fields of endeavour requires that the manifest and inherent contradictions of the position be disregarded. It presents the social reality of the world of work as 'manageable' but only in an imagined world, an ideological projection of how the world should be, could be; a fantasy. The Review seeks to oblige educators to ensure that students serve a national interest defined solely by neoliberal values even though it dishonestly fabricates an authoritative voice of industry according to its ideological predisposition, fails to comprehend the dialectic complexity of social interaction in business, advocates a distorted concept of creativity and treats individual creative identity as a commodity.

OUTCOMES: THE APOTHEOSIS OF NEO-LIBERALISM IN HIGHER EDUCATION?

Has the process that began with the election of May 1970 been brought to a climax by the election of May 2010? This may appear to be a convenient construction but the emergence of the policy direction of the Conservative Government, aided and abetted by elements of the Liberal Democrat Party leadership committed to neoliberal values, may come to be cited as the moment when the contradictions of neoliberalism became clearly identifiable. All areas of social cooperation to be found in painfully, painstakingly established institutions are under threat but the site of the hottest ideological contest must be Education. For many years the discursive space has been dominated by neoliberal partisans promoting the entrepreneurship agenda, in effect paving the way for the Browne Report on Higher Education Finance. New labour's complicity in this agenda is now plain to see. Browne is merely the latest in a succession of corporate insiders to pronounce on public services and with the publication of his report the programme has reached its climax.

The Conservative Government response has brought the significance of the Cox Review into sharp focus as an important text which facilitates the entry of the entrepreneurship agenda, the carrier of neoliberal values, into education. Schumpeter, it seems, has been proved correct in his critique of corporatism and the inevitable detachment of capitalism as a concept from people's perception as a mechanism that will provide the 'Good Life' for the mass of the population. The deception and greed at the heart of neoliberalism has resulted in a class of managers in both private and public sectors, particularly in Higher Education, reaping rewards that separate them from the mass of people, including students and their parents, who cannot even imagine the lifestyle these salaries bring. The explicit link, established by Browne and Conservative Government policy, between individual investment in education and future employment will necessarily become the measure of what is legitimate knowledge despite the fact that there can never be a guarantee of such a simple causal relationship, makes this separation of Senior Managers from the rest of the education community deeply concerning. The savage cuts to the teaching budget fulfil two purposes; first to attack those areas of academic research and teaching that are not amenable to neoliberal values, where alternative discourse originates and where the history of prior discourse is retained; second, to entrench the explicit link between individual student education investment and future employment revenue that will inevitably restrict teaching and learning to that which is deemed necessary to fulfil the education / employment contract.

The ideology represented by this move reduces us to a state of unconnected individuals whose only right to act is as homo-econimus, merely as a consumer of services, not as homo-agens, an autonomous individual acting socially with others within the complex constraints of multiple and competing contexts. Once the concept of education for the sake of the individual and the wider community detached from any particular ideological discourse has been eradicated it is a short step to defining legitimate and illegitimate knowledge and legitimate and illegitimate behaviour. Behaviour will be contextualised by the market and the intended entrenchment of these values in our education system, excluding any alternative competing narrative, represents the imposition of narrow concepts of thought whose legitimacy rests in neoliberal values creating a division in our society which evokes unfortunate echoes from the past.

My specific concern is for those young people who hope to make their way in communication media. Given the importance of autonomy and professional ideology of objectivity in communication media for the functioning of a democratic public sphere the implications are alarming. Construction of identity within the wider media 'Habitus' is intrinsic to learning in this context. Professionally, managing the tension between individual agency and autonomy and institutional authority requires a high level of critical independence, a capacity to comprehend multiple contexts and an awareness of subjective positions, one's own and others. Cox represents an ideology that potentially drives out those things that cannot be justified in commercial terms and articulates an entrenchment of subordination of the individual which shifts an already unequal power relationship decisively in favour of established commercial and political elites that advance a neoliberal agenda.

The scale and audacity of this move is matched only by its dishonesty. An institution which is based on a principle of societal good, which once embodied concepts of democracy and respect for divergent views and discourse, is transformed into a market supposedly governed by individual choice as part of an ideology of deception. But we know that markets are not benign, neutral or efficient but rigged, unfair and prone to catastrophic failure due to abuse on a colossal scale by the same corporate elite that promotes the market in education. Not content with brazenly demanding that the public, through taxation, finance the inculcation of neoliberal values in the education system they now expect young people and their parents to fund their indoctrination. At the behest of this coalition of the greedy education ceases to be a site of learning and becomes a realm of propaganda and, employing economic blackmail, coercive behaviour modification of the most offensive form.

CONCLUSION

The Cox Review appears to be an open and discursive text, inviting interpretation and a creative response, however, the position articulated is designed, I maintain, to preclude a response outside its parameters. This is not to say that the creative process and innovation are not essential factors in life generally and in commerce and industry particularly; nor to deny the nation state, the necessity of entrepreneurial activity, the effects of globalisation, the politics of employment and employability or even the potential of Schumpeter's theories. However, the selectivity, partiality and lack of complexity evident in the text represent a culture that excludes critique and alternative and competing theory. Popper's assessment of followers of Hegel might be applied to Cox and the ideology he represents; "Hegel's fame was made by those who prefer a quick initiation into the secrets of this world to the laborious technicalities of a science which, after all, may only disappoint them by its lack of power to unveil all mysteries. "(Popper 1943 31) The issue with the Cox Review is not business or creativity, as such, but integrity, evidenced by the parroting of cant from the ERT, CBI and other representatives of corporate interest as "the best available thinking..." which, it argues, should exercise primary influence in education. Democratic collective strategic action is excluded by the articulation of this concept in terms of authority and subservience within an exclusively commercial context. It represents the neoliberal incursion into cultural and social spheres, an imposition of an authoritarian hegemonic rationality even as its values are undermined by economic calamity. Cox, markets a simple concept of the 'Creative' as commodity to be exploited by established business with an oppressive fervour redolent with Hegelian historicist fantasy, a narrow, determinist and self serving policy perspective enacted through government and its agencies which, potentially, fatally distort the educative environment.

The market experiment in finance, commerce and industry has been a catastrophic failure. The solution for the Conservative Government, it seems, is to continue the experiment until every aspect of our society and culture is laid waste. It will be interesting to see whether a market in which providers, Universities and Colleges, seek to sell a tainted product, neoliberal indoctrination masquerading as an education, can survive but the cost of the trial is, I fear, too great. At present there is no political party that will articulate opposition and an alternative narrative to the neoliberal perspective that unites the Conservative and Liberal Democrat Parties. It is to the Labour Party leadership's shame that under Blair and Brown they allowed themselves to be first seduced and then to wholly give themselves to this neoliberal fantasy. For the sake of our pluralist democracy, even at this late stage, we need a mainstream political leadership that will critique and oppose what can only be described as neoliberal totalitarianism, denying any voice that tries to act collectively and democratically, denying the capacity to act socially, denying any acknowledgement that the narratives of others are interwoven with our own.

BIBLIOGRAPHY

Apple, M. W. (1995). Education and Power. London, UK: Routledge.

Apple, M. W. (2006). Educating the "Right Way": Markets, Standards, God and Inequality. Taylor Francis Group, llc.

Ball, S. (2001). Labour, learning and the economy: A 'policy sociology' perspective. In M. Fielding (Ed.), Taking Education Really Seriously (p. 260). London, UK: Routledge Falmer.

Ball, S. (2007). Education Plc: Understanding Private Sector Participation in Public Sector Education. Abingdon, UK: Routledge.

Ball, S. (2008). Performivity, privatisation, professionals and the state. In B. Cunningham (Ed.), Exploring Professionalism (pp. 50–72). London, UK: Bedford Way papers.

Beck, U. (1992). Risk Society: Towards a New Modernity. London, UK: Sage.

Bentley, T., & Seltzer, K. (1999). The Creative Age: Knowledge and Skills for the New Economy. London, UK: Demos.

Bradshaw, T. (2006). Innovation and Public Procurement (p. 16). London: Confederation of British Industry.

Buras, K. L. (2006). Tracing the core knowledge movement: History lessons from above and below. In M. Apple & K. L. Buras (Eds.), The Subaltern Speaks: Power, Curriculum and Educational Struggles (p. 294). Abingdon, UK: Routledge.

Burke, J. (2010). India fury over us 'double standards' on BP and Bhopal. In The Guardian. Manchester, UK: Guardian News and Media ltd.

Couldry, N. (2010). Why Voice Matters. London, UK: Sage.

Cox, G. (2005a). The Cox Review of Creativity in Business: Building on the UK's Strengths (p. 47). London, UK: HM Treasury.

Cox, G. (2005b). The Cox Review; Questionnaire for Business. 19 DOI: http://213.219.8.102/pdfs/dti/innovation/cox_review.pdf

Croteau, D., & Hoynes, W. (2006). The Business of Media: Corporate Media and the Public Interest. London, UK: Sage.

Curran, J. (2002). Media and Power. London: Routledge.

Curran, J. & Gurevitch, M. (Eds.). (2005). Mass Media and Society. London, UK: Hodder Arnold.

Curran, J., & Seaton, J. (1981). Power without Responsibility: The Press, Broadcasting and New Media in Britain. London, UK: Routledge.

Dolowitz, D. P. (2004). Prosperity and fairness? Can new labour bring fairness to the 21st century by following the dictates of endogenous growth? British Journal of Politics and International Relations, 6(2), 213–239.

Frank, T. (2000). One Market under God: Extreme capitalism, Market Populism and the End of Economic Democracy. New York, USA: Anchor Books.

Friedman, M. (1962). Capitalism and Freedom. Chicago: Chicago University Press.

Gibb, A. (2005). Towards the Entrepreneurial University: Entrepreneurship Education as a Lever for Change (p. 46). Durham: University of Durham.

Habermas, J. (1992). The Structural Transformation of the Public Sphere. Cambridge, UK: Polity Press.

Hallin, D. C., & Mancini, P. (2004). Comparing Media Systems: Three Models of Media and Politics. New York, USA: Cambridge University Press.

Harris, P. (2011). Arianna Huffington: The cheque's in the post. In The Observer. London, UK: Guardian News and Media Limited.

Hatcher, R. (2001). Getting down to business: Schooling in the globalised economy. Education and Social Justice, 3(2), 45–59.

Hay, C. (Ed.). (2006). Managing economic interdependence: The political economy of New Labour. In Developments in British Politics. Basingstoke, UK: Palgrave Macmillan.

Hayek, F. (1944). The Road to Serfdom. Abingdon, UK: Routledge.

Held, D. (2006). Models of Democracy. Cambridge, UK: Polity Press.

Herman, E. S., & Chomsky, N. (1994). Manufacturing Consent. London, UK: Random House.

Herrmann, K., Hannon, P., et al. (2008). Developing Entrepreneurial Graduates: Putting Entrepreneurship at the Centre of Higher Education (p. 40). Durham, UK: National Council for Graduate Entrepreneurship.

Hirtt, N. (2000). The 'Millennium Round' and the liberalisation of the education market. Education and Social Justice, 2(2), 12–18.

Janssen, D. (1998). Job Creation and Competitiveness through Innovation. Brussels, Belgium: The European Round Table of Idustrialists.

Jessop, B. (1993). Towards a Schumpeterian Workfare State? Preliminary remarks on post- fordist political economy. Studies in Political Economy, 40(spring), 7–39.

Jessop, B. (2007). New Labour or the Normalization of Neo-liberalism? British Politics, 2(2), 290–293.

Jones, D. (2005). The Business of Education Improvement: Raising LEA Performance through Competition (p. 44). London: Confederation of British Industry.

Kenny, M., & Smith, M. (1997). (Mis)understanding Blair. The Political Quarterly, 68(3), 220–230.

Lambert, R. (2003). Lambert Review of Business-University Collaboration. http://www.hmtreasury.gov.UK/d/lambert_review_final_450.pdf

Leitch, S. (2006). Prosperity for All in the Global Economy - World Class Skills. London, UK: H.M.Treasury. H.M.S.O.

Lorenz, A. (2005). The World's Toxic Waste Dump: Choking on Chemicals in China. Spiegel online. Berlin: Germany, der Spiegel 48/2005.

McAnulla, S. (2007). New Labour, old epistemology? Reflections on political science, new institutionalism and the Blair government. Parliamentary Affairs, 60(2), 313–331.

McCarthy, C., & Pitton, V., et al. (2009). Movement and stasis in the neoliberal reorientation of schooling. In M. Apple, W. W. Au, & L. Gandin (Eds.), The Routledge International Handbook of Critical Education (pp. 36–50). Abingdon, UK: Routledge.

McChesney, R. W. (2004). The Problem of the Media. New York, USA: Monthly Review Press.

Moreland, N. (2006). Entrepreneurship and higher education: An employability perspective. In M. Yorke (Ed.), Learning & Employability (p. 24). York, UK: The Higher Education Academy.

Newman, J. (2000). Beyond the new public management? In J.Clarke, S. Gerwitz, & E. McLaughlin (Eds.), Modernising Public Services. New Managerialism, New Welfare? London, UK: Sage.

Olssen, M. (1996). In defence of the welfare state and of publicly provided education. Journal of Education Policy, 11(3), 337–362.

Osborne, G. (2010). Budget Statement by the Chancellor of the Exchequer, the Rt Hon (G. Osborne MP, Ed.). London, UK: H. M. Treasury.

Perkin, H. (1989). The Rise of Professional Society. Abingdon, UK: Routledge.

Popper, K. (1943). The Open Society and Its Enemies. Abingdon, UK: Routledge.

Popper, K. (1943). The Open society and Its Enemies. Abingdon, UK: Routledge.

Pryce, V. (2005). Creativity, Design and Business Performance (p. 76). DTI economics paper no. 15. London, UK: Department of Trade and Industry.

Roberts, P. (2006). Nurturing Creativity in Young People: A Report to Government to Inform Future Policy (p. 22). London, UK: Department for Culture, Media and Sport.

Robertson, S. L., & Dale, R. (2009). The World Bank, the IMF, and the possibilities of critical education. In M. Apple, W. W. Au & L. Gandin (Eds.), The Routledge International Handbook of Critical Education (pp. 23–35). Abingdon, UK: Routledge.

Robinson, K. (1999). All our Futures: Creativity, Culture and Education. C. M. Sport. London, UK: H.M.S.O.

Rogers, C. R. (1961). On Becoming a Person. London, UK: Constable & co, ltd.

Sainsbury, D. (2003). Competing in the Global Economy: The Innovation Challenge (p. 148). DTI. London, UK: Department of Trade and Industry.

Saltman, K. J. (2009). Corporatization and the control of schools. In M. Apple, W. W. Au & L. Gandin (Eds.), The Routledge International Handbook of Critical Education (pp. 51–63). Abingdon, UK: Routledge.

Santome, J. T. (2009). The Trojan Horse of curricular contents. In M. Apple, W. W. Au & W. Gandin (Eds.), The Routledge International Handbook of Critical Education (pp. 64–79). Abingdon, UK: Routledge.

Schudson, M. (1995). The Power of News. Cambridge, USA: Harvard University Press.

Schudson, M. (1999). What public journalism knows about journalism and doesn't know about "Public". In T. Glasser (Ed.), The Idea of Public Journalism. New York, USA: The Guilford Press.

Schudson, M. (2003). The Sociology of News. New York, USA: W. W. Norton & co. Inc.

Schumpeter, J. A. (1943). Capitalism, Socialism and Democracy. Abingdon, UK: Routledge.

Smith, T. (2003). Something old, something new, something borrowed, something blue: Themes of Tony Blair and his government. Parliamentary Affairs, 56(4), 580–596.

Strauss, A. (1997). Mirrors and Masks. London, UK: Transaction Publishers.

Thompson, C., Mitterbauer, P., et al. (2000). In Search of Quality in Schools: The Employers' Perspective (p. 19). London, UK: Confederation of British Industry.

Thompson, J. B. (1995). The Media and Modernity: A Social Theory of the Media. Cambridge: Polity Press.

Von Mises, L. (1946). Human Action: A Treatise on Economics. San Francisco, USA: Fox & Wilkes.

Wayman, M., & Brown, B. (2007). Creating entrepreneurship: Entrepreneurship education for the creative industries. The Higher Education Academy Art Design Media Subject Centre & National Endowment for Science, Technology and the Arts, 127.

Whitfield, D. (1999). Private finance initiative: The commodification and marketisation of education. Education and Social Justice, 1(2), 2–13.

Wring, D. (2005). The Politics of Marketing the Labour Party. Basingstoke, UK: Palgrave Macmillan.

Yorke, M., & Knight, P. T. (2006). Embedding employability into the curriculum. In M. Yorke (Ed.), Learning and Employability (p. 32). York, UK: The Higher Education Academy - Enhancing Student Employability Co-ordination Team.

AFFILIATIONS

Stephen Colwell
Ravensbourne

SOPHIE PARK

6. THE INDUSTRIALISATION OF MEDICAL EDUCATION? EXPLORING NEOLIBERAL INFLUENCES WITHIN TOMORROW'S DOCTORS POLICY 2009

INTRODUCTION

This policy is crucial to understanding developments within UK medical education, the National Health Service (NHS) and beyond. No policy is ever created in isolation (Bowe, 1992; Taylor, 1997) and there are, no doubt, commonalities between this and many other policies influencing the work of being a doctor, or indeed a patient. This policy relates to the UK undergraduate curriculum of medicine and represents, therefore, the first and formative steps in the career of a doctor. Medical students are learning during this time, not only about the relevant facts and application of science, but establishing their own identity as doctors and exploring the complexities within the doctor-patient relationship (Hafferty, 2009; Hunter, 1991). Political emphases, language and in turn delivery of this policy document are likely, then, to affect the way in which doctors are encouraged to practise medicine in the future, redefining what it is 'to be professional' and to 'be' a doctor.

Tomorrow's Doctors (TD) was first published in 1993. It was, at the time, a landmark document, setting out radical changes in the priorities and focus of undergraduate medical education. Acknowledging the pre-existing 'factual overload' (GMC, 1993, p. 7), it recommended a core curriculum aimed at preparing students for their first professional posts. This slim twenty-eight page document was the first of its kind in medicine to express national curricular standards, 'more rigorously defined than had been customary' (GMC, 1993, p. 7). TD 1993 had broad objectives, encouraging an integrated, systems-based approach with greater emphasis on human, communication and public health aspects of the curriculum; acknowledging the importance of primary care in teaching; and recommending a core curriculum for diverse professional opportunities in medicine (GMC, 1993). TD has since been revised in 2003 and 2009. In March 2009, an extensive, internet-based consultation period began around this latest

M. Lall (ed.), Policy, Discourse and Rhetoric: How New Labour Challenged Social Justice and Democracy, 121–140.

'modernised' edition and its related 'impact document' (Jessop, 2009; McGraw, 2009; MPS, 2009; MSC, 2008; PMETB, 2009; RCGP, 2009; RCP, 2009). TD 2009 was then published in its final form on 1st September 2009 (GMC, 2009). Its stated aims are to set out 'the standards, knowledge, skills, attitudes and behaviours that medical students should learn at UK medical schools' (GMC, 2008, p. 3).

Overtime these revisions have been influenced by wider global discourses, shaping much of the style, priorities and absent areas of content within this policy document. A particular picture, lens or mode of creating meaning in language, can become a dominant window or 'discourse' through which to both express and perceive the world, becoming difficult to resist or create alternative meaning. TD is published by the General Medical Council (GMC) which has facilitated an enormous shift within its published literature and recommended practice towards regulation and patient safety. The GMC is financed directly by an annual registration fee for all practising doctors in the UK. While historically the GMC largely represented self-regulation by the profession, it now comprises lay and non-medical professionals, acting on behalf of the state both to inform and bring about policy change as a state regulatory body of the profession. Unlike the British Medical Association (BMA) whose explicit purpose is to support, inform and defend the profession itself, the GMC emphasises its primary role as protector of the patient focusing upon registration and regulation duties of doctors.

The GMC is also, however, responsible for setting the standards and monitoring delivery of undergraduate medical education. In April 2010, following the recommendations of the Tooke Report to centralise the continuum of medical education regulation throughout doctors' careers (Tooke, 2008), the GMC also took over responsibility from the Postgraduate Medical Education and Training Board (PMETB) to include postgraduate medical education. The concepts of standardisation and regulation have, therefore, become culturally synonymous with education'. This relationship, of course, has potential advantages and disadvantages (Tooke, 2008). This chapter will examine some of the potential effects this may have and how, through this apparent conformity with the culturally dominant ideologies of modernisation and neoliberalism, a new hegemony is being created (Fraser, 1992), changing the nature of medical education towards industrial training, rather than meeting the wider vocational demands for independent and critical practitioners.

This chapter is divided into three sections exploring the context of influence, practice and spaces for political strategy (Bowe, 1992). Throughout, we consider some of the contextual interplay between the NHS as 'employer' and undergraduate medical education as 'workforce supplier', in tension with wider educational aspirations for medical students and their patients. Within the first section, we will explore some of the global ideologies which have influenced the creation and acceptance of this policy. Next, we will focus upon how the interpretation, or attributed meaning of language, influences action and, by association, can be used to maintain a particular dominant position (Rizvi, 2007).

Finally, we consider more broadly, how specifying the particular through policy can be problematic and look for ways, as individuals, that we can engage the responsibility to raise our own awareness of discourses in action, and make informed choices about those we are able to reinforce or reject in our own language use and action.

CONTEXT OF INFLUENCE

This section allows us to explore some of the structures and discourses peripheral to a policy document, exerting influence upon the document and its possible interpretations. The commissioning of a policy document, its construction and interpretation are all likely to be affected by desires to favour or change existing ideologies, both within and beyond its context. Bourdieu uses a theory of relationality to describe the continual development and mutual influence between a particular entity, or 'habitus' and surrounding environmental factors, or 'the field' (P. Bourdieu, 1993; C. Brosnan, 2009). It is therefore useful to briefly examine the wider context of medical education, health and indeed globally dominant discourses, in order to understand the culturally normative values in which TD 2009 has been delivered and received. We can then begin to examine particular aspects of the policy document to better understand its conscious and subconscious motives and potential implications. This chapter focuses upon the era of 'New Labour' and early 'Coalition' governments. Both have embraced the discourse of 'modernisation' in their policy-making, particularly within public sector institutions (Harris, 2007) challenging the welfare state and the professions within, affecting their identities, relationships and working practices (Jensen, 2008). Modernisation includes the discourses of individualism (neo-conservatism), marketisation (neoliberalism) and national governance (or 'the third way') (Jensen, 2008). One powerful way in which these ideologies can be incorporated into practice is the use of curriculum (Apple, 2006). We will examine each of these in turn, using examples in the wider fields of health and medical education.

New Labour 'third way' policies have been responsible for promoting an enormous increase in national governance, or surveillance of control (Harris, 2007). This has developed within the increasingly dominant industrial discourse of 'managerialism' which prioritises accountability, standardisation, transparency and outcomes (Hill, 2009), (S. J. Ball, 1990b; Harris, 2007; Jensen, 2008). This transforms the perception of education towards a 'delivery system', with teachers as its technicians or operators (S. J. Ball, 1990b, p. 154; Iliffe, 2008), conceptualising individuals not as subjects, but objects (S. J. Ball, 1990b, p. 156). This growth in managerial demand for standardisation of practice necessitates the need for audit to monitor adherence to the standards set. Of particular importance to this culture, drawing parallels with Bentham's panoptican prison (Foucault, 1995), is the engagement of the participating individuals to fulfil the obligation to monitor both themselves and each other (S. J. Ball, 1990c). This technology of 'performativity' focuses upon outcomes, rather than process, allowing comparison of performance to be made, creating an artificial method for value judgements of success or failure to determine subsequent rationing (S. J. Ball, 1990b, p. 163). This process tends to marginalise the concerns of the individual, depersonalising and reducing responsibility within practice (S. J. Ball, 1990b, p. 157). New normative assumptions are created, often presented as a neutral and 'common sense' mechanism in order to achieve better efficiency. Any resistance to associated change or performance measures are rejected as 'contradiction of conformity that must be achieved' (S. J. Ball, 1990b, p. 160), promoting commitment to managerial measures as 'more professional' (S. J. Ball, 1990b, p. 162).

Increasingly students and higher education institutions have also been subjected to the concept of commercialisation and the 'shopping mall society' (S. J. Ball, 1994; Shields, 1992), one of the key neoliberal beliefs being that 'consumer choice' is a guarantor of democracy (Harris, 2007). Within UK healthcare delivery, the 'choose and book' system has been introduced requiring patients to state their preference for referral options between primary and secondary care, conceptualising a patient as a consumer with a number of purchasable treatment option choices. Within education, knowledge itself, has in fact, become conceptualised as an economic and 'purchasable' commodity, motivating many of the New Labour policies to increase access to Higher Education in the UK (Barnett, 2010; Guile, 2006). Increasingly under the New Labour government, students developed an altered relationship with their institutions of study, reinforcing the concept of the 'knowledge economy' and education as a tangible outcome, product or investment for future reward (Peters, 2005). Coalition policies to calibrate tuition fees with subsequent income reinforce this further, increasing a perception that knowledge should be immediately transferable into a purchasable commodity, in terms of acquired knowledge and expertise. This undoubtedly affects the relationship and power dynamics between tutor, institution and student, with an increased focus upon explicit 'value-add' factors of educational endeavours requiring measurable and explicit outcomes of learning which are valid in the employment market.

'Marketisation', or neoliberalism has been introduced steadily into the (just still) NHS through a number of recent government policies (Pollock, 2004). The UK, since 1948, has supported one of the few national health services in the world which is free at the point of access, providing universal and comprehensive care. This has become an increasing financial burden on the state with concurrent increases within western culture in medical specialisation and consumerism, prioritising 'want' rather than 'need' (Iliffe, 2008). Prioritising the individual, rather than the group and a demand (particularly in response to the media) for short-term satisfaction of the voters' desires, has made the concept of rationing particularly challenging to tackle. Increasingly, both New Labour and Coalition governments have been tempted to embrace the private sector as a short-term provider and solution (Pollock, 2004).

One of the most recent examples of neoliberal ideology within government policy is 'Liberating the NHS': the first white paper for health to be produced by the coalition government. This document, even prior to parliamentary approval, has rapidly changed practice. It's ideologies have already been embedded in previous New Labour policies such as *'The New NHS: Modern Dependable'* (State, 1997), promoting commissioning and a drive to increase competition between healthcare providers. 'Liberating the NHS' makes explicit the already dominant neoliberal assumption that economic rationality is paramount (Harris, 2007) and assumes that the only way to 'solve' the NHS challenge is through encouraging the introduction of market-forces within the NHS and the associated concept of competition between providers. The white paper decentralises power and financial responsibility, placing in particular general practice at the forefront of rationing decision-making. This is likely to make the transactional elements of the relationship between doctor and patient entirely explicit to 'users' impacting upon both patients' and doctors' understandings of the nature of professionalism, moving further towards neoliberal definitions and priorities.

Reference to planning of education and training within the White Paper are remarkably minimal, given the potential enormity of the changes. The document highlights the enmeshed relationship between workforce planning and education, and calls for greater transparency and accountability in the payment for educational endeavours. Some positive change may therefore result if, for example, the traditionally opaque funding of education allows a fairer distribution of money from previously over-resourced tertiary teaching hospitals to district generals and general practices. The document fails, however, to address two important issues. Firstly, what the competing private providers' obligation will be in respect of educational provision. Secondly, the potential detrimental impact the introduction of these ideologies, embedded within the commissioning proposals, into the NHS may have. Although UK medical school institutions currently receive funding for teaching, its direct impact upon frontline staff is often tacit. Despite a stipulation within GMC recommendations, that all doctors should be willing to contribute to teaching duties (GMC, 2006), in reality, the vast majority of clinician-led teaching is reliant upon the goodwill of teachers to contribute time and effort of themselves. The introduction of explicit markets into the NHS results in doctors' working practices becoming methodically compartmentalised, priced and their provision competitively negotiated between 'providers'. This challenges functioning relationships between primary and secondary care, but also threatens to create a cultural shift in attitude and expectation of professional reward, altering the acceptable values for prioritising aspects of work. Amid increasing emphasis upon competition and measurement of cost-labelled service provision, motivations and opportunities for involvement in education face a fragile future.

CONTEXT OF PRACTICE

> Language is not only an instrument of communication or even of knowledge,
> but also an instrument of power. One seeks not only to be understood but also
> to be believed, obeyed, respected, distinguished.' (Bourdieu, 1977, p. 648)

This section illustrates how awareness of language *use* can facilitate our understanding of policy. Wittgenstein, in his careful attention to the subtleties of language, initiated what later became known as 'linguistic philosophy' exploring the nature and function of language (Clack, 1999, p. 1). His concern surrounds what it takes for language to be meaningful or to have sense; or 'the relation of language to the world' (Clack, 1999, p. 4). In his first work exploring the function of language, the *Tractatus Logico-Philosophicus,* he developed the 'picture theory of meaning' (Wittgenstein, 1974). This contends that language has sense only insofar as it serves to picture possible facts. In his second book, *Philosophical Investigations*, Wittgenstein moves beyond this positivist and 'objective' understanding of language towards a more dynamic model of language to include its relation to gesture and expressive behaviour, defining meaning not as description of fact, but as *use* (Wittgenstein, 1953). This provides the basis for a body of qualitative enquiry, seeking to uncover what a person means when they say something and to what use a sentence is being put (Clandinin, 2000). Within the context of policy, this understanding of textual production as revealing meaning (both conscious and unconscious), has enormous potential to penetrate deep into both explicit and implicit meanings within documents.

The word 'context' means *con* together and *text* to weave (OED, 2010). By definition then, text is not read as an object, but is an interweaving of meaning and interpretation between writer and reader. Interpretation of a particular policy document will depend, therefore, in part upon the fore-position of the reader and institutional cultures in which they function. By extension, the process of writing an analysis is of course also situated within its own set of assumptions and political positions. A text can, within limits, control the extent to which it facilitates either 'writerly' co-authorship and creative involvement in policy enactment or 'readerly' control over meaning, resulting in a much more passive readership (Belsey, 1980; Bowe, 1992). The style of text production is likely to reflect the ideologies and attitudes of those producing it, or wider cultural ideologies which have created the conventions of a particular time.

If we first consider the overall structure and presentation of TD 2009, we already witness conformity to an audit-style culture. This document is divided into 'outcomes for graduates' and 'standards' (GMC, 2009). Each 'standard' has a number of 'criteria' describing how the standard should be interpreted and the means by which it should be met. There is, therefore, evidence of an explicit aspiration, typical within a modernising managerial discourse (S. J. Ball, 2008) (Harris, 2007) to control the *application* of policy in order to standardise the results in practice. This creates a tension within the purpose of this document between its role as a policy; reference of standards for future monitoring of adherence to policy; and actual curriculum. Although there will be some variation in the local interpretation and priorities of each medical school, the way in which this document is written and delivered and its adherence monitored, is likely to result in near conformity across the UK, despite an enormous breadth in culture between students and their patient populations.

The purpose and intentions of this policy are closely related to what the imagined 'product' of a medical curriculum should be. What is the desired function of these educational endeavours? This document was written by a variety of authors who, in turn, attempted to incorporate a selection of available literature and opinion. There are, therefore, differing and competing interests at play within the contributions to and construction of this document, which is perhaps why certain areas of the document lend themselves, to a lesser of greater extent, to a particular discourse. Does this document seek to 'inspire relations of authority, obedience and orderly discipline' required for later roles as supervised, compliant industrial-style workers, or to 'encourage independence, self-reliance, creativity and initiative' (Burbules, 1994, p. 3618), fulfilling some of the broader and more creative aspirations of education. While some students in the short-term will favour a spoon-fed approach to practice with reliance on guidelines and segmented competency-based curricula, most, as they progress, will favour the latter educational expectations, aspiring to an independent practice to address the holistic needs of their patients. TD 2009 appears to be strongly influenced by the former model of education towards an industrial framework and expectation of learning.

> 'Since Hippocrates, a dozen precepts have provided guidance for medical education and professionalism. Not so any more. The UK's General Medical Council (GMC) has specified 300 standards for undergraduate education and behaviour in two reports ... With so many requirements, the relative merit of each is lost, as is the broader goal of education.' (Lancet, 2009)

The degree of specificity (and therefore centralised control) within this document varies considerably. Attempts at standardisation of practice have been welcomed by some (McGraw, 2009; MPS, 2009; MSC, 2008; PMETB, 2009; RCP, 2009) and rejected by others (Jessop, 2009; Lancet, 2009; RCGP, 2009) during the consultation process. While areas such as 'The Doctor as a Scholar and Scientist' are markedly writerly in construction, providing overarching direction with little direct guidance, the specification of competences required for practical procedures for graduates is extraordinarily detailed and precise (GMC, 2009). This may represent the status and assumed trust which different aspects of the curriculum represent. Following the publication of TD 1993, a neo-conservative discourse of derision has evolved in relation to the 'adequacy' of students' scientific knowledge. Knowledge required for medical practice comprises both scientific and experiential or practical form (Hunter, 1991) (Friedson, 2001). The tension between these forms of knowledge and their associated status has, essentially, continued from the first conversations between barbers and apothecaries defining what a doctor is. Practical knowledge is often 'codified' knowledge and acquired implicitly. TD *1993* emphasised the importance of this latter form of knowledge, reducing the amount of science-based theory required at undergraduate level and prioritising a more patient-focussed form of learning.

This has resulted in a number of phenomena. In a sense, a 'golden age' has been created 'pre-TD 1993' with a subsequent 'lack of knowledge problem' in graduates becoming increasingly accepted and neutralised as an obvious issue to 'solve' (S. J. Ball, Goodson, I.F. and Maguire, M., 1994; Habermas, 1985, p. 91). This was acknowledged by those responsible for postgraduate training at the time of the consultation, celebrating the reclamation of 'indoctrination' of factual knowledge by the undergraduate curriculum (PMETB, 2009). Secondly, neoliberal ideology has been used in an attempt to make practical implicit knowledge explicit, measurable and, therefore, 'monitorable'. Patients are by definition varied, non-standardised and difficult to control which makes them problematic within a neoliberal discourse as both 'consumers' and sources of learning. This has been addressed in a number of ways including a strong emphasis within TD 2009 and surrounding GMC guidance on 'patient safety', continued close support for both evidence-based medicine (EBM) and competency based learning, and recommendations for the use of simulation as an alternative to patient contact.

The principle of patient safety has received a prominent position within this and many other GMC documents (GMC, 2006, 2009, 2010). It is emphasised in TD 2009 as the first responsibility of both the GMC and medical schools beyond any other approach or concern.

'Protecting patients and taking appropriate steps to minimise any risk of harm to anyone as a result of the training of their medical students.' (GMC, 2009)

This immediately sets an assumption of a 'problem' which the document seeks to address, namely the protection of patients. The notion of patient safety embodies an industrial conception of the human nature of clinical practice. Acknowledging the fallible nature of doctor as 'potential wrong-doer', enormous efforts have been focussed upon constructing standardised routines to avoid 'human error'. While this has some obvious attractions, the converse position of machine providing medical care highlights the mistakes which can also be potentially made, *without* the benefit and flexibility of human judgement. In effect, this moves professional ideals towards an authoritarian mode of regulation using fear of penalty from rule deviance. This contrasts strongly with a more liberal educational philosophy, seeking to achieve right human relations through approaches including respect, role modelling and an expectation of trust and responsibility towards the learner. Pioneers of 'patient safety' often utilise tragic examples of 'mistakes' and a desire for the professional body to learn from these is obviously desirable. However, the culture of fear and legalistic dimension which this adds to the interaction (or even potential *possibility* of interaction) between teacher, doctor or student and patient is, for many, uncomfortable.

The 'industrial agenda' for both patient safety and standardisation in teaching and learning has been manifest in many ways through the technology of simulation. At first glance, simulated technologies provide an appealing label to mark investment in 'modern learning'. However, while there are, of course, benefits for the novice in rehearsing practical techniques away from the patient context, the potential disadvantages for unconsidered use are immense. It is also interesting to note at this point, the potential contradictions within this document in supporting patient-centred learning. TD 2009 does, for example, state that 'the curriculum must include early and continuing contact with patients (pt 103)' and promotes a curriculum which is structured to provide 'a balance of learning opportunities ... to integrate the learning of basic and clinical sciences, enabling students to link theory and practice (pt83)' (GMC, 2009). It also has a dedicated section on 'student assistantships' promoting experiential learning towards the rather 'safer' end of the final year. These ambitions are, however, competing with a number of paradoxical tensions promoting patient safety, standardisation and simulation.

Simulation is promoted at a number of places within the TD 2009 document. For example, 'Medical schools should take advantage of new technologies, including simulation, to deliver teaching (pt 100) and 'Opportunities should be provided for students to learn with other health and social care students, including the use of simulated training environments with audiovisual recording and behavioural debriefing' (pt102) (GMC, 2009). This latter sentence promotes quite a sophisticated form of simulation and in many schools simulation has been used until now as 'the next best thing' to patient contact to rehearse procedures and also compensate for the high student numbers and subsequent limited patient access[24]. Moreover, simulated skills and consultations are widely used in both undergraduate and postgraduate exams. Consequently, many essential elements and processes of 'doctoring' receive little attention for study in students' desire to rehearse 'performable' knowledge, if they are not measurable or related to assessment outcomes (Bleakley, 2006). The popularity of simulated learning and assessment is largely due to its perceived qualities as both standard and reliable. Ironically, the more reliable an exam becomes, the less valid for patient-based clinical practice it risks becoming.

Chair of the GMC, Peter Rubin, does acknowledge in his opening foreword the presence of uncertainty and complexity in clinical practice (GMC, 2009). The question remains, however, whether the style and dominant ideological position of this document allows for these demands to be fulfilled. There is, of course, wide variation between the requirements and approaches of various specialities within medical practice. All, however, encounter uncertainty, be it surrounding boundaries of knowledge, the nature of the doctor-patient relationship, or the presence of conceptual tensions within the consultation involving rationing or policy implementation (Beresford, 1991). Much of a doctor's skill involves listening to a patient's story and being able to 'problem set' (Schon, 1983), even if no immediate solution is available. A managerial paradigm judges these encounters as 'failure' if they achieve no measurable outcomes. All consultations to an extent require an acknowledgement of uncertainty concerning the human condition and require a bond of trust between patient and doctor. Many of the more 'modern' documents and GMC policies about clinical practice, embodying notions of industrialisation and neoliberalism, were created after various media scandals expressed a lack of trust in the profession (Kennedy, 2001; Redfern, 1999; Smith, 2004) with a subsequent demand to regain that trust through 're-professionalisation'. The industrial discourse of managerialism in this context, offering standardisation, accountability and managerial regulation (from both external and internal sources), holds an inviting appeal.

This shift of trust from the individual professional to external sources can also be witnessed more widely within the NHS in the exponential use and production of 'evidence-based medicine' (EBM). Such cultural norms are likely to influence students' learning and their developing sense of professional priorities and preferences. Many clinicians are prepared to accept uncertainty within their practice, supporting a reflective model of clinical practice which facilitates the development of problem-setting as well as problem solving skills, dependent upon critical, reflexive analysis of a clinical situation. A contrasting (and increasingly dominant) position however, holds that uncertainty is, in fact, a 'solvable problem' through the appropriate commissioning and dissemination of research findings (Harrison, 2002). This has, of course, had the indirect result of supporting only research which has an obvious practical relevance (Hammersley, 2007). Within clinical practice, this has resulted in development of criteria enabling some consumer judgement about treatment options. This produces an associated shift in responsibility surrounding shared decision-making with patients, and an expectation for patients to comprehend the complex relevance to themselves of statistics produced in controlled and often limited circumstances. Secondly, EBM has provided a source of 'scientific' outcome measures to inform managerial control of medical procedure through standardisation and production of guidelines (Cliffe, 2008). Research which, incidentally, has been judged predominantly through a positivist lens, resulting in a 'hierarchy of evidence' which favours randomised controlled trials above more qualitative enquiry (Greenhalgh, 1997; Sackett, 2000).

Whole institutions have been created based upon these ideological conceptions. The National Institute of Clinical Excellent (NICE), for example, works to disseminate the findings of clinical research in the form of practical guidelines and protocols, with the assumption that doctors' practice will be influenced accordingly (Berg, 1997). The chances of adherence have been maximised through, for example, the Commission for Health Improvement (CHI) monitoring clinicians' use of NICE guidelines as a performance measure of 'good practice', dictating the success of an NHS organisation, through publication of comparative performance information (S. J. Ball, 2008; Harrison, 2002). Similarly, the Quality and Outcomes Framework (QOF) has been devised to measure the performance activity of GPs, determining their associated income (Iliffe, 2008). By extension professional practice deviating from these consensus, are likely to be deemed 'unprofessional' and require determined justification.

The industrial aspirations of standardisation extend within the TD 2009 impact document to calls for more formal consistency across medical schools in the form of a national exam (GMC, 2008). Response has varied from resistance (Lancet, 2009; RCGP, 2009) to a classic neoliberal 'common sense' acceptance of managerial change stating that there is 'no justification for there *not* to be a common assessment system in medical schools' ' (McGraw, 2009, p. 7). This suggestion is supported by a survey demonstrating variation in medical school assessment (McCrorie, 2008). While the impact document does acknowledge that 'variety creates scope for development and avoids the creation of 'identikit' doctors', it expresses a concern, strongly situated within neoliberal ideology, of a problematic difficulty comparing 'the equivalence of standards and graduates' (GMC, 2008, p. 9). It further postulates that the range of assessment tools and 'variable academic rigour' (McCrorie, 2008) will result in varying knowledge, skill and proficiency between graduates (GMC, 2008, p. 9). It is further proposed, that this variation is, in part, due to the 'high level nature of guidance on assessment' in TD 2003, supporting a national exam as a solution to promote 'consistency in outcomes, confidence, efficiency gains and fairness in recruitment' (GMC, 2008, p. 10). These statements may have contributed to the readerly and prescriptive, curricula-like detail of some sections within TD 2009.

In the UK postgraduate arena, Modernising Medical Careers (MMC) has already introduced an explicitly competitive selection system between medical students, determining both the career speciality options and location available to medical graduates based on a national ranking grade, replacing the traditional system of *curriculum vitae* and interviews (MMC, 2005). Students, therefore, already perceive relevant assessments a high stakes priority, together with the fulfilment of any activity worthy of a 'point' within the established scoring system. Contrary to calls for collaboration and teamwork between trainees, many staff have subsequently observed highly competitive strategies between students negotiating their learning opportunities, in efforts to achieve the best grades within their set. While this system has satisfied neoliberal calls for standardisation and, by association, 'fairness' across the job market allocation, it has tangibly changed students' perceptions towards learning strategies, competition with colleagues and of most concern, their sense of self as a number within an industrial system, rather than possessing a sense of control and autonomy over their professional careers (Tooke, 2008).

While there is scope for passive or active interpretation of a curriculum (White, 1993), a national exam is likely to exacerbate these competitive behaviours and changes in sense of professional identity. Informal hierarchies between medical schools based upon, for example, their length of establishment, emphasis on science or patient-based learning and type of curricula, are in existence (C. Brosnan, 2010), but are still flexible and open to interpretation dependent upon the onlooker's position. A national exam, contributing to ratings for future employment as in the United States (US), would be a clear priority in the minds of both students and teachers, driving change towards a generic learning experience. As in the US, once established, an obvious development is to formally compare and rate individual and institutional outcomes using a single frame of judgement, in a form similar to existing UK school leagues tables. Gross performance measures will inevitably lead to the definition of some schools as 'successes' and others 'failures' (S. J. Ball, 1990b; Swanson, 2007).

This development of a 'quasi-market' (S. J. Ball, 2008, p. 44), while apparently spurred by a drive for consistency between graduates, is likely to have the reverse effect. Once explicit league tables of 'performance' exist, students of 'high' academic performance are likely to self-select certain schools, rejecting others, attaching minimal value to qualities other than those explicitly measured (S. J. Ball, 1990a; Gewirtz, 1995). The assessment and curricula will, therefore, serve ideological and political function in formally sorting students into categories, each with different intellectual skill or disposition. These will be judged and ranked, serving to perpetuate existing structures and prejudice within society (Apple, 2006; Phillips, 1998). Implicit within these recommendations is the concept that diversity between students is *problematic* equating variation with medical error. The obvious progression, then, is to eradicate this (or at least making non-conformity easier to identify and eliminate) (S. J. Ball, 1990a), through the use of a national exam. Given the breadth and diversity required within medicine, plus the importance of variety in learning styles and approaches for different individuals (Honey, 1995), this could have disastrous consequences.

CONTEXT OF POLITICAL STRATEGY

The last section has examined how the use of certain language and structure within a policy document, can be used to support a particular ideology. Historically, meaning in language has changed over time, supporting particular dominant lenses or 'discourses' for interpreting reality or experience. Within this chapter, we have observed how the current dominant ideologies of modernisation and neoliberalism have been supported within TD 2009 through its overall emphasis upon highly

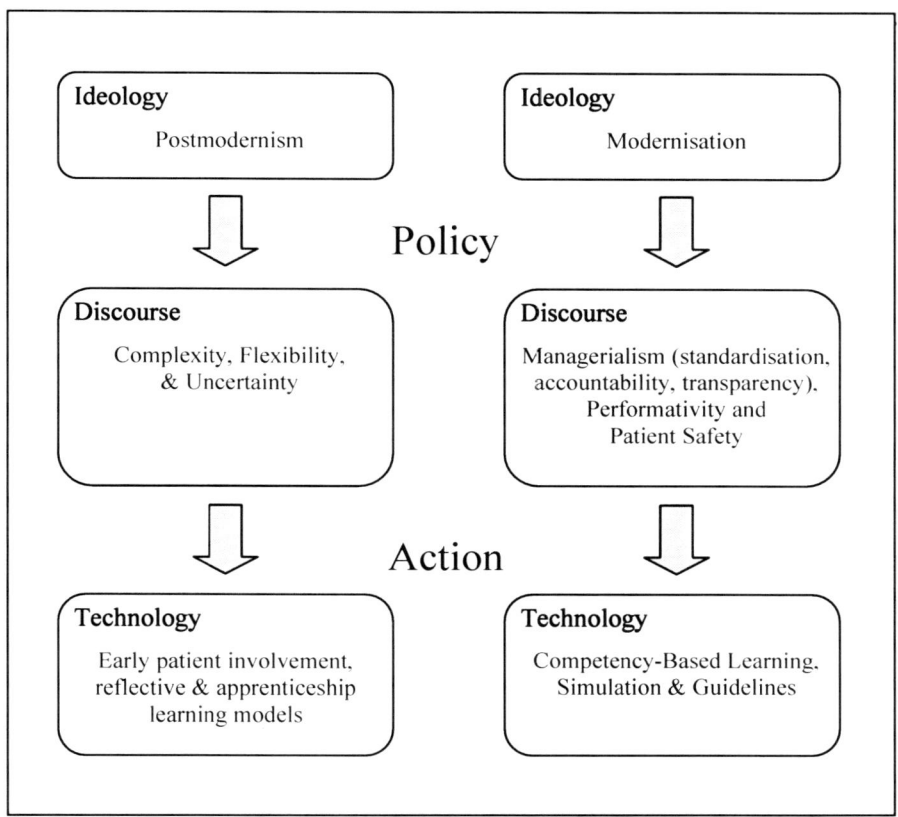

Figure 1. Examples of the competing tensions influencing the relationship between policy and action within TD 2009.

specific standards and outcomes, notions of patient safety and technologies such as simulation, proposals for a national exam and, more widely, evidence based medicine. We have highlighted the moral assumptions and tensions between the constraints of 'technical rationalism' (S. J. Ball, 1998, p. 79) and more human-orientated concepts of medical practice, embracing the possibilities for uncertainty and complexity in patient care. Further, we have explored the potential contradictions within the overarching nature and content of the guidance in TD 2009, which embeds a modernising and neoliberal philosophy likely to dominate over any discussions and efforts surrounding alternative approaches and agendas.

Linguistic practices, however, inevitably 'depend for their survival upon the continuing will of individuals to participate in them' (Rizvi, 2007, p. 218). This next section, then, emphasises not only the importance of gaining a deeper understanding of the cultural implications of policy through heightened awareness of language use, but also the need for reflection concerning our own use of language (Rizvi, 2007, pp. 212–213) (Wittgenstein, 1974) and opportunities for choice to demonstrate complicity or initiate change. It offers two alternative spaces in which to operate (Wallace, 1990) using reflection and engagement with human goodness and authenticity. Rubin's first sentence in his foreword states that 'Doctors must be capable of regularly taking responsibility for difficult decisions in situations of clinical complexity and uncertainty' (GMC, 2009). This aspiration for 'the professional' appears to lie in tension, as we have seen, with much of the dominant structure and content of the document. What is required in order that this alternative perspective might be fulfilled?

Firstly we consider the process of reflection and its facilitation of professional learning (Moore, 2004). Reflection is crucial in allowing us to link our practical experience with theory and develop the capacity to act creatively and responsively in previously unencountered situations. By developing this professional reflexivity, we can articulate our existing knowledge (Furlong, 2000) and adapt it to allow for practical variance (Moore, 2004). This 'intuitive knowing' (Schon, 1983) or 'professional authenticity' (S. Ball, 2004, p. 2), then allows us to manage uncertainty, changing contexts (Grimmett, 1994) and contradictory roles, using imagination to appropriately adapt clinical management plans. The process of reflection can itself be coloured by neoliberal interpretations, reducing it to a ritualistic, standardised check-list or technical process (S. Ball, 1998). The TD 2009 section on reflection, for example, encourages audit-type documentation of reflective learning in written portfolios (pt 21) (GMC, 2009). Meaningful reflection is, however, not guaranteed by these formal procedures (Moore, 2004), requiring an intellectual commitment to facilitate the critical application of theory to practice, both during and after clinical experience (Eraut, 1994), creating the possibility for alternative action.

Related, a second proposal for space engages both theory and philosophy to challenge our practice and associated responsibilities as professionals. The word 'profess' means to openly declare a belief, knowledge, vow or oath (OED, 2010). This is not a call for religious practitioners, but a question of 'goodness' in practice; an engagement beyond the intellectual towards a mortal involvement in the 'nature of practice' and human condition, reaching far beyond technical protocols and planned events (Standish, 2003). If to be professional is to mean more than ticking a list of achieved outcome competencies and standards, we accept a responsibility to profess the truth. This must reach beyond terms of correctness and adherence to codes of practice, to a subjective truth as 'revealing', involving a responsible and active projection of the 'goodness' in practice (Standish, 2003).

The role of medical educators, as both professionals and teachers, is then more than the purely constantive statement of how things are or description of 'what is' in terms of competence or proficiency (Standish, 2003). Professionalism implies a responsibility to 'profess' an openness, beyond a predetermined range of categories to the 'impossible possible' (Standish, 2003). Such a leap in level of professional engagement demands much more of the professional in terms of human commitment. Patients and professionals, however, require more than effective adherence to performance measures in order to satisfy the greater demands of human frailty. Where technical rationality has projected our focus to the demands of generalisability; adherence to institutional practice; transparency; and accountability, we have a professional responsibility to balance this approach, engage the 'professing ion' and to help maintain an awareness of the fragile individual and human condition for ourselves and tomorrow's doctors.

Wenger speaks of a 'learning revolution', transforming the function of learning institutions from 'controllers of the curriculum', to more flexible and accessible places of guidance for self-directed learners (Wenger, 1998). While there still has to be some consistency as to what 'a doctor' can be expected to 'be', perhaps we should be striving to embrace more fully the 'self' within the learner, rather than imposing increasingly restrictive curricula? This implies a redistribution of power and responsibility between learner and institution. It also raises questions of accountability in training, this broader model requiring an authenticity from the learner to engage themselves in their learning, more akin to the values of a 1960s' understanding of professional accountability (Harris, 2007). Whether learners, patients, managers and teachers, immersed in society's global neoliberal hegemony (Harris, 2007) are prepared to make this leap, remains to be seen.

CONCLUSION

Policies do not usually attempt to 'tell you what to do' (S. J. Ball, Goodson, I.F. and Maguire, M., 1994b, p. 19). They create circumstances in which the range of options available are narrowed and particular goals or outcomes are set (S. J. Ball, Goodson, I.F. and Maguire, M., 1994b). This policy has been produced through a number of collaborative and consultative processes and therefore displays a variety of ideologies and aspirations. However, its overall commanding structure using standards, criteria and outcomes and much of its content, particularly surrounding practical areas of the curriculum, represent ambitions to carefully control the behaviour of its subjects. Whereas a broader, more abstract text would allow writerly interpretation for individual medical schools, this text is very explicit in its expectations of adherence for medical schools and those monitoring their performance. In doing so, the overarching ideologies of modernisation and neoliberalism are embedded, focussing particularly on producing measurable and demonstrable outcomes to ensure a 'competent workforce'. These aspirations for control and associated industrial standardisation and accountability may, however, in fact limit the possibilities for nurturing a set of professionals who are genuinely 'fit for practice' in meeting patients' needs.

Aristotle writes about the dilemmas of policy-making related to the unique and individual nature of practice, which he calls *phronesis* (Beresford, 1991).

This includes the ethical and political reflection and self-understanding which helps citizens of a free society to practice the 'ethically good life'(MacIntyre, 1981, p. 220).

> 'Among statements about conduct, those that are universal are more general but the particular are more true – for action is concerned with particulars, and statements must harmonise with these.' (Aristotle, 1953)

Traditionally, policies are by their very nature general and the guidance they offer to decision-making less than precise. Our current example, is trying to defy this by adding specific detail of outcomes to be attained cementing a modernising and neoliberal ideology into both medical practice and its educational acquisition. Aristotle gives three basic reasons why general rules (or policies) are unable to give us the sort of precise guidance that would provide effective certainty in specific situations (Beresford, 1991). Firstly, criteria designed in advance can only anticipate what has been seen before. Secondly, Aristotle explores the 'indefinable character of the practical', fitting appropriate choices to a complex array of options and considerations (Beresford, 1991, p. 11). Rules either do too little, in that they can never address the concrete particular of a context, or too much, because they imply a normative rule, which impinges on flexible good practice. Thirdly, the concrete case may contain unique, non-repeatable elements (Beresford, 1991).

Within this document, policy-makers are trying to overcome these dilemmas by specifying the particular as a general rule. As Aristotle predicts, this constrains the flexibility required for broader definitions of 'good practice' and infers normative rules of judgement, not necessarily relevant or helpful to a particular case. A desire to impose an industrial model of practice upon medicine and medical education, illustrates these inevitable tensions and highlights the need for attention to the individual patient and context in practice. While a managerial discourse exists within our global society, there will be continued challenges towards the professional mode of medical practice, seeking standardisation and accountability. If Wittgenstein is right, and we can change moral policy through our considered use of language (Rizvi, 2007), then perhaps we should begin to engage with a freer and more reflective body of communication in an initial effort to support a more human and creative generation of tomorrow's doctors.

REFERENCES

Apple, M. W. (2006). *Educating the "Right" Way: Markets, standards, God, and Inequality (2nd ed.).* London: Routledge.

Aristotle. (1953). *Nichomachean Ethics* (pp. 29–32). London: Penguin.

Ball, S. (1998). Educational studies, policy entrepreneurship and social theory. In R. Slee, G. Weiner, & S. Tomlinson (Ed.), *School Effectiveness for Whom? Challenges to the School Effectiveness and School Improvement Movements* (pp. 70–83). Falmer Press.

Ball, S. (2004). *Education Reform as Social Barberism: Economism and the End of Authenticity.* Paper presented at the SERA Lecture at the Scottish Educational Research Association Annual Conference.

Ball, S. J. (1990a). *Industrial Training or New Vocationalism? Structures and Discourses Politics and Policy Making in Education: Explorations in Policy Sociology* (pp. 70–99). London: Routledge.

Ball, S. J. (1990b). Management as moral technology. In S. J. Ball (Ed.), *Foucault and Education: Disciplines and Knowledge* (pp. 153–166). London: Routledge.

Ball, S. J. (1994). *Education Reform: A Critical and Post-Structural Approach.* Buckingham: Open University Press.

Ball, S. J. (1998). Educational studies, policy entrepreneurship and social theory. In R. Slee, G. Weiner, & S. Tomlinson (Ed.), *School Effectiveness for Whom? Challenges to the School Effectiveness and School Improvement Movements* (pp. 70–83). Falmer Press.

Ball, S. J. (2008). *The Education Debate.* Bristol: The Policy Press.

Ball, S. J. (Ed.). (1990c). *Foucault and Education: Disciplines and Knowledge.* London: Routledge.

Ball, S. J., Goodson, I. F., & Maguire, M. (1994). *Post-structuralism, Ethnography and the Critical Analysis of Education Reform Education Reform: A Critical and Post-structual Approach* (pp. 1–13). Buckingham: Open University Press.

Ball, S. J., Goodson, I. F., & Maguire, M. (1994b). *What is Policy? Texts, Trajectories and Toolboxes Education Reform: A Critical and Post-structural Approach* (pp. 14–27). Buckingham: Open University Press.

Barnett, R. (2010). *Being a University.* Oxon: Routledge.

Belsey, C. (1980). *Critical Practice.* London: Methuen.

Beresford, E. B. (1991). Uncertainty and the shaping of medical decisions. *The Hastings Center Report, 21*(4), 6–11.

Berg, (1997). Problems and promises of the protocol. *Social Science and Medicine, 44*(8), 1081–1088.

Bleakley, A., & Bligh, J. (2006). Students learning from patients: Let's get real in medical education. *Advances in Health Sciences Education.*

Bourdieu. (1977). The economics of linguistic exchanges. *Social Science Information, 16*(6), 645–668.

Bourdieu, P. (Ed.). (1993). *Introduction and The Field of Cultural Production.* Cambridge: Polity.

Bowe, R., Ball, S. J., & Gold, A. (1992). *The Policy Process and the Processes of Policy Reforming Education and Changing Schools: Case Studies in Policy Sociology.* London: Routledge.

Brosnan, C. (2009). Pierre Bourdieu and the theory of medical education: Thinking 'relationally' about medical students and medical curricula. In C. Brosnan & B. Turner (Ed.), *Handbook of the Sociology of Medical Education* (pp. 51–68). London: Routledge.

Brosnan, C. (2010). Making sense of differences between medical schools through Bourdieu's concept of "field". *Medical Education, 44*, 645–652.

Burbules, N. C. (1994). *Marxism and Educational Thought International Encyclopedia of Education* (2nd ed.). Oxford: Pergamon.

Clack, B. R. (1999). Ludwig Wittgenstein: His life and philosophies. In B. R. Clack (Ed.), *An Introduction to Wittgenstein's Philosophy of Religion* (pp. 1–26). Edinburgh: Edinburgh Univeristy Press.

Clandinin, D. J., & Connelly, F. M. (2000). *Narrative Inquiry: Experience and Story in Qualitative Research.* San Francisco: Jossey-Bass.

Eraut, M. (1994). *Professional Accountability and Outcomes for Clients Developing Professional Knowledge and Competence* (pp. 223–241). London: Falmer Press.

Foucault, M. (1995). *Discipline & Punish: The Birth of the Prison* (A. Sheridan, Trans., 2nd ed.). New York: Random House.

Fraser, N. (1992). Rethinking the public sphere: A contribution to the critique of actually existing democracy. In C. Calhoun (Ed.), *Habermas and the Public Sphere* (pp. 109–142). Cambridge MA: MIT Press.

Friedson, E. (2001). *Professional Knowledge and Skill Professionalism: The Third Logic* (pp. 17–35). Cambridge: Polity.

Furlong, J., Barton, L., Miles, S., & Whitty, G. (2000). *Teacher Education in Transition*. Buckingham: Open University Press.

Gewirtz, S., Ball, S. J., & Bowe, R. (1995). *Markets, Choice and Equity in Education*. Buckingham: Open University Press.

GMC. (1993). *Tomorrow's Doctors: Recommendations on Undergraduate Medical Education*. London: Education Committee of the General Medical Council in pursuance of section 5 of the Medical Act 1983.

GMC. (2006). *Good Medical Practice*. from http://www.gmcuk.org/guidance/good_medical_practice/GMC_GMP.pdf

GMC. (2008). Impact assessment. Tomorrow's Doctors 2009: a draft consultation. Retrieved April 2009.

GMC. (2009). *Tomorrow's Doctors*. Retrieved September 28, 2009, from www.gmc-uk.org/education/documents/GMC_TD_2009.pdf

GMC. (2010). *Regulating Doctors, Ensuring Good Medical Practice*. from http://www.gmc-uk.org/

Greenhalgh, T. (1997). *How to Read a Paper*. London: BMJ Books.

Grimmett, P., & Neufeld, J. (1994). *Teacher Development and the Struggle for Authenticity*. New York: Teachers College Press.

Guile, D. (2006). What is distinctive about the knowledge economy? Implications for education. In H. Lauder, P. Brown, & A. H. Halsey (Ed.), *Education, Globalization and Social Change* (pp. 355–366). Oxford: Oxford University Press.

Habermas, J. (1985). Neoconservative culture criticism in the United States and West Germany: An intellectual movement in two political cultures. In R. J. Bernstein (Ed.), *Habermas and Modernity*. Cambridge: Polity Press.

Hafferty, F. W., & Castellani, B. (2009). The hidden curriculum: A theory of medical education. In C. Brosnan & B. Turner (Ed.), *Handbook of the Sociology of Medical Education* (pp. 15–35). Oxon: Routledge.

Hammersley, M. (Ed.). (2007). *Educational Research and Evidence-based Practice*. London: SAGE.

Harris, S. (2007). *The Governance of Education: Hoe Neo-liberalism is Transforming Policy and Practice* (1st ed.). London: Continuum.

Harrison, S. (2002). New labour, modernisation and the medical labour process. *Journal of Social Policy, 31*, 465–485.

Hill, D., & Kumar, R. (2009). Neoliberalism and its impacts. In D. Hill & R. Kumar (Ed.), *Global Neoliberalism and Education and its Consequences* (pp. 12–29). Abingdon: Routledge.

Honey, P. (1995). *Using Your Learning Styles*. London: Peter Honey.

Hunter, K. (1991). *A Science of Individuals: Medicine and Uncertainty Doctors' Stories: The Narrative Structure of Medical Knowledge* (pp. 27–48). Princeton, NJ: Princeton University Press.

Iliffe, S. (2008). *From General Practice to Primary Care: The Industrialisation of Family Medicine*. Oxford: Oxford University Press.

Jensen, K., & Walker, S. (2008). *Education, Democracy and Discourse*. London: Continuum.

Jessop, V., & Johnson, O. (2009). Tomorrow's Doctors: A global perspective. [Letter]. *The Lancet, 373*(9668), 1523.

Kennedy, I., Howard, R., Jarman, B., & Maclean, M. (2001). The gradual shift towards an interest in standards and in monitoring learning from Bristol: The report of the public inquiry into the management of care of children receiving complex heart surgery at the Bristol Royal Infirmary 1984 – 1995. http://www.bristol-inquiry.org.uk/

Lancet. (2009). Medical education and professionalism. [Editorial]. *The Lancet, 373*(9668), 980.

MacIntyre, A. (1981). *After Virtue*. London: Duckworth.

McCrorie, P. A., & Boursicot, K. (2008). *Variety in Medical School Graduating Examinations: Is It Tenable?*

McGraw, M. (2009). *Tomorrow's Doctors 2009 Consultation*. London: Royal College of Paediatrics and Child Health.

MMC. (2005). *Modernising Medical Careers*. Retrieved December 12, 2010, from http://www.mmc.nhs.uk/

Moore, A. (2004). *The Good Teacher*. London: Routledge Falmer.

MPS. (2009). *Consultation Response to GMC Consultation on Tomorrow's Doctors 2009*. London: Medical Protection Society.

MSC. (2008). *Consensus Statement on the Role of the Doctor*. Medical Schools Council.

OED. (2010). *Oxford English Dictionary*. Retrieved December 7, 2010, from http://oxforddictionaries.com/view/entry/m_en_gb0175040#m_en_gb0175040

Peters, M. A., & Olssen, M. (2005). 'Useful Knowledge': Redefining research and teaching in the learning economy. In R. Barnett (Ed.), *Reshaping the University: New Relationships between Research, Scholarship and Teaching* (pp. 37–48). Maidenhead: Open University Press.

Phillips, D. C. (1998). Epistemology, politics and curriculum construction. In D. Carr (Ed.), *Education, Knowledge and Truth* (pp. 159–173). London: Routledge.

PMETB. (2009). *Tomorrow's Doctors 2009 - Consultation*. London: Postgraduate Medical Education and Training Board.

Pollock, A. M. (2004). *NHS Plc: The Privatisation of Our Health Care*. London: Verso.

RCGP. (2009). *General Medical Council Consultation: A Draft Tomorrow's Doctors 2009*. London: Royal College of General Practice.

RCP. (2009). *Policy Responses and Statements*. Edinburgh: Royal College of Physicians.

Redfern, M., Keeling, J., & Powell, E. (1999). *The Royal Liverpool Children's Inquiry Report*.

Rizvi, F. (2007). Policy analysis as practical reason. In S. J. Ball (Ed.), *Education, Globalisation and New Times*. Oxford: Routledge.

Sackett, D. L., Straus, S., Richardson, W. S., Rosenberg, W., & Haynes, R. B. (2000). *Evidence-Based Medicine: How to Practise and Teach EBM* (2nd ed.). Edinburgh: Churchill Livingstone.

Schon, D. (1983). *The Reflective Practitioner: How Professionals Think in Action*. Hants: Ashgate Publishing Limited.

Shields, R. (1992). *Lifestyle Shopping: The Subject of Consumption*. London: Routledge.

Smith, D. J. (2004). The General Medical Council's New Fitness to Practise Procedures Fifth Report - Safeguarding Patients: Lessons from the Past - Proposals for the Future.

Standish, P. (2003). *Profession and Practice: The Higher Education of Nursing* (pp. 109–126).

The New NHS: Modern, Dependable(1997).

Swanson, D. (2007). *Relationship between Scores on US Medical Liscensing Examinations and Performance on Speciality Board Certifying Examinations*. Paper presented at the Recruitment into Foundation and Specialist Training Programmes in the UK.

Taylor, S. (1997). Critical policy analysis: Exploring contexts, texts and consequences. *Discourse: Studies in the Cultural Politics of Education, 18*(1), 23–35.

Tooke, J. (2008). *Aspiring to Excellence: Findings and Final Recommendations of the Independent Inquiry into Modernising Medical Careers*. from http://www.mmcinquiry.org.uk/Final_8_Jan_08_MMC_all.pdf

Wallace. (1990). *Coping with Multiple Innovations in Schools*. Bristol: School of Education, University of Bristol.

Wenger, E. (1998). *Communities of Practice: Learning, Meaning and Identity*. Cambridge: Cambridge University Press.

White, C., & Crump, S. (1993). Education and the Three Ps: Policy, Politics and Practice. A Review of the Work of S.J. Ball. *British Journal of Sociology and Education, 14*(4), 415–429.

Wittgenstein, L. (1953). *Philosophical Investigations*. Oxford: Blackwell.

Wittgenstein, L. (1974). *Tractatus Logico-Philosophicus*. London: Routledge

NOTES

[24] Numbers of medical students have been increased markedly since the introduction of the European Working Time Directive. Some school now have over 400 students per year

Sophie Park is a general practitioner (GP) and teaches at UCL Medical School

MICHAEL W. APPLE

AFTERWORD ON NEOLIBERALISM, THE CURRENT CRISIS, AND THE POLITICS OF HOPE

CHANGING COMMONSENSE

This book comes at exactly the right time. As I write this Afterword, I have just returned from a series of lectures in Spain. The economic crisis there is extremely serious. The media in Europe and the United States are filled with stories about political battles involving "bail-outs" of economies such as Spain, Portugal, Greece, and other nations. What is less often reported—at least in the mainstream media in the United States and Britain—is the damage that is being done to real people, to the lives and hopes of millions, to the effects of the neoliberal policies that are being imposed by the IMF and other international and national financial agencies, and the destruction of hard-won gains in social welfare, health, and education. The crisis is all too easy to miss if one keeps to the tourist areas. Yet these areas are skin-deep. Scratch beneath the surface in Madrid and similar cities and the realities become ever more visible. That a conservative government is predicted to win the forthcoming elections there says something important about the ways in which rightist movements have been able to creatively build a discursive environment that privileges their messages about the causes of the crisis and the increasing levels of impoverishment that have ensued.

For conservative governments in places such as Madrid—and London, major cities and entire states in the United States, and so many other places—the crisis, the impoverishment, and the loss of identifiable people's possibilities, can only be solved by the religion of the market. Shrink the state, remove the safety net, establish market discipline, fire public employees, make people more insecure by removing the right to affordable health care, slash pensions, cut funding for education, lay off teachers, and I could go on enumerating the areas of pain. In Stephen Ball's words, "The public sector must be remade in order to respond to the exigencies of globalization and to play its part in the economics of global competition. Individual and institutional actors and their dispositions and responses are tied to the fate of the nation in the global economy" (Ball, 2008, p. 15). Education is clearly not immune to these intense pressures.

M. Lall (ed.), Policy, Discourse and Rhetoric: How New Labour Challenged Social Justice and Democracy, 141–150.

I purposely have used the term "religion" in the first sentence of the previous paragraph, since the positions pushed forward often seem to be immune to counter-factuals. It is as if the glasses that are worn by those who hew to the positions associated with the neoliberal agenda make all of the pain invisible. Education policy is one of the arenas in which the limitations of these glasses are particularly evident.

Across the political spectrum, it is widely recognized that there is a crisis in education. Nearly everyone agrees that something must be done to make it more responsive and more effective. Of course, a key set of questions is: Responsive to what and to whom? Effective at what? And whose voices will be heard in asking and answering these questions? These are among the most crucial questions one can ask about education today.

Let us be honest. The educational crisis is real—especially for the poor and oppressed. Dominant groups have used such "crisis talk" to shift the discussion onto their own terrain.

One of the major reasons for the continuation of dominant discourse and policies is that the very nature of our commonsense about education is constantly being altered. This is largely the result of the power of particular groups who understand that if they can change the basic ways we think about our society and its institutions—and especially our place in these institutions—these groups can create a set of policies that will profoundly benefit them more than anyone else. Dominant groups are actively engaged in a vast social/pedagogic process—what Antonio Gramsci would call "a war of position" (Gransci, 1971) —one in which what counts as a good school, good knowledge, good teaching, and good learning are being radically transformed.

In the face of the neoliberal and neoconservative interpretations that circulate so widely both nationally and internationally, however, there is a growing body of literature in educational policy studies that critically examines the conceptual and ideological underpinnings and the ethical, political, and empirical realities of the major reforms that are currently travelling throughout the world. As I show in *Educating the "Right" Way* (Apple, 2006), we cannot understand why these policies have such power unless we go more deeply into the creative ways in which the Right has worked at changing our commonsense so that the meanings of key words that have what might be called "emotional economies" are radically transformed (see, e.g., Williams, 1976). The "thick democracy" of full participation is being replaced by the "thin democracy" of markets and consumption practices. Education is being commodified. Choice on a competitive market replaces the collective creation and recreation of our fundamental institutions. Words such as democracy and freedom become eviscerated, drained of their critical histories and of the social movements that established them as key elements in the formation of more progressive social and educational policies (see Foner, 1998). And this has occurred not only when conservative governments have been in power. New Labour in the UK and the Democratic Party in the United States, and similar parties in other nations, have been more than a little instrumental in sponsoring such shifts.

BUILDING THE CONSERVATIVE ALLIANCE

As I have also documented, in order to do justice to the complicated ideological assemblage behind the movement toward thinner versions of democracy, we also need to direct our attention to a wider set of groups. Within the complicated alliance of *conservative modernization* are four groups: neoliberals, neoconservatives, authoritarian populist religious conservatives, and members of an upwardly mobile fraction of the professional and managerial new middle class (Apple, 2006). The relative power of these groups often differs by region and nation, but it is important to realize that—although neoliberal impulses and policies are usually in leadership—they also usually exist in tandem with a number of other tendencies. Thus, neoliberalism does not stand alone. It exists in relation to other conservative tendencies. It is also important to recognize that there are not only multiple groups and tendencies within this conservative alliance, but there are also multiple relations of power that are being fought out—not only class relations, but those of gender and race (Apple, 2006; Apple, 2010; Apple, Au, & Gandin, 2009).

Some very impressive work has been done recently on the ways in which race and racialising dynamics are exceptionally powerful in current neoliberal and neoconservative educational reforms for example (see, e.g., Lipman, 2010, Gillborn, 2008; Buras, 2008). Similar analyses on the class basis and effects of such reforms are available as well (see, e.g., Ball, 2003; Power, Edwards, Whitty, & Wigfall, 2003) and of the inter-relations among multiple dynamics such as gender, sex, class, and disability (Lynch, Baker, & Lyons, 2009; Lynch & Lodge, 2002). Such work certainly complements the chapters of the collection that Marie Lall and her co-authors have produced and allows us to deepen our understanding of who benefits from the policies on which they focus their critical attention.

Let me say more about this process. I noted above that in a large number of countries, a complex alliance and power bloc has been formed that has increasing influence in education and all things social. The first and the strongest element of conservative modernization is the one to which this book rightly directs most of its attention—neoliberalism. It includes multiple fractions of capital who are committed to neoliberal marketised solutions to education, health care, social welfare, indeed to all aspects of the state (see also, Clarke & Newman, 1997). For them, private is necessarily good and public is necessarily bad. Democracy—a key word in how we think about our institutions and our place in them (Foner 1998)—is reduced to consumption practices. The world becomes a vast supermarket, one in which those with economic and cultural capital are advantaged in nearly every sector of society. Choice in a market replaces more collective and more political actions. *Thin* democracy replaces *thick* democracy. This demobilizes crucial progressive social movements that have been the driving force behind nearly all of the democratic changes in this society and in our schools (Apple & Buras, 2006).

In education, this position is grounded in the belief that the more we marketise, the more we bring corporate models into education, the more we can hold schools, administrators, and teachers feet to the fire of competition, the better they will be. There actually is very little evidence to support this contention—and a good deal of evidence that it increases inequality and acts as an arena in which those with socially valued economic, social, and cultural capital are privileged (see Apple 2006; Lipman 2011; Ball, 2003; Power, Edwards, Whitty, & Wigfall, 2003; Gillborn & Youdell, 2000). But neoliberalism continues to act as something like a religion in that it seems to be impervious to empirical evidence, even as the crisis that it has created in the economy and in communities constantly documents its failures in every moment of our collective and individual lives. The book you are reading does a fine job of showing what this nearly religious commitment means to an entire array of policies, institutions, programs, and real people's lives

The second most powerful group in this alliance is neo-conservatives who want a "return" to higher standards and a "common culture." In the face of diasporic populations who are making the United States, Britain, and many other nations a vast and impressive experiment in continual cultural creation, they are committed to a conservative culturally restorative project, pressing for a return to an imposed sense of nation and tradition that is based on a fear of "pollution" from the culture and the body of those whom they consider the "Others." That there is a crucial and partly hidden (at least to some people) dynamic of race at work here is not unimportant to say the least (Lipman 2011; Gillborn 2008; Leonardo 2009). Neoconservatives assume something that isn't there, a consensus on what should be "official" knowledge and a "common culture". They thereby evacuate one of the most significant questions that should be asked in our schools: What and whose knowledge should we teach? In their certainty over what a common culture is supposed to be, they ignore a key element in this supposed commonness. What is common is that we disagree. Indeed, what needs to be "the common" is the constant democratic and deliberative process of asking the question of what is common (Williams 1989; Apple, 2000).

A third key element in conservative modernization in many nations, one that is growing in influence, is composed of authoritarian populist religious conservatives who are deeply worried about secularity and the preservation of their own traditions. They too wish to impose a "common." For them, "the people" must decide. But there are anointed people and those who are not. In the United States, for example, for this increasingly influential group only when a particular reading of Christianity is put back in its rightful place as the guiding project of all of our institutions and interactions will we be able to once again claim that this is "God's country." In the process, they inaccurately construct themselves as the "new oppressed," as people whose identities and cultures are ignored by or attacked in schools and the media. It is not an accident that one of the fastest growing educational movements in the United States right now is homeschooling. Two million children have been taken out of public schools, most often for conservative ideological and religious reasons, and are being schooled at home. While the homeschooling movement is varied, these decisions are often driven by conservative attacks on public schools, on the public sphere in general as a source of danger and pollution, and once again by fear of the "Other" (Apple & Buras 2006; Apple 2006). Like the connections between neoliberalism and neoconservativism, the alliance that authoritarian populist religious conservatives have built with neoliberals is increasingly powerful in both the political and educational arenas and has had a decided influence on educational and social policies.

Finally, a crucial part of this ideological umbrella is a particular fraction of the professionally and managerially oriented new middle class. This group is made up of people who are committed to the ideology and techniques of accountability, measurement, and the "new managerialism," to what has been called "audit culture" (Apple 2006; Leys 2003). They too are true believers, ones who believe that in installing such procedures and rules they are "helping." For them, more evidence on schools', teachers', and students' performance—usually simply based on the limited data generated by test-scores—will solve our problems, even though once again there is just as much evidence that this too can create as many problems as it supposedly solves (Valenzuela 2005; Gillborn and Youdell 2000). Demonstrating that one is "acting correctly" according to externally imposed criteria is the norm. "Perform or die" almost seems to be their motto. New Labour's positions on these kinds of procedures and on the ideological assumptions that underpin them are among the clearest embodiments of such policies. They are also clear in the United States and a number of other nations where performance pay for teachers, where teachers' pay is based on the test scores of their students, has been instituted, often under the rhetoric of "value added" measures. Not only is this a deeply problematic understanding of the complex labour of teachers (and doctors, nurses, social workers, and others employed in the public sector), value added technologies themselves have proven to be decades away from being technically sophisticated enough to even come close to dealing with such complexity, to say nothing of their fundamentally flawed neglect of the realities of and importance of the work of care, love, and solidarity that underpins so much of the labour in schools, hospitals, home care, and elsewhere (Lynch, Baker, & Lyons, 2009).

As Lall makes very clear in her introductory chapter, the state itself—what it does, how it is organized and controlled, how its labour is controlled, paid, and (dis)respected—all of this is being radically transformed by the various elements in this alliance (see Clarke & Newman, 1997 and Jessop, 2002). While there are clear tensions and conflicts within this alliance, in general its overall aims are in providing the educational conditions believed necessary both for increasing international competitiveness, profit, and discipline and for returning us to a romanticized past of the "ideal" home, family, and school.

This new alliance has integrated education and other areas of social policy into a wider set of ideological commitments. The objectives in education are the same as those which guide its economic and social welfare goals. They include the dramatic expansion of that eloquent fiction, the free market; the drastic reduction of government responsibility for social needs; the reinforcement of intensely competitive structures of mobility both inside and outside the school; the lowering of people's expectations for economic security; the "disciplining" of culture and the body; and the popularization of what is clearly a form of Social Darwinist thinking.

The seemingly contradictory discourse of competition, markets, and choice on the one hand and accountability, performance objectives, standards, national testing, and national curriculum on the other has created a situation in which it is hard to hear anything else. Even though these seem to embody different tendencies, as I demonstrate elsewhere they actually oddly reinforce each other and help cement conservative educational positions into our daily lives (Apple 2006).

THE IMPORTANCE OF THIS BOOK

The increasing influence of this new hegemonic bloc in nearly every part of our daily life makes the book you are reading even more important. Marie Lall has brought together a number of authors who have lived the results of the transformations in policies and the common-sense that guides them. This book gives clear and compelling evidence of what is happening in so many contexts and institutions. Each of the chapters provides us with a critical analysis of the hidden (to some people) costs of the policies that are being followed by governments and elites.

The use of specific case studies is also a wise choice. While important, too many critical interrogations of the assumptions and effects of neoliberalism remain at a general level. Yet neoliberalism has *specific effects* at *specific sites*. And in order to truly understand what it does, we need to get close up to these sites.

Yet a focus on specific sites needs to be integrated into the larger picture as well. Thus, the choice to focus on the entire Policy Cycle provides the reader with a clearer picture how and why a set of policies comes to be, who the actors were and are, how policies move within the state and where they may originate outside the state, and what happens when they reach their "targeted audience." Of course, Stephen Ball's work on this complex set of dynamics is of considerable importance here (see, e.g., Ball, 2008) and Lall and her colleagues are very wise to employ it as a key part of their guiding framework. The framework is reminiscent of a key text in cultural studies as well, what Richard Johnson has so nicely called the "circuit of cultural production"—the production of texts and policies, their distribution, and their reception (Johnson, 1986). What is crucial is our ability to historicize these policies to trace out their paths and their determinate effects in real and varied institutions. The authors included in this book provide us with significant narratives and analyses of this very process.

HOPE AS A RESOURCE

Elsewhere, I have argued that there are many tasks that the "critical scholar/activist" must perform (Apple, 2010; see also, Apple, Au, & Gandin, 2009; Apple, Ball, & Gandin, 2010). One of the most important is the following. She or he must "*bear witness to negativity.*"[25] That is, one of our primary functions is to illuminate the ways in which educational policy and practice are connected to the relations of exploitation and domination—and to struggles against such relations—in the larger society.[26] Another task is to help illuminate what can be done to alter these relations. This task is a collective one of course. After reading this book, the crucial significance of this latter task is made even more visible.

Yet I have also noted other critical tasks of the critical scholar/activist if we are to be more effective in challenging dominance and also putting in place more thickly democratic policies and practices that actually *work*. One of these tasks is to do our critical analyses with an eye toward locating the contradictions in existing policies and practices, to find the spaces of possible counter-hegemonic work. Finding spaces does not stand alone however. It needs to be accompanied by something that is equally important. This is to document the successful struggles against dominant educational policies and practices, in essence to act as "critical secretaries" of those people and movements who are now filling those spaces, who are actually now building these counter-hegemonic alternatives. It is crucial that successes are documented (see, e.g., Buras, 2010, et al., 2010, Apple & Beane, 2007; Apple, 2010).

There are places to which we can turn both for strategies for engaging in these tasks and for concrete examples of programs and strategies of interruption that build off of the fine critical analyses that forms the core of this book. For example, The Centre for Equality Studies at University College, Dublin has been at the centre of research and action that stresses not only poverty and inequality, but movement towards equality in a time of conservative resurgence (Baker, Lynch, Cantillon, & Walsh, 2004). The same is true for CREA, an interdisciplinary research centre at the University of Barcelona that is a model of how to build a research agenda and then create policies and programs that even in a time of severe crisis in so many of our institutions and communities empower those who are economically and culturally marginalized in our societies (Flecha, 2011; Gatt, Ojaja, & Soler, 2011; Alexiu & Sorde, 2011; Aubert, 2011; Christou & Puivert, 2011; Flecha, 2009).

The lasting educational reforms in Porto Alegre in Brazil also provide a paradigm case of how social and educational policies can be joined so that impoverished citizens can and do take charge of their own lives and how the educational institutions and struggles over them play essential roles in changing the identities of the poor and disenfranchised in truly progressive ways (see, e.g., Gandin and Apple, 2003; Gandin & Apple, in press). Similar powerful self-formative movements, this time among women in very poor communities, that act directly against the impoverishing condition imposed by neoliberal national and international agendas, are visible in other material as well (see Apple, 2010). At the level both of individual schools and classrooms and of powerful critically democratic work by socially committed teachers and administrators over policies and practices in schools, there are also compelling accounts of successes (see, for instance, Apple & Beane, 2007; Watson, 2011; Swalwell, in press. See also the journal *Rethinking Schools*).

Yet there are other resources for substantive transformative actions that are available in addition to those to which I have pointed above. In this regard, we can also turn to the history of struggles against dominant interests inside and outside of education. Britain has an extensive tradition of counter-hegemonic educational movements, mobilizations, and institutions. While space does not allow me to go into detail here, a number of recent analyses have attempted to restore the collective memory of some of these movements, mobilizations, and institutions (see, for example, Gerrard, 2011; Fielding & Moss, 2011).

I bring these to your attention not simply because in general it is significant to ground oneself in the history of past moments, although that is indeed important. But I have two other particular reasons for doing this. First, one of the successful tactics of rightist alliances is to engage in a dual strategy of creating *historical amnesia* and rewriting the past to delegitimate alternative narratives. If alternatives and oppositional movements are seen as historical failures and as merely the voices of "special interests," this has major effects on a society's self-understanding. Second, and equally significant, historical amnesia makes us less apt to think that more socially responsive and just possibilities are indeed possible. Cynicism and demobilization are the results of such an outlook, a disaster in a time of radical reconstructions of education, health care, social services, and the entire public sector. This is something we cannot afford to let happen. As Raymond Williams (1989) reminded us, a crucial resource in times of crisis is *hope*. The fact that there is such a long history of successful progressive movements in so many sectors in all of our countries provides a necessary resource when we are constantly being told that the neoliberal agenda is the only solution to the crisis that it itself created.

I am not asking us to be romantic. But let us remember that the Right would not be so angry at the public sector, would not want to radically transform our institutions and our basic ways of thinking and acting in them, if there had not been major victories cemented in place in these very same institutions and in our understandings and identities. This book helps us recognize what is at stake if these lose understandings and identities. What happens next is up to all of us.

REFERENCES

Alexiu, T. M., & Sorde, T. (2011). How to turn difficulties into opportunities: Drawing from diversity to promote social cohesion. *International Studies in Sociology of Education, 21,* 49–62.

Apple, M. W. (2000). *Official Knowledge: Democratic Education in a Conservative Age* (2nd ed.). New York and London: Routledge.

Apple, M. W. (2006). *Educating the "Right" Way: Markets, Standards, God, and Inequality* (2nd ed.). New York and London: Routledge.

Apple, M. W. (Ed.). (2010). *Global Crises, Social Justice, and Education.* New York and London: Routledge.

Apple, M. W. & Beane, J. A. (Eds.). (2007). *Democratic Schools: Lessons in Powerful Education.* Portsmouth, NH: Heinemann.

Apple, M. W. & Buras, K. (Eds.). (2006). *The Subaltern Speak: Curriculum, Power, and Educational Struggles.* New York and London: Routledge.

Apple, M. W., Au, W., & Gandin, L. A. (Eds.). (2009). *The Routledge International Handbook of Critical Education.* New York and London: Routledge.

Apple, M. W., Ball, S., & Gandin, L. A. (Eds.). (2010). *The Routledge International Handbook of the Sociology of Education.* New York and London: Routledge.

Aubert, A. (2011). Moving beyond social inclusion through dialogue. *International Studies in Sociology of Education, 21,* 63–75.

Baker, J., Lynch, K., Cantillon, S., & Walsh, S. (2004). *Equality: From Theory to Action.* New York: Palgrave Macmillan.

Ball, S. (2003). *Class Strategies and the Education Market.* New York and London: RoutledgeFalmer.

Ball, S. (2008). *The Education Debate.* Bristol: Policy Press.

Buras, K., Randels, J., Kalamu ya Salaam, K., & Students at the Center. (Eds.). (2010). *Pedagogy, Policy, and the Privatized City: Stories of Dispossession and Defiance from New Orleans.* New York: Teachers College Press.

Christou, M., & Puigvert, L. (2011). The role of "other women" in current educational transformations. *International Studies in Sociology of Education, 21,* 77–90.

Clarke, J., & Newman, J. (1997). *The Managerial State.* Thousand Oaks, CA: Sage.

Fielding, M., & Moss, P. (2011). *Radical Education and the Common School: A Democratic Alternative.* New York and London: Routledge.

Flecha, R. (2009). The educative city and critical education. In M. W. Apple, W. Au, & L. A. Gandin (Eds.), *The Routledge International Handbook of Critical Education.* (pp. 327–340). New York: Routledge.

Flecha, R. (2011). The dialogic sociology of education. *International Studies in Sociology of Education, 21,* 7–20.

Fraser, N. (1997). *Justice Interruptus.* New York and London: Routledge.

Foner, E. (1998). *The Story of American Freedon.* New York: Norton.

Gandin, L. A., & Apple, M. W. (2003). Educating the state, democratizing knowledge: The citizen school project in Porto Alegre, Brazil. In M. W. Apple, et al. (Eds.), *The State and the Politics of Knowledge* (pp. 193–219). New York and London: RoutledgeFalmer.

Gandin, L. A., & Apple, M. W. (in press). Can democracy last? Porto Alegre and the struggle for 'thick' democracy in education. *Journal of Education Policy,* in press.

Gatt, S., Ojala, M., & Soler, M. (2011). Promoting social inclusion counting with everyone: Learning communities and INCLUDE-ED. *International Studies in Sociology of Education, 21,* 33–47.

Gerrard, J. (2011). Class, community and education: Cultures of resistance in socialist sunday schools and black supplementary schools. *Gender and Education, 23*(6).

Gillborn, D. (2008). *Racism and Education: Coincidence or Conspiracy.* New York and London: Routledge.

Gillborn, D., & Youdell, D. (2000). *Rationing Education.* Buckingham: Open University Press.

Gramsci, A. (1971). *Selections from the Prison Notebooks.* New York: International Publishers.

Jessop, B. (2002). *The Future of the Capitalist State.* Cambridge: Polity Press.

Johnson, R. (1986). What is cultural studies anyway? *Social Text, 16*, 38–80.

Leonardo, Z. (2009). *Race, Whiteness, and Education.* New York and London: Routledge.

Lynch, K., Baker, J., & Lyons, M. (2009). *Affective Equality: Love, Care, and Injustice.* New York: Palgrave Macmillan.

Lynch, K., & Lodge, A. (2002). *Equality and Power in Schools: Redistribution, Recognition, and Representation.* New York: RoutledgeFalmer.

Leys, C. (2003). *Market-driven Politics.* New York and London: Verso.

Lipman, P. (2011). *A New Political Economy of Urban Education.* New York and London: Routledge.

Power, S., Edwards, T., Whitty, G., & Wigfall, V. (2003). *Education and the Middle Class.* Buckingham: Open University Press.

Swalwell, K. (in press). *Educating Activist Allies: Social Justice Pedagogy with the Suburban and Urban Elite.* New York and London: Routledge.

Valenzuela, A. (Ed.). (2005). *Leaving Children Behind.* Albany, NY: State University of New York Press.

Watson, V. (2011). *Learning to Liberate: Community-based Solutions to the Crisis in Urban Education.* New York and London: Routledge.

Williams, R. (1985). *Keywords: A Vocabulary of Culture and Society.* New York and London: Oxford University Press.

Williams, R. (1989). *Resources of Hope.* New York and London: Verso.

NOTES

[25] I am aware that the idea of "bearing witness" has religious connotations, ones that are powerful in the West, but may be seen as a form of religious imperialism in other religious traditions. I still prefer to use it because of its powerful resonances with ethical discourses. But I welcome suggestions from, say, Muslim critical educators and researchers for alternative concepts that can call forth similar responses. I want to thank Amy Stambach for this point.

[26] Here, exploitation and domination are technical not rhetorical terms. The first refers to economic relations, the structures of inequality, the control of labor, and the distribution of resources in a society. The latter refers to the processes of representation and respect and to the ways in which people have identities imposed on them. These are analytic categories, of course, and are ideal types. Most oppressive conditions are partly a combination of the two. These categories map on to what Fraser (1997) calls the politics of redistribution and the politics of recognition.

Michael W. Apple is John Bascom Professor of Curriculum and Instruction and Educational Policy Studies at the University of Wisconsin, Professor of Educational Policy Studies at the Institute of Education, University of London, and World Scholar and Distinguished Professor of Educational Policy Studies at East China Normal University in Shanghai. Among his recent book are *The Routledge International Handbook of Critical Education* (2009), with Wayne Au and Luis Armando Gandin, *The Routledge International Handbook of the Sociology of Education* (2010), with Stephen Ball and Luis Armando Gandin, and *Global Crises, Social Justice, and Education* (2010).

Lightning Source UK Ltd.
Milton Keynes UK
UKOW03●658050712

195507UK00002B/144/P